DIY MEDIA

Colin Lankshear, Michele Knobel,
and Michael Peters
General Editors

Vol. 44

PETER LANG
New York • Washington, D.C./Baltimore • Bern
Frankfurt • Berlin • Brussels • Vienna • Oxford

DIY MEDIA

CREATING, SHARING AND LEARNING WITH NEW TECHNOLOGIES

EDITED BY
MICHELE KNOBEL & COLIN LANKSHEAR

PETER LANG
New York • Washington, D.C./Baltimore • Bern
Frankfurt • Berlin • Brussels • Vienna • Oxford

Library of Congress Cataloging-in-Publication Data

DIY media: creating, sharing and learning with new technologies /
edited by Michele Knobel, Colin Lankshear.
p. cm. — (New literacies and digital epistemologies; v. 44)
Includes bibliographical references and index.
1. Educational technology. 2. Media literacy.
I. Knobel, Michele. II. Lankshear, Colin. III. Title: Do it yourself media.
LB1028.3.D59   371.33—dc22   2009025888
ISBN 978-1-4331-0634-7 (hardcover)
ISBN 978-1-4331-0635-4 (paperback)
ISSN 1523-9543

Bibliographic information published by **Die Deutsche Nationalbibliothek**.
Die Deutsche Nationalbibliothek lists this publication in the "Deutsche
Nationalbibliografie"; detailed bibliographic data is available
on the Internet at http://dnb.d-nb.de/.

© 2010 Peter Lang Publishing, Inc., New York
29 Broadway, 18th floor, New York, NY 10006
www.peterlang.com

Printed in the United States of America

To our dear friend Harvey Sheppard of Bottle Cove, Newfoundland.

Table of Contents

Part 2: Still Media

Part 3: Moving Media

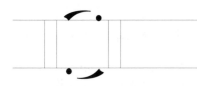

Acknowledgments

The editors and authors would like to thank the following for giving permission to use their images within the chapters of this book: Yahoo! for permission to use the screen shots from Flickr appearing in Figures 4.1, 4.2, 4.3, 4.4, 5.1, and 5.5; Guy Merchant for permission to use his photographs in Chapter 4; John Potter for permission to use his photographs in Chapter 5; Heather Armstrong for the screenshot from her blog, *dooce.com,* appearing in Figure 5.2; Go Squared Ltd. (htp://www.gosqu ared.com) for permission to use the icon set titled "40 Image Editing Icons" (currently available at http://www.gosquared.com/liquidicity/ar chives/384) and shown in Figure 5.3, and in particular, James Gill of Go Squared Ltd., who created the icons appearing in Figure 5.3; Alice Potter for all images appearing in Figures 5.4a, 5.4b, 5.4c, and 5.4d; Alexandro Nuñez for his original artwork for a Machinima storyboard appearing in Figure 6.1; Shinywhitebox.com for the screenshot from iShowU appearing in Figure 6.2; Anim8 Stop Motion creator, Michael Mallon, for his time and responses to interview questions; Keegan and Greg Twigg (twiggarts on YouTube) for the image appearing Figure 7.1; and Martin Waller for his detailed comments about using stop motion in his Year 2 classroom, and for permission to use the image appearing in Figure 7.6 in this volume.

The editors particularly thank the authors for their contributions to this book. We know they all lead busy and demanding lives, and are deeply appreciative of the time, effort and expert insights they have given to this project. We have learned a great deal from each of them.

Caitlin Curran is due special thanks for her administrative, behind-the-scenes work on this manuscript, including help with formatting, proof-reading, obtaining permissions, among other, often tedious, tasks. Requests for assistance were always met with a smiling "Sure!" and tasks were meticulously done and completed well ahead of schedule. We are very grateful for her contributions to this book.

The editors' warm thanks are also due to Harvey Sheppard and Vera Joyce of Lark Harbour, Newfoundland, for offering "whenever" access to their computer and the internet during the summer of 2009 while we were writing the introduction to this book (ostensibly "on vacation" and "away" from "all that stuff"). They also contributed directly to our thinking about DIY culture and ethos in everyday people's lives.

We thank the various universities, colleges and schools employing the contributing authors for supporting their research and publishing activity. In our own case as editors, we thank the following universities for their ongoing support of our work: Montclair State University, James Cook University, Mount Saint Vincent University, and McGill University.

We also thank everyone at Peter Lang Publishing for making this such an easy project to administer. Quick answers to our queries, the right forms to fill in at the right time, and important advice regarding formatting and figures are just some of the valued input we received. In particular, we'd like to thank Bernadette Shade and Chris Myers for their usual patience, goodwill and good humor throughout this writing project.

Chapter 1

DIY Media: A contextual background and some contemporary themes

COLIN LANKSHEAR AND MICHELE KNOBEL

Introduction

This book aims to introduce do-it-yourself—DIY—media to educators and caregivers who are aware that young people are doing a lot of "digital media" work on a day-by-day basis and who would like to know more about what this work involves. Its audience includes teacher educators, in-service teachers and teachers in training, educators involved in professional development and after-school programs, librarians, parents, and other caregivers who want a better understanding than they currently have of what many young people are doing with digital media. The following chapters explore what is involved in creating media—and learning how to create media—from the standpoint of participating in a range of DIY media practices, such as podcasting, music remixing, creating flash animations, making machinima movies, and so on.

The book takes a *practice* approach to its subject matter. Each chapter addresses its particular form of media engagement in ways that illuminate it as a sociocultural *practice*. Practices are socially recognized ways of using tools and knowledge to do things (Scribner & Cole, 1981; see also, Gee, 2004, 2007; Hull & Schultz, 2001; Lankshear & Knobel, 2006). Podcasting, for example, involves using particular kinds of tools, techniques and technologies to achieve the goals and purposes that podcasters aim to achieve, and to use them in the ways that people known as podcasters recognize as appropriate to their endeavor in terms of their goals and values. We think that understanding what many young people are doing with digital media is a matter of understanding what it is they are intent on *doing and being* when they engage with media as DIY creators/producers. This is a matter of knowing something about their goals and aims and purposes; their tools and how they use them; the knowledge they draw on and seek to obtain in crafting their production to a personally satisfying level of expertise; the values and standards they recognize as relevant to good practice.

The audience we envisage for this book is one that seeks a better understanding of young people's DIY engagement with media for *educational* reasons—in a broad sense of "educational." They are not just curious about what kids are doing. Rather, they want to be able to make meaningful and respectful connections to these practices; connections that will contribute to learning in ways that will enhance young people's prospects of living well in the present and the future. In some cases, making these connections might simply involve coming to appreciate the complex skills and understandings inherent in these pursuits, instead of worrying about DIY media tinkering and experimentation as nothing more than a waste of time or as eating into students' attention to homework. In other cases, it might be a matter of seeing how connections can be made between classroom curricular requirements and what children and young people are doing-for-themselves with digital media. This is *not* to suggest that teachers should suddenly turn around and import each and every DIY media practice directly into the classroom. The point is, rather, to understand how key learning principles and systems of appreciation (Gee, 2007) tied up in these practices can be used to inform sound teaching practices (e.g., how the principles of effective video editing developed from creating machinima can be translated into editing written narratives or play scripts).

Developing this latter kind of understanding is not a matter of just reading about DIY media practices in the abstract. It requires, more than anything, some kind of embodied, hands-on engagement in the practice. And this, in turn, extends well beyond simply coming to grips with the technical aspects of a given DIY media practice (e.g., how to move the playhead to where you want to clip a movie, how to add searchable tags to your photos within Flickr.com), although this dimension is important. It also necessarily includes a commitment to obtaining a sense of "insider" perspectives on the practice by spending time participating in, and even contributing to, relevant affinity spaces. Affinity spaces are "specially designed spaces (physical and virtual) constructed to resource people tied together . . . by a shared interest or endeavor" (Gee, 2004, p. 73). These spaces can extend across online archives or artifact hosting websites (with provision made for leaving review comments, etc.), discussion boards, face-to-face events, paper-based and online guides, and the like—all of which support people in accessing and sharing knowledge "that is distributed and dispersed across many different people, places, Internet sites and modalities" (ibid.). In the case of creating a stop motion animation, for example, this might include spending quite some time browsing the videos archived at StopMotionAnimation.com or on YouTube.com and reading review comments in order to generate a sense of what constitutes a "good" stop motion animation (e.g., photo display timing is set to ensure a sense of fluid motion, lighting remains constant from photo to photo within a single scene). Watching a good number of videos hosted at either site soon shows which themes, topics and storylines are done to death in the world of stop motion animation, and which are fresh and innovative. Reading interviews with stop motion animators about what got them started and what keeps them involved at sites like Anim8StopMotion.com also affords useful insights into trends within DIY stop motion animation creation as well as helps to identify what are considered to be landmark videos that contribute to setting the benchmarks for judging innovative animations (see Chapter 7, this volume). A focus on *practice* therefore includes the technical dimensions of the practice, as well as the insider perspectives on what it means to create something well (or well enough to be personally satisfying or to meet a given purpose).

Accordingly, each chapter in this book begins with a section that discusses the particular media practice in focus (e.g., podcasting, music remix, photosharing) from the standpoint of insiders to that practice. The authors consider some of the cultural knowledge and cultural ways that members of that practice—or sharers of that affinity (Gee, 2004)—recognize, contribute to, honor and strive to maintain and develop. The authors present their perspectives in ways that will provide newcomers or "strangers" to the practice with a sense of who the people are who participate in the practice, what is in it for them, and how they interact with others within this practice. At the same time, the authors' points of view engage those of other people participating in the practice whose views may vary on some points (e.g., around future trends and directions), thereby opening up possibilities for further reflection, debate and growth.

The middle section of each chapter is a "how to get started" statement, designed for people who want so far as possible to "learn by doing" (and "create while learning") in the area of DIY media, but who would also like a ready reference to augment the support they can get face-to-face from expert others, or that they can access online by running Google searches, trawling sets of relevant "frequently asked questions" (FAQs) and answers, accessing discussion forums, and so on. We firmly believe that in order for "outsiders" or newcomers to begin to move towards becoming "insiders," they need to begin by *participating* somewhere. This is much the same as it is, say, for ethnographers who want to study a culture different from their own. Ethnographers need to begin participating in events—typically in everyday events that have discernible steps such as food preparation or religious ceremonies—before they can start understanding these events as an insider might. Observation alone is insufficient for understanding any culture. Working at "getting on the inside" of a practice has two dimensions—as we've already alluded to above: the hands-on dimension, and the culture/affinity dimension. The aim of the middle section in each chapter, therefore, is to give newcomers support in "having a go" at a range of DIY media practices. Each chapter includes within this section reference to key sites within the practice that help mobilize affinities (e.g., Machinima.com for machinima makers, AnimeMusicVideos.org for AMV remixers), along with other recommended sites for obtaining technical help and other resources. Many chapters also include references to online how-to guides or structured walkthroughs that act as direct props for newcomers to use to support getting stuck in and "mucking around" with producing a media artifact of one kind or another.

The final part of each chapter is intended to contribute to the evaluative, reflective, critical dimension of social practices from an educational standpoint. It poses "so what?" questions about media practices in relation to educational purposes. This involves negotiating a tricky tension between intrinsic and more instrumental purposes. There is a world of difference, for example, between the intrinsically motivated pursuits and efforts of *bona fide* fans of media phenomena (Jenkins, 1992, 2006a, 2006b)—who engage in the practice because it is integral to their cultural interests, peer relationships and identities—and the pressures felt by many educators and teachers in training that they should "get up to speed" on 21st century media and skills; that they should pursue some "insider-like" proficiencies and appreciations of new media practices in order to make better teaching and learning connections with digital age learners and with contemporary shifts in theories and practices of learning (Buckingham et al., 2004; Ito et al., 2009; Jenkins et al., 2006). We are sensitive to this tension because we feel it ourselves on a day-to-day basis. To the extent that we ourselves can make the time and create the space, we revel in "mucking around," "tinkering," and creating media artifacts for the sheer intrinsic pleasure of doing it and the sense of fulfillment it generates when something "comes off" at a level or standard we are content with (all too rarely, of course!). For us, this is the heart and soul of DIY media—people doing it because they can't *not* do it. At the same time, we are acutely aware of the extent to which we have only "got into this stuff" because we have felt we "had to" in order to do the best job we can as educators. As editors, this book is very much grounded in our own experiences of contradictions: contradictions that the chapter authors have been recruited to explore and, we suspect, that they experience to varying degrees themselves on a continuing basis.

Our brief to the chapter authors was to write for a wide range of users, including relative newbies through to those who are very much at home using their computers. This caveat reflects our own teaching experiences; in graduate courses we have taught teachers who needed to ask their neighbor over to help them find the "on" button on their new laptop computer, teachers who only recently opened their first email account, and teachers who had long been using blogs and digital movie editing processes in their classrooms. Computer-savvy teachers are likely to find the historical background in each chapter provides useful contextualizing information; newbies are likely to find the step-by-step guides and suggestions for finding additional support and trouble-shooting advice online most helpful to begin with. All readers are likely to find something of interest in the suggestions for teaching each author provides. This collection is designed to be dipped into on a just-in-time-and-place basis, and the chapters can be read in no particular order, as can the sections within each chapter. When all is said and done, however, it is only an introduction to each of the eight DIY media practices showcased across the chapters. And it is certainly not an exhaustive accounting of all the possible DIY media practices currently engaged in around the world. In sum, this book offers a series of how-to guides, but it is no substitute for immersing oneself in the social practices associated with creating a digital media artifact well and *doing it yourself*. Hopefully, however, it may help to encourage at least some readers to throw themselves into "mucking around" with one or more of the cultural practices and associated digital media described, according to personal preferences and interests.

DIY and DIY media

As terminology in common usage, "DIY" or "do-it-yourself" is usually traced to the early mid-1950s U.S. scene (Merriam-Webster.com cites 1952; dictionary.com cites 1950–1955). Early uses made particular reference to people (by implication, mainly males) undertaking maintenance, repair or modification work on major investment items like homes and vehicles, without (necessarily) having the specialized training or expertise associated with that work. In such cases, individuals believed they could do the work in question sufficiently well to be able to bypass the paid (often costly) services of specialist personnel (such as "professionals" or tradesmen). Benefits from doing this include saving money, convenient completion times, personal satisfaction, having it done the way one wants, and so on. The rise of DIY coincided historically with the growth of the suburbs and suburban lifestyles in the U.S. and elsewhere throughout the western world. It moved established forms of domestic activity and self-reliance—such as farmers fabricating their own implements and/or repairing commercially produced implements, and women knitting or sewing garments for the family—onto new terrain, and onto a new scale. Furthermore, it also allowed the domestic producers of long established "home-made" artifacts to aspire to a different quality of production. Whereas "home-made" traditionally implied products that were "folksy" or otherwise visibly not "commercially produced," DIY-ers could now aspire to a more professional look and feel to their production.

The "tasks, tools and knowledge" framework derived from the concept of social practice provides a useful way of understanding this phenomenon. The new "home-made" of post-1950s DIY emerged as more specialized *tools* and *knowledge* became more readily accessible (i.e., available to "non-specialist" people at affordable prices), allowing ordinary people to entertain the idea of pursuing what had hitherto been specialized *tasks*. In the area of home improvement, for example, this involved the emergence of small scale but sophisticated power tools, along with locally available night courses, hobby classes, magazines and other DIY publications, kitsets and their included step-by-step guides. Much the same applied in areas like sewing, knitting, and cooking/catering or home entertaining, as new knowledge resources akin to those available for home improvement emerged alongside increased access to sophisticated programmable sewing and knitting machines, overlockers, and professional grade ovens and food mixers, and the like.

It has subsequently become common to talk about a DIY ethic, and to extend talk of DIY far beyond its most common early referents.

> The DIY ethic . . . refers to the ethic of being self-reliant by completing tasks oneself as opposed to having others who are likely more experienced complete them. The term can indicate "doing" anything from home improvements and repairs to health care, from publication to electronics (Wikipedia, 2009a, no page).

At the level of an "ethic," DIY has been linked to a range of antecedents and values systems. These include a late 19th century Arts and Crafts movement associated with figures like William Morris, which sought to keep traditional arts and crafts alive in the face of displacement by escalating industrial/mass production processes and/or to reject a growing industrial aesthetic (Wikipedia, 2009b).

More recently, DIY has been associated with a range of 1960s–1970s philosophies and countercultural trends, including anti-consumerist, anti-corporatist, environmental, self-reliance, self-actualization, New Age, and subsistence values and practices (see, for example, Lavine & Heimerl, 2008; Spencer, 2005; Wikipedia, 2009b). For example, the work of Ivan Illich (1971, 1973a, 1973b, etc.) provided an especially sophisticated and forceful account of how professionalized institutions, from the church to the school, have disabled people, forcing them to become dependent on those professionals who alone are sanctioned or authorized to provide various services. The logic of enforced consumption of professional services through manipulative institutions (Illich, 1973a) conditions people to confuse the process of realizing values with the process of consuming commodities. What people can do perfectly well for themselves has been rendered illegitimate, and, to the extent that legitimate services come at a price, what is readily available in principle has become economically scarce in practice. The result is a profound and disabling "disempowerment," which includes being robbed of the opportunity to discover what one might in fact be able to do for oneself and, in many cases, do better and more to one's personal tastes and beliefs than is "delivered" by a professionalized institution or bureaucracy. Illich went so far as to describe school—"the age-specific, teacher-related process of full time attendance at an obligatory curriculum" (1973a, p. 32)—as "the reproductive organ of the consumer society," and was a key informant (along with people like John Holt and Everett Reimer) for the emergent homeschooling and unschooling movements of the 1970s.

Many commentators (e.g., Spencer, 2005; Tiggs, 2006; Wikipedia, 2009b) highlight the influence of 1970s punk on the evolving DIY ethic and on the subsequent direction of DIY media in particular. They talk of a substantial DIY subculture grounded in anti-corporate and anti-consumerist values having impacted DIY music and (online) self-publishing and encouraged personal styles of self-presentation, self-expression, and identity work.

With respect to self-publishing, punk amplified the orientation and scale of zines, or "cut and paste publishing" (Knobel & Lankshear, 2002). These short-run magazines—"zines" for short—were originally typed texts that were cut and pasted by hand into booklet form and copied. Some writers date zines as an identifiable cultural form back to the 1940s (Chu, 1997; Duncombe, 1997, 1999; Williamson, 1994). Personal zines—perzines—are more recent, achieving "critical mass" in the mid-1980s. These zines grew out of the 1970s punk rock scene as fans put together "fanzines" about their favorite bands, focusing on biographical details, appearance dates and venues, album reviews, and the like. According to a Wikipedia (2009b) entry, the "burgeoning zine movement took up coverage of and promotion of the underground punk scenes, and significantly altered the way fans interacted with musicians" (no page). These zines were distributed during concerts or via networks of friends and fans. They soon evolved into more personalized locations of expression and their topics and themes ranged far beyond the punk rock scene. They nonetheless retained their roots in a DIY ethic, becoming a key "gateway to DIY culture" and generating "tutorial zines showing others how to make their own shirts, posters, magazines, books, food, etc." (Wikipedia, 2009b). Increasingly, zines are published on the internet (sometimes referred to as "ezines"). Conventional paper zine production now also often involves computers in the production process, although today's zinesters typically retain the DIY ethos and the look and feel of original zines; for example, using computers to key and markup the text, then cutting and pasting texts and images onto each page after they have been printed, and then scanning or copying these pages as they are.

Of course, punk subculture nurtured the development of DIY music, whereby legions of bands generated audiences, created fan bases, recorded their music and produced merchandise outside the ambit of corporate labels and the kinds of constraints imposed by "commercial considerations." This created "opportunities for smaller bands to get wider recognition and gain cult status through repetitive low-cost DIY touring" (Wikipedia, 2009b). Above all, perhaps, so far as subsequent DIY music media is concerned

> punk taught people that you don't have to be virtuoso to . . . make music. Similarly, the computer-based music phenomenon has taught people they don't need instruments or other people to make music. Remix, as a particular form of that [DIY] principle, teaches people that anybody can comment on or interpret already existing music. Finally, as with punk, the expectation is not that you are remixing to secure immortality. The idea is that doing it yourself (DIY) is a worthwhile activity in and of itself (Jacobson, p. 32, this volume).

Other important DIY media practices and influences ran alongside punk in the 1970s (and earlier), like dance music and fan video remixing, but were not explicitly countercultural or ideological in the sense that punk was. Dance music remix dates to Jamaican dance hall culture in the late 1960s and the wish to customize existing music to suit the tastes and needs of different kinds of dance audiences. Drawing on the potentials of particular tools and technologies (e.g., turntables, magnetic tape, audio tape recording) DJs and individuals with access to recording equipment began using homespun techniques to remix songs. DJs used twin turntables so that they could play different versions of the same song simultaneously whilst manually controlling for speed (beats to the minute). Others edited tape recordings to meet their purposes, by sampling and splicing tapes, often literally "cutting and pasting" them, and by combining different tracks from one or more multi-track recordings. Remixers produced speedier versions of a song, a more stripped back sound, elongated songs to keep people dancing longer, and so on (Hawkins, 2004; Jacobson, this volume; Seggern, no date). When digital sound became the norm, all kinds of "sampling" techniques were applied, using different kinds of hardware devices or software on a computer.

The important point here is the innovative "make do" and "invent on the fly" character of this kind of remixing and modification of existing music. In the absence of specialist tools, techniques and knowledge for achieving certain purposes, people invented their own. In many cases they contributed to developing techniques and defining tasks that record companies subsequently took up. In this way they anticipated present day digital media developments where, for example, video games fans have developed innovative and cost-effective ways of producing videos using game engines and screen-capture recording software, in a process known as machinima. The various aesthetic and video techniques employed in machinima have influenced role-play video game design itself (especially with respect to the increasing sophistication of cut-scenes between game segments or levels), along with commercial media, including television advertising (e.g., Volvo's "Game On" and Coca-Cola's "Coke side of life" commercials) and commercial entertainment (e.g., the "Make Love not Warcraft" episode of *South Park* and MTV's machinima music videos) (see also Knobel & Lankshear, 2008; Picard, 2006; Chapter 6, this volume).

Similarly to the case of music remixing, access to analogue video recorders and commercial videos led to the emergence of fan-based video remixing, using footage recorded from television or videos. This was a linear and often tedious process that typically required many hours of manually working two analog video recorders. DIY music videos were especially popular, and the first Anime Music Videos (AMVs) were made by fans using analogue tools.

One VCR would play the source footage tape while the other would record the footage onto the AMV tape. The creator would record a piece of footage, pause the AMV tape, find the next piece of footage to use, record, and continue to repeat the slow, tedious process through the whole AMV. Music was put in at the end, often recorded off of a CD or tape (Springall, 2004, p. 22).

By the mid-1980s, DIY media were already a well-established popular cultural pursuit across a range of analogue formats: notably, zines, music remixing, self-published comics and fan fiction, and video remixing, film-making, and groups recording their own music. The ease, scale, quality and social organization of engagement in DIY media have, however, undergone a quantum change from the mid 1980s, as digital electronic tools, production techniques, and electronically networked communications have become increasingly accessible (for detailed accounts see, for example, Benkler, 2006; Burgess & Green, 2009; Bruns, 2008; Jenkins, 2006a, 2006b; Lankshear & Knobel, 2006; Leadbeater & Miller, 2004).

The DIY media scene today

In the sense we are using it here, "DIY media" comprise digital entertainment and expressive media—animation, live action video, music video, music, spoken voice tracks, other artistic works—produced by everyday people to meet their own goals and personal satisfactions. These goals and satisfactions might be associated with fanship in some larger phenomenon, affiliation with some social group, or interest in something particular, or might simply emerge out of having the opportunity to tinker with and explore the means for producing a media artifact of one kind or another.

DIY media in this sense are very much characterized by people being able to produce their "own" media—whether they be radio-like podcasts, "original" remixed music, animated video shorts, music videos, etc.—by making use of software, hardware and "insider" skills, techniques and knowledge that were previously the domain of highly-trained experts who had access to specialized and typically very expensive media production know-how, resources and spaces.

The increasing availability of free or almost free image, video and sound editing software, the increasing affordability of computers and digital still and video cameras (including free availability of such resources in a growing number of public libraries and community media centers), and the relative ease of finding online how-to guides, trouble-shooting help, raw resources (e.g., source video, sound effects) collectively make it possible for everyday people to become media *producers* rather than merely media consumers (Leadbeater & Miller, 2004; Shirky, 2008).

Axel Bruns (2008) takes this analysis further to argue for the emergence of "produsers." He explains how conventional distinctions between producers and consumers no longer hold within an online, networked economy and argues instead for recognizing a new hybrid: the *produser*. A produser, according to Bruns, is an "active" and "productive" user (p. 23) of content created, developed, modified, and shared by a community. That is, produsers *use* rather than consume (i.e., "use up") artifacts, knowledge, information, content and other resources (p. 14). Within this model of active and productive use, content or artifacts "prodused" by a community are always available to others and open to revision or reworking in ways, ideally, "which are inherently constructive and productive of social networks and communal content" (p. 23). The concept of produser captures how digital, distributed networks make possible non-hierarchical and open participation in online communities, the rapid sharing of ideas and resources, how users are able to tap into the collective intelligence of a group or community to contribute in small, modular ways to larger projects, and how knowledge can be used and shared among peers and experts. Bruns emphasizes the importance of internet-mediated networks and services—such as blogs, wikis, video-hosting sites, etc.—in helping make this possible.

Indeed, the genuine sophistication of even the most basic audio and editing programs and the possibility of drawing on existing media to resource DIY media projects mean it is quite possible for the everyday person to create a polished product without necessarily being "artistic" (i.e., able to draw well, sing beautifully, play a musical instrument, take museum-quality photos, etc.). For example, as mentioned earlier, free screen-recording software (like Fraps), role-playing video games or 3D virtual worlds that provide characters and scenes, and free video editing software can be used to produce machinima (see Chapter 6, this volume). Previously, this kind of animated video typically required numerous key frame and in-betweener artists, expertise in animation and general film effects and techniques, and/or access to and facility with computers designed especially for creating or editing the animation (costing tens of thousands of dollars), studio space, musicians to create the video soundtrack, voice actors, expertise in the areas of animation and filmmaking, serious funding, and so on. Now, it is perfectly possible for someone without any formal training in film or animation techniques, and who cannot "draw to save him/herself," to create an engaging animation in their home office or bedroom.

A sense of the sheer scale and range of DIY media engagement today can be gauged from looking at the proliferation of user-content management websites that have sprung up online since the early 2000s. These kinds of service sites do not create their own content but, instead, make it possible for everyday users to post their own content online. Massive sites like YouTube, OurMedia.org, Stickam, Blip.tv, Flickr, Picasa, Photobucket, PodcastAlley, Podomatic, and LibSyn, to name just a few, fall into this category. Not all of the content posted by users to such sites is DIY—a good deal of it is taken directly from television, DVDs, radio, or from other online spaces (e.g., photos of celebrities, other people's music remixes), although Eric Garland (2008), who is involved in the online measurement business, argues that user *redistributed* content should be considered an important part of DIY media. At the time of writing, the video hosting service, YouTube, is attracting over a billion views a day; the photohosting site, Flickr, hosts more than a billion images; and the podcast-hosting site, Podcast Alley, hosts 4.7 million podcast episodes.

In addition to these massive sites, numerous more specialized online sites exist that have been purpose-developed for hosting particular kinds of DIY media. Typical examples, among many others, include:

- Machinima.com—with over 26,000 unique visitors in September 2009—for hosting machinima videos and spanning a large number of types of machinima—categorized according to the game engine they use, and searchable by the kind they are—drama, comedy, thriller, romantic, fantasy, sci-fi, etc.

- AnimeMusicVideos.org, or AMV.org—with over 23,000 unique visitors in September 2009—is devoted to hosting anime music videos (video remixes that use predominantly anime footage and are set to music). As with Machinima.com, AMV.org enables viewers to search for videos by type (drama, comedy, romance, etc.) and by anime series (e.g., *Naruto, Great Teacher Onizuka, Evangelion,* etc.).

• Aniboom.com—with close to 68,000 unique visitors in September 2009—and Newgrounds.com—with 1.3 million unique visitors in September 2009—which host flash animations and flash games.

• StopMotionAnimation.com—with roughly 16,000 unique visitors in September, 2009—which hosts stop motion animations, spanning everything from claymation, doll and figurine animation, line-drawing animation, sand-based animation (2D and 3D), live action stop motion, everyday object stop motion, and so on.

DIY media creators often have a good sense of the professional standards typically applied to the media they themselves are creating (cf., comments by Matt in Chapter 9, this volume). This doesn't mean that working to professional standards is always a consideration in DIY media creation; the outcomes of rudimentary explorations of a new technique are often satisfying and sufficient. Morover, there are ample instances on YouTube of cellphone videos showing friends riding their bikes off piers or bridges into deep water (and all kinds of similar fare) to suggest that DIY media creation is often more concerned with maintaining social relationships than with exercising any will to production quality or conceptual sophistication. At the same time, accomplished DIY media creations reveal "amateurs working to professional standards" (Leadbeater & Miller, 2004, p. 9). Prior to the explosion of DIY media creation, knowledge of these professional standards was often confined to those who were highly trained in the area. These days, online how-to guides, dedicated open discussion forums where experts and novices alike can participate, help boards and blogs, user-created media content review and comment spaces, and ready access to what are regarded as exemplary models of the target media artifact make many elements of "professional standards" explicit and accessible to the everyday person (e.g., amateur anime music video makers committed to professional standards know that good quality AMVs don't include clips that are subtitled or have different screen resolutions from one another, that they avoid clichéd transitions between clips, and so on).

DIY media as a window on the contemporary

Part of our interest in DIY media stems from how experiences of creating and learning to create new media through participation in popular cultural pursuits employing new technologies within a range of "affinity spaces" (Gee, 2004) can be seen as instantiating and illuminating some important current trends to do with "how we identify ourselves, participate with others, connect with others, mobilize resources and learn" (Hagel & Seely Brown, 2005, p. 3). DIY media provide a window on some distinctively contemporary ways of "being in the world." In this section we will briefly address some aspects of identity, participation, resource mobilization and learning.

Identity

Identity is widely identified as a key to understanding entrée into and sustained participation in cultural practices of creating and sharing digital media within such pursuits as fanfiction writing, video game building or modding, creating movie trailers for fictional movies, music remix, and so on (see, for example, Alvermann et al., 2007; Alvermann & Heron, 2001; Black, 2007, 2009; Burn, 2008; Chandler-Olcott & Mahar, 2003; Gustavson, 2008; Hull, 2004; Lam, 2000; Pleasants, 2008; Thomas, 2007a, 2007b). In his recent discussion of "the digital society," Allan Martin (2008) presents a helpful line of argument for understanding why identity work has become such a visible focus of activity within contemporary daily life. Martin builds on work by people like Bauman (2000), Beck (1992), and Giddens (1999) to argue that under current conditions within societies like our own—where "the classical industrial order" prevalent from the mid-19th century has gradually dissolved into a society "of uncertainty and risk"—constructing individual identity has become "the fundamental social act" (Martin, 2008, p. 153). The declining significance of industry (and social class categories tied to types of employment), nation state, and institutionalized religion, which were "the three pillars of the 'modern' order," has robbed individuals of the "certainties . . . of work, order and belief" that they had long provided (ibid.). The idea of "the long term" has become increasingly meaningless, and for people enduring these *post*-modern conditions "life has become an individual struggle for meaning and livelihood in a world that has lost its predictability" (ibid.). As Martin puts it:

> The taken-for-granted structures of modern (i.e. industrial) society–the nation-state, institutionalized religion, social class–have become weaker and fuzzier as providers of meaning and, to that extent, of predictability. Even the family has become more atomized and short-term (2008, p. 153).

In the face of these conditions, says Martin, constructing individual identity "becomes the major life project" (ibid.), and within the daily pursuit of this end, consumption, community-building, and digital culture converge in interesting ways. Ways and styles of consuming—such as owning particular artifacts, or being a fan—become "badges of order" (p. 153) that offer at least some temporary or provisional sense of normality and existential safety. Since we can no longer take "the community" (as we previously knew and experienced it) "as a given that confers aspects of identity" (ibid.), the processes of building communities and actively finding communities to become involved and participate in have become "conscious action-forming parts" of constructing individual identity. Digitally-mediated participation in affinities and communities assumes major proportions in this context, including, of course, becoming involved in creating and sharing digital media. Martin notes that within societies like our own, digital tools have become an almost ubiquitous means for people to present themselves to society at large. They can do this

> by creating and broadcasting statements (developing blogs or personal websites, contributing to online fora, sending email, texting, presenting a curriculum vitae, etc.) or multi-media objects (mounted on social collection sites). [Digital tools] also enable social identity development, making oneself in interaction with others, members of "strong" groups such as family or friends, or "weak" groups such as online "communities" (2008, p. 155).

From this perspective, the nature and significance of high-investment participation in digital media affinities for doing identity work can be understood as an integral and radically coherent dimension of being a contemporary person living a contemporary life. We think it is especially important for educators and caregivers to consider this perspective when reflecting on (or worrying about) the kinds of investments young people make in pursuits like creating, sharing, and otherwise interacting around digital media creation and the kinds of preferences and priorities they exercise with respect to activities they choose to engage in most energetically and enthusiastically.

Participation

The phenomenon that Henry Jenkins identifies as an emerging *participatory culture* is crucial to understanding contemporary social and cultural life. Participatory culture is what happens when "consumers take media into their own hands" and become actively involved in contributing to cultural development through creating media, sharing it, and responding to it (Jenkins, 2006, p. 132; see also Benkler, 2006; Bruns, 2008; Chapter 3, this volume). Participation, in this sense, describes how consumers themselves can be media producers, side-stepping, or, at least, reconfiguring traditional relationships with broadcast media companies that previously placed consumers in passive, receiver roles. Jenkins claims that "[t]he power of participation comes not from destroying commercial culture but from writing over it, modding it, amending it, expanding it, adding greater diversity of perspective, and then recirculating it, feeding it back into the mainstream media" (Jenkins, 2006, p. 257; see also Bruns, 2008, p. 93). To participate in this kind of culture is to be both a consumer *and* a producer who contributes actively—albeit to varying degrees and in varying ways according to interest, time, resources, etc.—to the media available for others to view, listen to, read and enjoy and use in turn.

In an influential occasional paper published jointly by MIT and the MacArthur Foundation, Jenkins and colleagues (2006, p. 8) explain the rise of participatory culture in terms of social and cultural responses to "the explosion of new media technologies that make it possible for average consumers to archive, annotate, appropriate, and recirculate media content in powerful new ways" (Jenkins et al., 2006, p. 8). They define a "participatory culture" as one:

1. With relatively low barriers to artistic expression and civic engagement

2. With strong support for creating and sharing one's creations with others

3. With some type of informal mentorship whereby what is known by the most experienced is passed along to novices

4. Where members believe that their contributions matter

5. Where members feel some degree of social connection with one another (at the least they care what other people think about what they have created). (Jenkins et al., 2006, p. 7)

In the context of a much larger discussion of media education for the 21st century, Jenkins and colleagues highlight the creative and innovative dimensions of participating in what Gee calls affinity spaces. They identify affinity spaces as "highly generative environments, from which new aesthetic experiments and innovations emerge" (2006, p. 9) and argue that participating regularly in affinity spaces develops a range of skills and proficiencies that are likely to prove valuable in the workplace, as well as for being able to most fully enjoy one's interests (ibid., p. 10). These include: being comfortable with communicating via a range of electronic modes, being able to multitask and make rapid decisions, being able to navigate and process information obtained from a range of sources, being able to collaborate with diverse others.

With respect to our focus on DIY media specifically, Rebecca Black illuminates this generative nature of participating in affinity spaces in her own study of fan fiction writers (e.g., Black, 2007, 2008). Black describes how three fans of anime (e.g., the *Card Captor Sakura* series) became successful writers of fan fiction (stories based on existing media narratives and written by fans). These writers—all of whom were English language learners—wrote fanfics which they posted to the website Fanfiction.net, the premier online fanfic-hosting website. Over time, based on feedback received from other writers, they enhanced their creative narrative writing prowess, and each developed a large following of readers. In these cases, the affinity space comprised commercial anime series, fan websites and discussion boards devoted to these series, FanFiction.net (where authors can be reviewers and reviewers authors, regardless of writing expertise or number of fanfics posted to the site), and the availability of all kinds of informal support services (such as beta-readers who will read a story before it's posted online for public reading to help with editing and smoothing the prose).

Black documents how obtaining reviews from strangers provided her three informants with powerful motivation to continue writing and posting to the site. She further explains how participating in this site encourages and supports writers in developing original and innovative storylines, even if many of their principal characters are taken from existing commercial media. For example, one of her study participants explained in an interview (Black, 2006, p. 16) that when she realized that many of her readers had little understanding of Chinese and Japanese history she wrote two fanfics in response. One combined elements of the movie, *Memories of a Geisha*, and the anime character, Sakura (from the *Card Captor Sakura* series). The other was "set in 1910 Kyoto, Japan, [and centered] on Sakura's struggles with an arranged marriage" (ibid.).

Mobilizing resources

In their introduction to a stimulating discussion of emerging models for mobilizing resources, John Hagel and John Seely Brown (2005, p.1) remind us that in the course of their daily lives people perceive and act on the basis of "'common sense' assumptions about the world around us and the requirements to meet our goals" (ibid.). Such assumptions collectively make up "common sense models" for judgment, decision-making and action within everyday routines. Hagel and Seely Brown claim that each major technology shift generates a new common sense model, and that in the context of contemporary technology innovations—notably, the microprocessor and packet-switched electronic networks dating from the 1970s—we are now "on the cusp of a shift to a new common sense model" that will reshape many facets of our lives (ibid.).

Interestingly, in terms of our focus in this book, Hagel and Seely Brown identify digital media as a key domain within which early signs can be found of an important shift toward a new common sense model of how best to mobilize resources under foreseeable conditions of uncertainty, and where a focus on sustainability of resources will become increasingly important. They describe this emerging new common sense model in terms of a shift away from "push" approaches toward "pull" approaches. This shift can in turn be understood in terms of a convergence between the twin needs to confront uncertainty (itself partly a consequence of recent technological innovations) and to promote sustainability, on the one hand, and the opportunities technological innovations offer for meeting these same needs, on the other. Hagel and Seely Brown's argument has particular relevance to educators, because education/learning is a major sphere of resource mobilization, and to the extent that the projected shift from "push" to "pull" plays out, education/schooling will be impacted in far-reaching ways.

Very briefly, throughout the 20th century the dominant common sense model for mobilizing resources was based on the logic of "push." Resource needs were anticipated or forecast, budgets drawn up, and resources pushed in advance to sites of anticipated need so they would be in place when needed. This "push" approach involved intensive and often large-scale planning and program development. Indeed, Hagel and Seely Brown see programs as being integral to the "push" model. They note, for example, that in education the process of mobilizing resources involves designing standard curricula that "expose students to codified information in a predetermined sequence of experiences" (p. 3). Education, in fact, is a paradigm case of the push model at work.

According to Hagel and Seely Brown we are now seeing early signs of an emerging "pull" approach within education, business, technology, media, and elsewhere, that creates *platforms* rather than programs: platforms "that help people to mobilize resources when the need arises" (p. 3). More than this, the kinds of platforms we see emerging are designed to enable individuals and groups to do more with fewer resources, to innovate in ways that actually create new resources where previously there were none, and to otherwise add value to the resources we have access to. Pull approaches respond to uncertainty and the need for sustainability by seeking to expand opportunities for creativity on the part of "local participants dealing with immediate needs" (p. 4). From this standpoint, uncertainty is seen as creating opportunities to be exploited. According to Hagel and Seely Brown, pull models

> help people to come together and innovate in response to unanticipated events, drawing upon a growing array of highly specialized and distributed resources. Rather than seeking to constrain the resources available to people, pull models strive to continually expand the choices available while at the same time helping people to find the resources that are most relevant to them. Rather than seeking to dictate the actions that people must take, pull models seek to provide people on the periphery with the tools and resources (including connections to other people) required to take initiative and creatively address opportunities as they arise . . . Pull models treat people as networked creators (even when they are customers purchasing goods and services) who are uniquely positioned to transform uncertainty from a problem into an opportunity. Pull models are ultimately designed to accelerate capability building by participants, helping them to learn as well as innovate, by pursuing trajectories of learning that are tailored to their specific needs (p. 4)

We see all this, *par excellence*, in contexts of participation within DIY media affinities. Affinity spaces are paradigm instances of the kinds of platforms Hagel and Seely Brown have in mind. Their expansive character in terms of creativity and innovation is precisely what Jenkins and colleagues (2006) mean when they identify affinity spaces as *generative* environments. Indeed, the logic of the "pull" platform is precisely the logic of "participatory culture," viewed from the standpoint of resources and creativity.

Hagel and Seely Brown describe the emergence of pull approaches within media production (see also Bruns, 2008). DIY media producers take existing media resources and customize them to their individual needs, tastes and purposes—often with collaborative support of others—thereby creating an expanded range of media choices for others (cf. Hagel & Seely Brown, 2005, p. 6). This occurs at different levels and intensities of interaction and engagement.

> At the most basic level, younger generations of customers are increasingly customizing media to better suit their individual needs. For example, rather than relying on music companies to pre-determine the mix of songs on a CD . . . music listeners are [increasingly] downloading individual tracks and assembling [and sharing] their own tailored sequence of songs. (ibid.)

At another level, podcasters are sharing "their customized selections of music from many different artists with friends and wider audiences" (ibid.). At still another level, machinima movies made using massively multiplayer online role-playing games can involve large-scale collaborations. Because of the distributed nature of much of this kind of collaboration it is possible that many of those involved never meet face-to-face during—or even after—the project. "Illegal Danish Super Snacks" is a well-known machinima made within the online role-playing game, *World of Warcraft* (see: http://machinima.com/films.php?id=1940), and was shortlisted for a U.S. Machinima Award in 2007. This 20-minute video was a collaborative effort involving around 100 individual players from several countries—each operating their own game character within a series of designated locations within the game—along with 10 voice actors. A number of participants never met each other or the director of the machinima.

DIY media creators, then, can be seen as early exponents of "pull" approaches to mobilizing, using, and expanding resources. This further affirms their presence at the leading edge of contemporary trends.

Learning

Scholars like Rebecca Black (2008), David Buckingham (2003), Andrew Burn (2009), Julia Davies and Guy Merchant (2009), James Gee (2003,

2004, 2007), Henry Jenkins (2006; Jenkins et al., 2006), Marc Prensky (2006), Will Richardson (2006), Katie Salen (2008), John Seely Brown and Richard Adler (2008), and Constance Steinkuehler (2008), among others, have discussed at length how online resources and popular cultural affinities have converged in ways that enable and sustain modes of learning very different from the predominantly "push" approach of conventional schooling. Seely Brown and Adler (2008) discuss this convergence in relation to how new technologies have helped leverage the potential of "social learning" and then consider how these technologies might further contribute to the development of a "demand" or "pull" approach to learning—Learn 2.0—that will "better serve the needs of twenty-first century students" (p. 20).

By "social learning," Seely Brown and Adler mean learning based on the assumption that our understanding of concepts and processes is constructed socially in conversations about the matters in question and "through grounded [and situated] interactions, especially with others, around problems or actions" (2008, p. 18). From a social learning perspective, the focus is more on *how* we learn than on *what* we learn. It shifts "the emphasis from the content of a subject to the learning activities and human interactions around which that content is situated" (p. 18). This is just the kind of engagement and process a DIY media creator experiences when, for example, s/he interacts with peers to resolve (what turns out to be) a file compatibility or file conversion problem in the course of creating an AMV or a machinima movie.

Social learning also puts the emphasis squarely on "learning to be" (Seely Brown & Adler, 2008, p. 18; Gee, 2007, p. 172). According to Seely Brown and Adler (2008, p. 19), mastering a field of knowledge involves not only "learning about" the subject matter but also "learning to be" a full participant in the field. This involves acquiring the practices and the norms of established practitioners in that field or acculturating into a community of practice.

In the case of Rebecca Black's fan fiction writers mentioned previously, they are not learning fan fiction content *per se* but, rather, learning to be proficient/better/successful fanfiction authors—and learning a lot *about* fan fiction as a social practice in the process. In Chapter 9, our co-author and informant, Matt, describes key aspects of his own endeavors in learning to be the best AMV creator he can be.

With respect to burgeoning Web 2.0 resources and the possibilities for a Learn 2.0 model grounded in a social learning ethos, Seely Brown and Adler (2008) claim that resources like blogs and wikis, mashups, social networks and social network sites like Facebook or Orkut, content-sharing sites, online affinity spaces and the like, exemplify

[a] new user-centric information infrastructure that emphasizes participation (e.g., creating, remixing) over presentation, that encourages focused conversation and short briefs (often written in a less technical, public vernacular) rather than traditional publication, and that facilitates innovative explorations, experimentations, and purposeful tinkerings that often form the basis of a situated understanding emerging from action, not passivity (p. 30).

In a parallel argument to that presented by Hagel and Seely Brown (2005) about approaches to mobilizing resources, Seely Brown and Adler argue that current and foreseeable challenges posed by uncertainty and sustainability portend a need to move from a "push" approach to learning—that builds up "an inventory of knowledge in students'" heads—to a "demand-pull" approach. A pull approach shifts the emphasis toward "enabling participation in flows of action," focusing on "'learning to be' through enculturation into a practice as well as on collateral learning" (Seely Brown & Adler, 2008, p. 30). Such an approach would involve "providing learners with access to rich (sometimes virtual) learning communities built around a practice"—and resourced as appropriate from the bounty of the internet. Learning would be "passion-based": that is, "motivated by the learner either wanting to become a member of a particular community of practice or just wanting to learn about, make, or perform something" (ibid.).

This, of course, is the kind of learning that participants involved in the kinds of pursuits described in this book *already* engage in on a daily basis. It is steeped in values, processes, and forms of interaction that many young people associate with their *norm* for learning.

Overview of the book

The DIY media practices in which young people engage are many and diverse. There is not space to deal with all or even a majority of them here. The following chapters address music remix, podcasting, photosharing, photoshopping, machinima, flash animation, stop motion animation, and anime music videos. This selection aims to provide readers with a general introduction to a set of DIY media practices that are currently popular among young people and that are also sufficiently straightforward and accessible for "newbies" to muck around with and explore. Furthermore, the practices selected for treatment here mean that much of the book's content transfers well to other kinds of DIY media. For example, the video editing techniques described in Chapters 7 and 9 can be applied to creating live action videos and video remixes. The audio editing techniques described in Chapters 2 and 3 can be used to create soundtracks for more complex audiovisual projects. Archiving and tagging photos—discussed in Chapters 4 and 5—can inform a range of complex DIY media projects, such as large-scale, collaborative photo narratives or a series of user-created comics. At the same time, we are conscious that a range of popular DIY practices have, of necessity, been omitted. These include making live action videos (popular among live action role-players and cosplayers); non-commercial newsblogs; wikis; blog fiction and fictional blogs; digital music creation; digital art; videoblogging; comics/graphic novels; video remixes of different kinds (such as those focusing on political commentary, satire, parody, spoofing, etc.); eyewitness videos about newsworthy events (e.g., Witness.org); live-casting online (e.g., using Yahoo Live, or Justin.tv); to name just a few. We hope that the combined efforts of the authors in this collection will stimulate others to pick up some of the options we have had to pass up here.

The book has been organized in three parts: audio media, still media, and moving media—which might equally well be described as focusing on the audio, the visual and the audiovisual. From the outset we aimed to ensure that the book did not become dominated by one type of DIY media. Thinking in terms of *types* of DIY media was useful in this respect. The order of the sections isn't important and does not imply, for example, that podcasting is "easier" or less sophisticated than, say, creating machinima. Rather, organizing the book the way we have is intended to encourage readers to begin to form their own folksonomies around different ways of thinking about types of DIY media.

Finally, despite their scale and significance within popular culture, a number of the practices addressed below, such as creating flash animation and machinima, have received little research and scholarly attention to date. This book aims to help bring them into the frame.

References

Alvermann, D. E., & Heron, A. (2001). Literacy identity work: Playing to learn with popular media. *Journal of Adolescent & Adult Literacy*, 45(2), 11–122.

Alvermann, D. E., Hagood, M. C., Heron-Hruby, A., Hughes, P., Williams, K. B., & Yoon, J. C. (2007). Telling themselves who they are: What one out-of-school time study revealed about underachieving readers. *Reading Psychology* 28, 1–19.

Bauman, Z. (2000). *Liquid modernity.* Cambridge: Polity Press.

Beck, U. (1992). *The risk society.* London: Sage.

Benkler, Y. (2006). *The wealth of networks: How social production transforms markets and freedom.* New Haven, CT: Yale University Press.

Black, R. (2006). Language, culture, and identity in online fanfiction. *E-Learning.* 3(2): 170–184.

Black, R. (2007). Digital design: English language learners and reader reviews in online fiction. In M. Knobel & C. Lankshear (eds.), *A new literacies sampler* (pp. 115–136). New York: Peter Lang.

Black, R. (2008). *Adolescents and online fanfiction.* New York: Peter Lang.

Black, R. (2009). Adolescents, fan communities, and twenty-first century skills. *Journal of Adolescent & Adult Literacy.* 52(8): 688–697.

Brown, J. Seely & Adler, R. (2008). Minds on fire: Open education, the long tail, and Learning 2.0. *Educause* (January/February): 17–32.

Bruns, A. (2008). *Blogs, Wikipedia, Second Life, and beyond: From production to produsage.* New York: Peter Lang.

Buckingham, D. (2003) *Media education: Literacy, learning and contemporary culture.* Cambridge: Polity Press.

Buckingham, D., with Banaji, S., Burn, A., Carr, D., Cranmer, S. & Willett, R. (2004). *The media literacy of children and young people: A review of the research literature on behalf of Ofcom.* London: Ofcom.

Burgess, J. & Green, J. (2009). *YouTube: Online video and participatory culture.* Cambridge, UK: Polity.

Burn, A. (2008). The case of *Rebellion:* Researching multimodal texts. In J. Coiro, M. Knobel, C. Lankshear, C. and D. Leu, (eds), *Handbook of research on new literacies* (pp. 151–178). Mahwah, NJ: Erlbaum/Taylor & Francis.

Burn, A. (2009). *Making new media: Semiotics, culture and digital literacies.* New York: Peter Lang.

Chandler-Olcott, K., & Mahar, D. (2003). Tech-savviness meets multiliteracies: Exploring adolescent girls' technology-mediated literacy practices. *Reading Research Quarterly,* 38, 356–385.

Chu, J. (1997). Navigating the media environment: How youth claim a place through zines. *Social Justice, 24*(3), 71–85.

Davies, J. & Merchant, G. (2009). *Web 2.0 for Schools: Learning and social participation.* New York: Peter Lang.

Duncombe, S. (1997). *Notes from the underground: Zines and the politics of alternative culture.* New York: Verso.

Duncombe, S. (1999, December). DIY Nike style: Zines and the corporate world. *Z Magazine.* Retrieved Jun. 30, 2009, from: http://www.zcommunications.org/zmag/viewArticle/12804

Garland, E. (2008). BigChampagne: Online media measurement. Panel presentation. 24/7 DIY Video Summit. Institute for Multimedia Literacy, University of Southern California. February 8.

Gee, J. (2003). *What video games have to teach us about learning and literacy.* New York: Palgrave.

Gee, J. (2004). *Situated language and learning.* New York: Routledge.

Gee, J. (2007). *Good video games and good learning: Collected essays on video games, learning and literacy.* New York: Peter Lang.

Giddens, A. (1990). *Consequences of modernity.* Cambridge: Polity Press.

Gustavson, L. (2008). Influencing pedagogy through the creative practices of youth. In M. Hill & L. Vasudevan (Eds.), *Media, learning, and sites of possibility* (pp. 81–114). New York: Peter Lang.

Hagel, J. & Brown, J. Seeley (2005). From push to pull: Emerging models for mobilizing resources. Unpublished working paper, October. Retrieved Jan. 4, 2001, from: http://www.edgeperspectives.com

Hawkins, E. (2004). *The complete guide to remixing.* Boston, MA: Berklee Press.

Hull, G. (2004). Youth culture and digital media: New literacies for new times. *Research in the Teaching of English, 38*(2), 229–233.

Hull, G., & Schultz, K. (2001). Literacy and learning out of school: A review of theory and research. *Review of Educational Research, 71*(4), 575–611.

Illich, I. (1971). *Celebration of awareness: A call for institutional reform.* New York: Anchor Books.

Illich, I. (1973a). *Deschooling society.* Harmondsworth, UK: Penguin.

Illich, I. (1973b). *Tools for conviviality.* New York: Harper and Row.

Ito, M., Horst, H., Bittanti, M., boyd, d., Herr-Stephenson, B., Lange, P., Pascoe, C., & Robinson, L., with Baumer, S., Cody, R., Mahendran, D., Martínez, K., Perkel, D., Sims, C. & Tripp, L. (2009). *Living and learning with new media: Summary of findings from the Digital Youth Project.* Chicago, IL: MacArthur Foundation.

Jenkins, H. (1992). *Textual poachers: Television, fans and participatory culture.* New York: Routledge.

Jenkins, H. (2006a). *Convergence culture: Where old and new media collide.* New York: New York University Press.

Jenkins, H. (2006b). *Fans, bloggers, and gamers: Exploring participatory culture.* New York: New York University Press.

Jenkins, H., with R. Purushotma, K. Clinton, M. Weigel, & A. Robison (2006). *Confronting the Challenges of Participatory Culture: Media Education for the 21ˢᵗ Century.* Occasional Paper. Boston, MA: MIT/MacArthur Foundation.

Knobel, M. & Lankshear, C. (2002). Cut, paste, publish: The production and consumption of zines. In D. Alvermann (Ed.), *Adolescents and literacies in a digital world* (pp. 164–185). New York: Peter Lang.

Knobel, M. & Lankshear, C. (2008). Remix: The art and craft of endless hybridization. *Journal of Adolescent & Adult Literacy.* 51(2): 22–33.

Lam, W. S. E. (2000). Literacy and the design of the self: A case study of a teenager writing on the Internet. *TESOL Quarterly, 34*(3), 457–482.

Lankshear, C. & Knobel, M. (2006). *New literacies: Everyday practices & classroom learning.* Maidenhead, UK: Open University Press.

Lavine, F. & Heimerl, C. (2008). *Handmade nation: The rise of DIY, art, craft, and design.* Princeton, NJ: Princeton Architectural Press.

Leadbeater, C. & Miller, P. (2004). *The Pro-Am Revolution: How enthusiasts are changing our economy and society.* London: Demos.

Martin, A. (2008). Digital literacy and the "digital society." In C. Lankshear & M. Knobel (Eds.), *Digital literacies* (pp. 151–176). New York: Peter Lang.

McClay, J., Mackey, M., Carbonaro, M., Szafron, D., Schaeffer, J. (2007). Adolescents composing fiction in digital game and written formats: Tacit, explicit and metacognitive strategies. *E-Learning.* 4(3): 274–285.

Picard, M. (2006). Machinima: Video game as an art form? *Loading . . .* 1(1). Retrieved Aug. 4, 2009, from: http://journals.sfu.ca/loading/index.php/loading/article/view /17/20

Pleasants, H. (2008). Negotiating identity projects: Exploring the digital storytelling experiences of three African American girls. In M. Hill & L. Vasudevan (Eds.), *Media, learning, and sites of possibility* (pp. 205–233). New York: Peter Lang.

Prensky, M. (2006). *Don't bother me Mom—I'm learning!* New York: Paragon.

Richardson, W. (2006). *Blogs, wikis, podcasts, and other powerful web tools for classrooms.* Thousand Oaks, CA: Corwin Press.

Salen, K. (2008). Toward an ecology of gaming. In K. Salen (ed.), *The ecology of games: Connecting youth, games, and learning.* (pp. 1–20). Cambridge, MA: The MIT Press.

Scribner, S. & Cole, M. (1981). *Psychology of literacy.* Cambridge, MA: Harvard University Press.

Seggern, J. (no date). *Postdigital remix culture and online performance* (Exhibition at Unversity of California at Riverside). Retrieved July 1, 2007, from ethnomus.ucr.edu/remix_culture/remix_history.htm (No longer available)

Shirky, C. (2008). *Here comes everybody: The power of organizing without organizations.* New York: Penguin.

Spencer, A. (2005). *DIY: The Rise of Lo-Fi Culture.* New York: Marion Boyers.

Springall, D. (2004). "Popular Music Meets Japanese Cartoons: A History on the Evolution of Anime Music Videos." Unpublished undergraduate Honors Thesis. Birmingham, Alabama: Samford University, 2004.

Steinkeuhler, C. (2008). Cognition and literacy in massively multiplayer online games. In J. Coiro, M. Knobel, C. Lankshear, & D. Leu (Eds.), *Handbook of research on new literacies* (pp. 611–634). Mahwah, NJ: Erlbaum.

Thomas, A. (2007a). Blurring and breaking through the boundaries of narrative, literacy and identity in adolescent fan fiction. In M. Knobel and C. Lankshear (Eds), *A new literacies sampler* (pp. 137-166). New York: Peter Lang.

Thomas, A. (2007b). *Youth online: Identity and literacy in the digital age.* New York: Peter Lang.

Tiggs, T. (2006). Scissors and glue: Punk fanzines and the creation of a DIY aesthetic. *Journal of Design History.* 19(1): 69–83.

Wikipedia (2009a). DIY ethic. *Wikipedia.* Available from: Retrieved Nov. 1, 2009, from http://en.wikipedia.org/wiki/DIY_ethic.

Wikipedia (2009b). DIY. *Wikipedia.* Available from: http://en.wikipedia.org/wiki/DIY (accessed July 1, 2009).

Williamson, J. (1994, October). Engaging resistant writers through zines in the classroom. *Rhetnet: A Cyberjournal for Rhetoric and Writing.* Retrieved Jan. 1, 2001, from: http://wac.colostate.edu/rhetnet/judyw_zines.html

Part 1: Audio Media

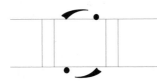

Chapter 2

Music remix in the classroom

Erik Jacobson

SECTION ONE

So what is music remix?

The idea of remix, taking an existing cultural resource and reshaping it, has at this point in time moved far beyond its origins in the world of music production. Indeed, the possibilities that digital technology and social networking software offer have led some to suggest that the concept of remix is a way to understand the current cultural moment (Knobel & Lankshear, 2008). This book itself is a testament to the kinds of interesting work people are doing today in a variety of media. This chapter will return to remix's origins in music to look at what it is, why people engage in remixing music, how to do it, and what the educational or developmental implications might be for using music remix in the classroom.

In some sense, remixing music is not a new idea. As long as people have been making music they have been taking the ideas of other musicians and reworking them into something they can call their own. A musician's interpretation of a song written by somebody else bridges the gap between the given and the created. For example, folk songs have been passed down over the years, reworked and adapted to the ears of subsequent generations. Many blues songs are built on the same basic bass lines and chord progressions, but blues musicians have been finding new ways to make songs and to put their spin on shared resources for over one hundred years. Jazz musicians can take a well-known melody and push it into new and interesting shapes (see Coltrane's version of *My Favorite Things* as an excellent example of how radical an interpretation can be while still being recognizable as a given song). However, the inherent malleability of music has come to be articulated differently in an age when technology allows people who cannot play any instruments themselves to rework and reshape previously existing songs. Reinterpretation can now be accomplished through the use of a computer, and increasing numbers of people create their interpretations or reinterpretations via digital technology.

How is remixing different from the creation of music using digital technology? One key difference is that remixing remains focused on reworking a given song (or songs). So, in contrast to digital music creation in which music is genuinely "composed" or where the musician takes bits of pre-existing songs (called sampling) to create a new song in which the source sounds are not necessarily recognizable (think of a dense collage of sounds), in remixes the source song(s) retain their identity in some recognizable form. Navas (2007a, no page) suggests that in remix, regardless of what is added or taken away, "the 'aura' of the original will be dominant." Thus, listeners should still recognize the elements of the original tracks on which a remix draws.

Thus, there is an inherent tension in remix, just as there is with any sort of (re)interpretation of an original or "source" song. While the "aura" of the original song might be dominant in a remix, it is always in danger of being lost in amongst the sounds added or subtracted to the final track. In this way, remix "challenges the aura of the original and claims autonomy even when it carries the name of the original" (ibid.). The question is how far can you go in remixing a song before it becomes something substantially new. Of course the question can also be asked at the other end of the continuum: How much has to be altered to constitute a remix? Is just adding an extra measure or chorus enough to justify adding "remixed by—" after the title of the source song? For amateur DIYers, such questions might not be so pressing, but for professional remixers such questions are currently hotly debated and difficult to resolve.

Another key difference between digital music creation and music remix is that remix tends to call attention to its own use of samples. "Samples" in this sense refer to discrete bits of music or sound taken from previously recorded materials that are placed in a new context (e.g., part of a drum rhythm, a guitar sound, a bit of a vocal). Remixers often expect their audiences to experience recognizing samples as part of the enjoyment and meaning making of listening. Indeed, part of the enjoyment of remixes is identifying how parts of the "original" sound within the context of the remix (e.g., spotting the music to *Dr Who* or *Inspector Gadget* when they are remixed with other songs). This recognition often draws on a shared nostalgia ("Do you *remember* that?!") and supports a sense of connection between the remixer and the audience. So for example, "Hip-hop producers, unlike pop producers, have therefore chosen not to mask the means of production and have often chosen to draw our attention to the fact that they have recontextualized elements from another artist's song" (Haupt, 2006, p. 110). In this way, sampling and remixing are posited as just as valid forms of interpretation as Coltrane's jazz improvisations using well-known songs.

Because the tension between the idea of an original and the autonomy of an interpretation is at the core of remixing, it allows remixes themselves to be commentaries on the process of creating meaning. For example, the drum tracks of James Brown's '60s funk masterpieces have long been a really rich resource that many remixers draw upon. When multiple remixers utilize the same sample (of *I Feel Good*, for example), the audience can reflect on how it is being used in each case. Each song becomes a lesson in remixing—"Oh, they started with that drum track, added the vocal, and then put in that guitar bit. . . ." Listeners can then decide if the assembled bits add up to a new meaning (that is, they appreciate the work that went into the remix and get something new out of the song) or are just so many parts that don't hang together ("Yeah, I get how they did it, but so what?").

Although avant-garde musicians began experimenting with editing tapes and using tape recorders as instruments as early as the 1950s, remixing really took off in popular music in the 1960s and the 1970s. Two common forms of remix from this era act as two ends of a remix continuum. At one end there are remixes in which the "aura" of the original is clearly dominant. At the other end are remixes that represent the limits of interpretation—they pose questions about how far a remix can go (as an interpretation of an original) without creating something entirely new.

Remixes that maintain a clear sense of the original are often created to be dance floor friendly. Remixers reshape aspects of the song to get people to move. At some level this represents remix at its most straightforward. For example, since the mid-1960s, DJs in Jamaica have been famous for taking the same instrumental track ("riddims") and laying new vocals over the top. In fact, you can purchase entire albums that consist of the same instrumental track played over and over. Each new vocal track creates another *version* (a Jamaican term for remix). Similarly, in the 1970s, producers took known songs (e.g., Blondie's *Atomic*), added additional percussion (or emphasized the beat in other ways) and extended the length of the track so it could be dropped into a seamless mix created by a club's DJ. Although this process was first associated with disco remixes of songs, it spread to other genres that were interested in getting people onto the dance floor, so that even punk bands like the Clash ended up with dance remixes of certain songs (see various mixes of their song *Magnificent Seven*, for example). Whether new vocals have been layered over an existing instrumental track or the beats under an existing vocal track have been altered, these types of remixes tend to be clearly recognizable as the song in the title.

At the other end of the continuum are remixes that exemplify a cut-and-paste aesthetic that challenges the idea of "the aura of the original." In these remixes songs are radically reshaped, sometimes with the use of multiple samples from a variety of sources. For example, the birth of hip-hop in the United States is grounded in DJs taking the drum breaks and other parts of funk and rock records (e.g., James Brown, Aerosmith, etc.) and using record scratching and sampling techniques to combine them while the MC rapped over the top. Unlike Jamaican riddims, hip-hop DJs didn't simply take one instrumental track and have their MCs rap over them—they created altogether new instrumental tracks from previously existing ones. Yet these instrumental tracks called attention to the source material and thus to themselves as a form of remix. For example, the first mainstream rap success, the Sugarhill Gang's *Rapper's Delight*, did not hide the fact that it was sampling from Chic's *Good Times*. In fact, hearing the Sugarhill Gang rap over the familiar guitar riff from *Good Times* was part of the fun of the song. This kind of sampling pushes the idea of remix to its logical extreme; the edge where the listener recognizes both the "aura" of the original source and the remix's call for recognizing something new. Thus, *Rapper's Delight* is a song in its own right, but it also would not exist without *Good Times*.

In the 1970s, remixing was happening both in the production studio (with high-end technology) and in the street (with turntables and mixers, electronic devices for combining different audio sources). By the mid-1980s cultural critics were suggesting that hip-hop represented the cutting edge of music creation, and that remixing was an art form that captured the zeitgeist. The idea of "remix" came to be seen as a cultural process more generally (rather than just limited to music), and the cut-and-paste aesthetic was seen as a claim to some new sorts of knowledge (see the flowering of postmodernist writing about culture, for example). At a more concrete level, what caught people's attention was that rather than reworking old forms like folk and the blues on traditional instruments, people engaged in remix were interpreting songs without actually using instruments.

By the late 1980s and early 1990s, remixing became part of the mainstream. In the studio, pop acts started using pre-existing recorded music as source material. While some of these artists focused on sampling a diverse array of sounds to create complex compositions (see the Beastie Boys' critically lauded album *Paul's Boutique*), others worked with just one or two recognizable bits of songs (see *Bittersweet Symphony* by The Verve, built on a sample from the Rolling Stones' *Sympathy for the Devil*, or MC Hammer's *U*

Can't Touch This, which basically consisted of him rapping over Rick James' *Superfreak).* Moby's album *Play* consisted of old gospel vocal tracks set to new electronic music compositions. Subsequent critical debate about *Play* focused on the nature of remix ("Who is the author of this?") as much as it did on ongoing arguments about the politics of cultural appropriation ("How does race factor into who gets recognized as an author/musician?").

Since that time, the advent of cheap music editing software has moved the creation of remixes from the production studio back into the hands of the people (as it was with the birth of hip-hop in the first place). Remixing now takes place in basements and bedrooms all across the globe. Websites provide samples for use and places to share remixes. Chat rooms allow for communication between people engaged in remixing. This period has also seen the advent of a popular form of remixing called mash-ups, in which two (or more) songs are combined to make one song in which both parts are still recognizable. A vocal track from one song might be placed over the music track from another song. Oftentimes this is done to make a point (e.g., "these songs are very similar despite being made by different artists possibly working in different genres") or in an attempt to be funny by using the sharp contrast between the songs (e.g., combining a Britney Spears' pop song with a heavy metal track by Metallica). Perhaps the most famous example of this is DJ Danger Mouse's *Grey Album*—a mash-up of the Beatles' *White Album* with Jay-Z's *Black Album.* These mash-ups are not legal, and not intended for sale but instead are circulated among those interested in the format.

There are many reasons for why people get involved in remixing music, but most seem to do so for pleasure, politics, or the intersection of the two. Just as is the case with traditional instruments, people simply like to create music. The fact that it can be done on computers using samples doesn't alter this pleasure. There is a creative and artistic urge satisfied by making remixes. For other people, there is a simple pleasure in working with new digital technologies to produce new music. Many people just like to play around with software or hardware by taking them for a test spin. Creating remixes is one way to see what they can achieve with the digital technology they have (which is also the case with other digital technologies discussed in this volume). Other people engage in music remixing because they are attracted to the ideological element of it. This can be as straightforward as adding a voice clip of a politician or public figure to an existing track (e.g., dropping samples of a speech by George Bush into a song). Some see the format and process of remix itself as ideological in nature and part of a larger cultural critique of ideas and assumptions about authorship or the ownership of art. For this reason, reworking parts of the existing music canon (e.g., a Beatles song, a Beethoven symphony) and re-envisioning it is seen as a political act. This idea finds support in the legal response to some high-profile examples of remixing. For example, the band Negativland was sued by U2 and others for a remix of *I Still Haven't Found What I'm Looking For* that sampled a weatherman reading the lyrics of the song and Casey Kasem making off-color off-air comments about U2 (see Negativland, 1995, for an account of the case). DJ Danger Mouse's *Grey Album* was never an official release, but the Beatles' record company sued to force him to stop distributing it. Interestingly, this act might have extended the life of this mash-up, as people interested in remix culture became involved, and the continued distribution of the recording became a political act (see Ayers, 2006, for an account).

Although the *Grey Album* is the most celebrated case of remix as a political act to date, many people involved in remix culture are interested in exploring new ideas about the ownership of intellectual or artistic creations. The open source software movement, shareware and copyleft all have analogies in the music production community. Many of those involved in remix culture reject traditional ideas about ownership. Like the open, collaborative service, Wikipedia, audio remix can be seen as a democratic ideal, in which anybody with a relevant set of software and hardware and access to samples (or songs that can be sampled) can become an artist. People create songs or samples and post them on the internet, with the expectation and hope that somebody else will pick them up and make something out of them in turn. Remix, in this way, is at the forefront of greater debates about what it will mean to create or to own a piece of artwork (cf. Lessig, 2008). It also extends some of the lessons of punk rock. Punk taught people that you don't have to be a virtuoso to get up on stage and make music. Similarly, the computer-based music phenomenon has taught people they don't need instruments or other people to make music. Remix, as a particular form of that principle, teaches people that anybody can comment on or interpret already existing music. Finally, as with punk, the expectation is not that you are remixing to secure immortality. The idea is that doing it yourself (DIY) is a worthwhile activity in and of itself.

There are a number of websites where you can explore the current world of music remix. The four listed below illustrate many of features discussed above:

(a) ccMixter (http://ccmixter.org)
The site describes itself in this way:

> ccMixter is a community music site featuring remixes licensed under Creative Commons where you can listen to, sample, mash-up, or interact with music in whatever way you want (ccMixter.org, 2008, main page)

The site contains samples and remixes that are available for use in remixing (this includes a cappella vocal tracks, too). The site also has editors' picks and playlists that highlight good work available via this site. Artists can upload profiles of themselves and samples of their work to this space. Data are included about which songs have been remixed. There are chat boards (http://ccmixter.org/forums/7) where people pose specific questions about the remix process, ask for compositional advice, or call for project participants. Sample topics include, "A call to all singers for a slow blues rock record," "How to make my mix sound professional," and "Compositional methods."

(b) Opsound: Open Sound Resource Pool (http://www.opsound.org)
The site describes itself in this way:

> Opsound is a gift economy in action, an experiment in applying the model of free software to music. Musicians and sound artists are invited to add their work to the Opsound pool using a copyleft license developed by Creative Commons. Listeners are invited to download, share, remix, and reimagine. (Opsound.org, 2008, main page)

The site has songs and remixes made available by artists under a Creative Commons Attribution Share Alike license.

(c) Remix Fight (http://www.remixfight.org)
This site was created to provide a chance for remixers to *compete* with each other. In a FAQ section they explain:

> Remix Fight is a remixing community open to everyone. We get people to send us source files for their songs and then make that source available for download. People download that source, make a remix, and then e-mail an mp3 of their mix to us. Then, we post all the mp3s we've received and set up a poll so that visitors to the site can listen to the mixes and vote on which one they like the best. At the end of the month, we close the poll and announce a winner. (Remix Fight, 2008, Frequently Asked Questions)

Remix Fight is a handy site for music remix beginners or "newbies" to spend time on, listening to good and bad quality remixes alike in order to obtain a sense of what can (and perhaps should not) be done.

(d) The Free Sound Project (http://www.freesound.org)
This site is focused on sounds and sound effects, rather than songs, but still encourages people to remix. For example, adding additional sounds to an existing song track can radically alter the mood of the song or even change its meaning.

SECTION TWO

How to make your own basic remix

There are many different software programs that can be used to create a music remix. Typically, remixing is done using the same programs that are used to create digital music. Some of these programs are proprietary and thus need to be purchased. There are products available only for Mac (e.g., GarageBand) and only for PCs (e.g., Fruity Loops, M-Audio Session Software). There are some programs that are available in two versions: the basic (or demo) one is free and the more advanced one needs to be purchased (e.g., AcidPlanet, Sound Studio). In addition to using software programs that are housed in the user's computer, remixing can also be done entirely on-line. For example, Remix Galaxy (http://www.remixgalaxy.com) is a website that has a sequencer and samples that can be used to create new remixes.

For each digital music or remix software program there tends to be online tutorials and chatrooms in which users can help each other out. In addition to the site noted above, there are some sites that provide general advice about remixing (e.g., http://www.teachdigital.pbwiki.com/digital-music). Regardless of which platform is being used, the process of remixing in each is basically the same. Multiple audio files are added as individual tracks which are then combined to form an integrated piece of music. These tracks can be used to add new sounds or to reshape elements of an existing song. The window of each music remix program provides a menu of editing options. For example, the user can change the volume, the pitch, or the tempo of the sounds they input into the file. Most procedures rely upon cut-and-paste processes. That is, the user highlights parts of a song they want to copy, copies this selection to the computer's clipboard, and then pastes the selection into a track in its new form. When possible, the vocal track can be separated from the instrumental track in the same way. More detailed or complex remixes take advantage of higher-end functions, but a user can create their first remix without having to master very many key strokes.

For the purposes of this chapter, we will look at remixing using Audacity, which is available free online (as part of a Creative Commons licensing agreement). There is a free user's manual for Audacity (http://audacity.source-forge.net/help/documentation) as well as a shorter online help guide (http://audacity.sourceforge.net/onlinehelp-1.2/reference.html). The directions given below for how to create a basic remix draw on both of these resources (see also, Chapter 3 in this volume). Although the examples presented are from Audacity, the steps covered will basically be the same for any kind of remixing and music remix program.

After selecting a song for remixing, you:

1. Create a File

2. Work with Samples

3. Build the Remix

4. Export the Song

Each of these will be reviewed in turn.

1. Create a File

In any remix software platform, you begin by creating a new file or project. For example, in Audacity, you begin a new project by moving the cursor to "File" on the menu bar on the top of the screen and selecting "New." This will create a new file without any tracks. To import a whole song, you move to "Project" on the menu and select "Import Audio." This will allow you to select the song you wish to start with, and will create a stereo audio track. In this case, I will be remixing *We Shall Not Be Moved* as performed by Mavis Staples, so I have imported this song intact. Figure 2.1 is a screen shot of what the project looks like at this point.

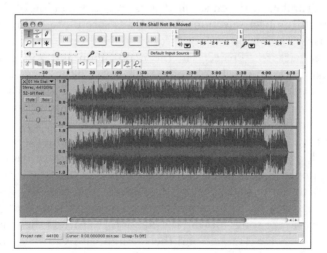

Figure 2.1: A song file imported into Audacity

The waveform display allows users to move around within the song file (e.g., for editing or sampling purposes) by using the "shape" of the track. By zooming in on the display (available under the "View" section of the menu), users can find pauses or breaks in the music, which is helpful when selecting samples. The user can also listen to any section of the file by moving the cursor, clicking on a location within the track, and hitting the "play" button on the upper part of the window. The other buttons (see Figure 2.1, top left-hand side) provide additional typical audio functions (record, pause, stop, fast forward, and rewind).

2. Work with Samples

Once the focal song has been imported, users can begin remixing by adding additional audio tracks. To do this, move to the menu bar and under "Project" select either "New Stereo" or "New Audio" track. This places a new track right below the already imported track (in the present example, Mavis Staples' *We Shall Not Be Moved*). Here you also can import samples, loops or other sounds (using "Input Audio" under "Project") or start working with pieces of the original song.

For example, for my project, the first decision I made was to take parts of the song itself to use in the remix. The beginning of this version of the song has a few measures of a slow drumbeat without any vocals. I liked this part and thought that I could layer some vocals from other sources on top of it. To create this sample I listened to the track again and stopped the cursor at the point where I wanted the sample to end (in time with a completed pattern of the drumbeat). I then scrolled back to the beginning of the song to highlight the drumbeat selection. When I was sure it was what I wanted, I copied it (using Command + C, or "Copy" in the drop-down "Edit" menu). Next I went back to "Project" in the main menu and added another—blank—audio track. In that blank audio track I pasted the copy of the sample I had just created (by using Command + V) (see Figure 2.2). This is a basic copy-and-paste procedure and it can be used throughout the process of making a remix with Audacity (as well as other remixing software).

As Figure 2.2 shows, the isolated sample of the drumbeat is very short. To create a longer passage that can provide a context for or background to new vocal samples, I have to paste multiple copies of the sample side-by-side within the same audio track. Once I have a sense that this new instrumental section is long enough, I can move the original source song back in its play track by selecting the song, moving the cursor forward, and then under "Project," selecting "Align Tracks," and then "Align with Cursor." This isolates the instrumental section so that I can easily add other samples to it. Figure 2.3 shows what my project now looks like on-screen at this point.

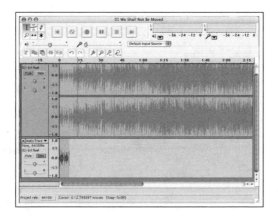

Figure 2.2: Small drumbeat sample in Audacity

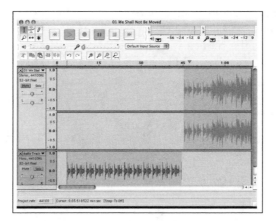

Figure 2.3: Adding a sample to a remix project

For my project, I wanted to add additional samples to the song. The easiest way to do this is to create new audio tracks into which you import samples. You can use the "Import Audio" function to import any sound files that you already have on hand (e.g., other songs, other sounds, etc.). Once they have been imported, you can edit them into the form you want (using the cursor and the function commands). If you have a large sample and you are going to delete most of, it might be easier to create a new project altogether and do the editing in that file before importing it into your current project. Copying-and-pasting works across project files as well as within them.

Of course, you can also create new sound files by recording directly into your project file. There is software that allows you to record whatever you are listening to on the computer (e.g., internet radio, sound files from web pages, etc.), but that is not required to do this. All you need are a few cheap cables from an electronics store to have your computer serve as both receiver and recorder. Most computers have a jack for headphones and an audio input jack (typically on the side of laptops and on the front of desktop computer harddrive boxes). By using a cable to connect the headphone jack to the audio input jack, you can have Audacity record whatever is coming out of the headphone jack. In order to hear and monitor the process, you can buy a cord that plugs into the headphone jack on one end and has two additional jacks on the other end. Your headphones can plug into one, and the cord connecting to the audio input jack can go into the other.

For this project, I am interested in grabbing a sample of Martin Luther King, Jr.'s last speech. I don't have a copy already on hand, but I know that it is available on YouTube. Once I locate it there, I create a new audio track within Audacity and click the record button on the top of the screen.

Then I hit play on the YouTube video. I listen as the whole track is recorded, and then I copy and paste to grab the samples I want for my remix. Figure 2.4 shows the section of the program I use for this part of the process. The record key is the button with the circle on it, and the chart to the right provides information about the volume of the input (see Figure 2.4).

Figure 2.4: Using Audacity to record sound playing on your computer

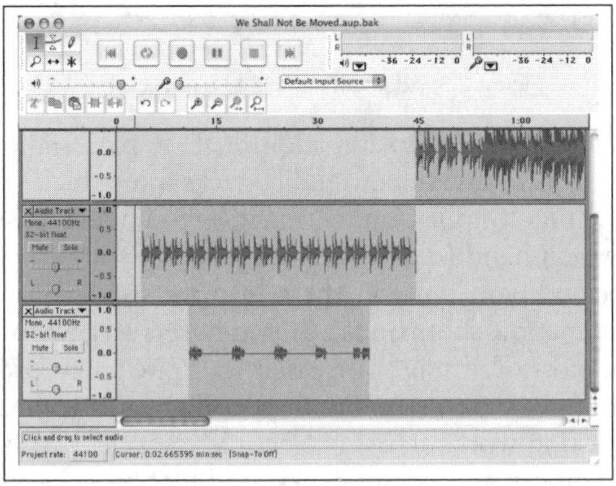

Figure 2.5: Creating a loop of audio plus stretches of silence

In my project, I want to use three sound samples from the video I've found, but I don't want them stacked up next to each another. I can create spacing in the Martin Luther King, Jr. sample track by adding the amount of silence I desire. To do this I go to "Menu," select "Generate," choose "Silence" and then input the number of seconds of silence I would like. Now I have created a larger loop or sample of Martin Luther King's words that I am going to add to my mix. I can copy and paste this loop throughout my project. Figure 2.5 shows how my project file now looks:

The project now comprises three "rows" of sounds. The track in the top row is the original song. The second track down is the drum instrumental, and the third track down comprises the Martin Luther King, Jr. samples.

To adjust the volume of each track, users can click on the "Audio Track" box, which appears directly to the left of the track (see the left-hand side of Figure 2.5). Moving the cursor up and down on the - / + scale changes the "gain" applied to the track. In my case, I increased the volume of the Martin Luther King Jr. samples (the third track in Figure 2.5) to make sure they would not get lost amongst the other elements of the mix. As you move through the creation of the remix, you will find yourself listening to certain sections over and over to hear if they are working.

3. Build the Remix

Once the initial track has been input, and new audio tracks have been created and added to the project, the remix process now involves repeating the same actions: Identifying samples and sounds that you would like to add, editing and reshaping the samples, and placing them in the appropriate place in a given track. In addition to cutting and pasting, loops and samples can be reshaped using tools built into the program. Under the "Effects" menu, there is a wide range of ways to work with the sounds that have been input. These include, for example, bass boost, fade in/out, wahwah, tremolo, reverse, change speed, and change pitch, among many others.

These are the kinds of things that are covered in the user guide, but perhaps are best learned through actually making your own music remix and by reading and participating in online remix chat-rooms or forums. The Audacity Wiki (http://wiki.audacityteam.org/index.php?title=Tutorials) provides step-by-step tutorials in:

- Reworking voice records

- Vocal removal

- Mixing stereo tracks to mono

- Audio restoration (e.g., click and noise removal)

Other support and feedback are offered at the sites mentioned in the first section of the chapter (e.g., ccMixter.org).

In terms of completing my "We Shall Not Be Moved" remix project, I did the following:

- Near the beginning of the song I added an introduction by Barbara Dane (from her own recorded version of "We Shall Not Be Moved")
- I continued to add samples from the Martin Luther King, Jr. speech throughout the project
- I added vocals from a Spanish-language version of the song ("No Nos Moverán") and several other versions of the song (by the Almanac Singers, the Seekers, and some un-attributed singers who were part of the civil rights movement in the U.S.)
- Finally, I added an "outro" by pasting the drum beat loop that I had created earlier on and used it to close my remix.

4. Export the Song

When the project is finished, you are ready to export the file. This means you save the song as a single file that can be burned to a disk, copied to an mp3 player, uploaded to the internet, and so on. Remix music programs by default save your file as a "project" that can *only* be played within the remix program itself. This is done so that you can continue editing your project. Once you export your remix file, you will no longer be able to pick it apart, copy and paste in new sections, or edit "inside" the file.

Depending upon the remix software you are using, exporting your song may be done in several different ways. Some software allows for directly exporting files into formats like mp3. Audacity does not. The Audacity User's Guide explains:

> Audacity cannot encode MP3 files by itself, because the MP3 encoding algorithm is patented and cannot be legally used in free programs. However, Audacity has been programmed to recognize other existing MP3 encoders that you can download separately. All you have to do is to obtain the appropriate MP3 encoder and then show Audacity where it is located. (Audacity, 2008, no page)

The Audacity website (http://audacity.sourceforge.net/) provides links to encoders that will run on Windows, Linux/Unix and Macintosh platforms. There will be similar information for other platforms at their own sites, or an internet search will help you find what you need.

Once completed and exported to a standard audio format (e.g., *.mp3, *.wav, *.aiff, *.ogg), the project is now transportable as a complete, stand-alone song.

SECTION THREE

The educational benefits of music remix

Hopefully the discussion in the opening section of this chapter has shed some light on why people engage in music remixing and how easily it can be done using readily available technology. The third and final question to be addressed in this chapter is how and why remix might be used in the classroom. There are (at least) three possible educational reasons to think about remix as a classroom activity: (1) its connection to other skills needed in the contemporary world; (2) the way it opens up discussions about the nature of artistic creation; and (3) the fact that it offers students a chance to discover and articulate their own ideas about hermeneutics, or text analysis and interpretation. Each of these is worthwhile on its own (that is, in relation to remixing music) but can also be applied usefully to other creative works (including those based on print) and academic disciplines. Each of these suggested educational benefits is addressed in turn below.

21ˢᵗ century skills

Recent studies have found that one in every two American teens have used digital technology to create media content and that one-third of them have shared this content on the internet (Lenhardt & Madden, 2005; cited by Jenkins, 2006, p. 3). No doubt many of these content producers are music remixers. On the surface this seems to indicate that students are doing fine without having these activities take place in the classroom. However, Jenkins (2006) suggests that while these adolescents are developing skills associated with content production and dissemination, they can still benefit from school-based pedagogical interventions. One reason for this is the existence of what has been called a "participation gap" in which there is "unequal access to the opportunities, experiences, skills and knowledge that will prepare youth for full participation in the world of tomorrow" (Jenkins, 2006, p. 3). This focus on "full participation" is different from long-standing concerns about gaps in access to computer technology itself (what has been called "the digital divide"). Although increasing numbers of students have access to computers and software, they may not have opportunities for meaningful participation in any of the various communities that digital technology and social networking platforms foster and support. It is *participation* in these communities that allows students to fully develop the range of skills required in the current digital age.

For example, beyond basic skills such as keyboarding and basic computer operations, Jenkins (ibid.) emphasizes the importance of the following "21st Century Skills."

- *Play:* The capacity to experiment with one's surroundings as a form of problem-solving

- *Performance:* The ability to adopt alternative identities for the purpose of improvisation and discovery

- *Simulation:* The ability to interpret and construct dynamic models of real-world processes

- *Appropriation:* The ability to meaningfully sample and remix media content

- *Multitasking:* The ability to scan one's environment and shift focus as needed to salient details

- *Distributed Cognition:* The ability to interact meaningfully with tools that expand mental capacities

- *Collective Intelligence:* The ability to pool knowledge and compare notes with others toward a common goal

- *Judgment:* The ability to evaluate the reliability and credibility of different information sources

- *Transmedia Navigation:* The ability to follow the flow of stories and information across multiple modalities

- *Networking:* The ability to search for, synthesize, and disseminate information

- *Negotiation:* The ability to travel across diverse communities, discerning and respecting multiple perspectives, and grasping and following alternative norms

This is not the place in which to go into detail about each of these skills (Jenkins' report is available online for readers who would like more detail), but it is worthwhile to note that engaging in remix depends upon the existence and development of a number of the skills identified. Certainly, remixing is an opportunity for play and performance (as is the production of any piece of music or art). Remixers work with new technologies and new sounds to explore the possibilities of each. Additionally, remix as a political act (whether by adding overtly ideological content to songs or by distributing freeware programs to facilitate remixing) is grounded in a deep praxis where one's philosophy is enacted and reflected upon as part of play and performance.

For example, in 2007 the musician M.I.A. released a song called *Paper Planes*. The base of the song is the melody and rhythm of the Clash song *Straight to Hell*, and M.I.A. raps over a remixed version (that includes the noise of cash registers and gun shots—the sound of money being made in ways legal and illegal). In the original song, the Clash used the generation of children fathered and abandoned by United States soldiers in Vietnam as a metaphor for the exploitative relationship between Western capitalist powers and oppressed populations in Southeast Asia. M.I.A., born in London to a politically radical Tamil family, spent most of her early life moving from country to country (including Sri Lanka, India, and back to England). In remixing *Straight to Hell*, M.I.A. stakes a claim as a member of the population the original song focuses on, directs her lyrics to what it takes to get by as an immigrant in an unwelcoming society, and adds a sonic overlay (e.g., the gun shots) that adds "street cred" and political commentary—this is the sound of life of people in the working-poor Diaspora. Many of our students are using their own homemade remixes to make similar commentaries about their own identities and border crossings. Indeed, this connection of remix technology to daily decisions around how we perform and/or resist cultural, economic, or gender identities means that we have to listen for the new ways in which our students are working through long-standing issues.

Indeed, what might be distinct about remix (compared to the traditional production of music) is how heavily it draws on some of the other "21st Century" skills identified by Jenkins. Most importantly, the technical or mechanical aspects of remix (e.g., finding the source song, identifying the sounds or materials that will be used in the remix, sharing the song on the internet) are both individual and communal in nature. To participate in online remix communities means to recognize where resources are stored, how to access them, and how to share them in return. Being an active member of a music remix chat room or discussion board means you are willingly sharing resources and are open to the idea that knowledge is an assemblage of ideas and experiences generated by novices and experts alike. This use of networking, distributed cognition and collective intelligence is the hallmark of online life and students must be comfortable with each of them for meaningful participation to occur. For some students, remixing might provide the perfect invitation to join this kind of communal work. It certainly can be argued that sharing music remixes (and advice about how to remix) is a much better use of social networking technology than page after page of photos of adolescents getting drunk or throwing faux gang signs. Remixing provides opportunities for the kinds of project-based, collaborative learning for which teachers strive.

Creation and dialog

Sharing information or content via online communities or through peer-to-peer networks has led many to wonder if this generation of students will develop "a changed attitude toward intellectual property" (Jenkins, 2006, p. 3). On the one hand, this "changed attitude" can be framed as negative (e.g., commonly expressed concerns about illegal file sharing or the "stealing" of music). From this perspective, young people who share commercial music without concern for copyright are described as parasitic, benefiting from the work of others without paying their fair share. However, this "changed attitude" toward intellectual property can also be framed as a positive if it is understood as escaping from the weight of privileged authorship and canonical tradition (compare, for example, 20th century movements in visual arts in which artists played with intellectual property, like Duchamp painting a moustache on a copy of the Mona Lisa). Remixing treats everything as fair game for reinterpretation and everything as a possible resource for crafting a (re)interpretation. Indeed, remixing music fits very well with Jenkins' definition of appropriation as "the ability to meaningfully sample and remix media content" (2006, p. 4). This is a creative act that depends on using pre-existing materials that might be somebody's "intellectual property." However, remixing is not simply taking somebody else's intellectual property and putting your name on it. Jenkins (2006) suggests that the skill of appropriation, which is a key dimension of remix:

> may be understood as a process that involves both analysis and commentary. Sampling intelligently from the existing cultural reservoir requires a close analysis of the existing structures and uses of this material; remixing requires an appreciation of emerging structures and latent potential meanings. Often, remixing involves the creative juxtaposition of materials that otherwise occupy very different cultural niches (p. 33).

Understanding appropriation as a creative act (of which music remix is just one example) calls attention to two key aspects of the creation of art. First, it supports the idea that no work of art is created *ex nihilo* or "out of nothing." Artists are always "sampling intelligently" from the resources to which they have access (e.g., historical and contemporary content, styles and themes). Second, appropriation understood as a creative response to other work exemplifies the kind of conversations we see happening in other art forms. Art implies, either explicitly or implicitly, a commentary on other art (and the world). One painter's work can be understood as a thoughtful rejoinder to another. Poets write and respond to other poets, and novelists do the same. People who create remixes engage in just these sorts of ongoing dialogues, reshaping previous works and expecting their own work to be reshaped or cut-up for use in another remix. Although this process is often addressed in art and English classes, it might seem so abstract that students don't get a sense of it in real-world terms. With well-structured pedagogical interventions, students and teachers can make productive analogies between music remix as commentary and appropriation in art (more generally) as commentary. Having students themselves engaging in the act of commenting through appropriation might make it clearer. For example, imagine asking students to remix a recording of a traditional English folk song. Then, at the same time, imagine providing students with information about the traditional plots, characters, themes, and tropes that Shakespeare had on hand before he started putting paper to pen. It takes nothing away from the genius of Shakespeare to suggest that he appropriated materials from the "existing cultural reservoir" (Jenkins, 2006, p. 33). Instead, it points to the very nature of that genius. Discussing with students why his particular tale of star-crossed lovers is so well loved above countless other versions of the same story encourages them to think deeply about his art and craft.

This analogy between remixing music and art as conversation also can be extended to the social sciences. For example, in some sense historiography is the study of History as sampling. That is, we can ask the same sorts of questions of historians as we do of musicians, writers and artists. For example, how do those telling or writing history select from available resources to shape the story that they want to tell? How is one "history" a commentary on another "history" of the same event? How many fresh elements or perspectives does a "history" have to have to constitute a new contribution (rather than simple plagiarism)? Like working with Shakespeare, it is not a large leap from having students articulate the process of (re)interpreting a song to them analyzing the interpretive work of historians. Remixing and the discipline of History are both ongoing conversations about meaning.

Finding hermeneutics

For the last few decades the following aphorism has made the rounds: "talking about music is like dancing about architecture." Its origin has been attributed to many different people (and thus is a kind of free-floating meme), but it typically carries the same meaning. That is, talking about music is counter-productive because spoken language cannot possibly capture or express the meaning found in music. For example, you can analyze the score, list the instrumentation and note the techniques the musicians are using, but these are experiences of a different order to listening to (or playing/singing) this music. (It is said that Tolstoy was once asked what *Anna Karenina* was about, and he replied that the questioner should start reading at the first word of the novel). Thus, talking about remix and sampling might serve to place us some distance from experiencing (and fully understanding) the meaning of any given remix. While playing a given piece, musicians have always been able to play passages or quotes from other songs within a piece to call attention to the dialogue in which they are engaging (jazz music is the perfect example of this). What is different about remixing is that rather than simply being copies or recreations of those passages, remixes of music often utilize samples that call attention to themselves as such. These are not exactly direct quotations, since the original performances are sampled and reshaped, but they have a distinct quality to them. They combine with traditional elements of music (e.g., instrumentation, timbre, volume, tempo, etc.) to create new opportunities and requirements for meaning making. As noted earlier, in remixing, meaning is often found in the juxtaposition of sampled elements. This requires a certain kind of mastery. In the case of complex remix—as distinct from mash-ups, which typically just take the vocals from one song and overlay it on the music of another—comprehension relies upon an understanding of the original sources of the samples used (and the contexts within which they were created) and a sense of the new context being created by the remix itself.

For example, in the remix project described in the preceding section of this chapter, the use of the Martin Luther King Jr. samples can resonate in multiple ways. His powerful voice and words heard against a somewhat martial drumbeat and the melody of *We Shall Not Be Moved* can evoke optimism and determination, it can evoke pessimism and grief that he did not live to continue the struggles he devoted his life to, or it can move the listener to other emotions. Of course, it could also leave them cold and uninterested either due to the topic or the piece of art itself. Finally, the remix described in the preceding section was created during the lead-up to the U.S. elections that saw for the first time an African American running for—and later elected as—president. This potentially adds another layer of meaning to this remix for listeners, regardless of their own political positions.

If remix is brought into the classroom, how do we avoid the pitfalls of "talking about music?" Clearly, to write a five-paragraph essay about a specific remix would drain the life from it ("What I meant to say with this remix . . ." would be as productive as "What I meant to say with this poem . . ."). Rather than writing down a list of "what makes a good remix," students can create their own remix to illustrate their ideas. Similarly, the best way to respond to a remix is with another remix. So for example, a student could comment on MC Hammer's rather lazy use of Rick James' work in *U Can't Touch This* by making a new remix that is more complex and richer in terms of potential interpretations. This activity is similar to a common classroom practice whereby students respond to poems by writing their own poems (see *Love That Dog* by Sharon Creech, 2001, for a story told in such a manner). Engaging in remix would deepen that experience. In each case, students should be allowed to develop their (sometimes unconscious) hermeneutic sense without being asked to "dance about architecture." Indeed, although I don't want to justify the use of music remix in the classroom primarily on the grounds that it is good for print literacy development, the play of sound and noise in music remix has clear analogies in poetry. Sometimes the sound of the words, instead of their content, is the point, and they can only be responded to with other sounds. Seriously engaging in remix is about exploring new philosophies of aesthetics, which we should welcome on the part of students regardless of the media.

Of course, sometimes the point is the content, and the meaning of the remix rests in the juxtaposition of elements that have clear ideological value. For example, a student could join the debate about Moby's appropriation of African-American culture by taking "Moby's" work and adding samples from speeches by Malcolm X or Toni Morrison in ways that address this issue. It is the use and the placement of the samples themselves that would carry the meaning, rather than any accompanying essay ("What I meant by including Malcolm X here is. . . ."). Activities like this would highlight connections between students' developing ideologies and hermeneutic skills (including transmedia navigation and judgment, as noted by Jenkins, 2006).

Although "talking about music is like dancing about architecture" is usually understood as a dismissive comment, it is possible to understand it in a positive light. Indeed, the goal of criticism lies in helping to uncover latent potential meanings that viewers, readers or listeners might not find at first. However, beyond the explicit use of oral or written language to shape interpretation (e.g., "What we hear in this piece . . ."), we can also imagine commenting on a work of art using another medium. For example, a dance in the public space of a building could call attention to the way the space is actually lived in and used (as opposed to the design on the blueprint or the intention of the architect). Here "dancing about architecture" might be a very productive activity. Likewise, in talking (or writing) about music remix, students and teachers might find new ways of looking at things. However, this requires a commitment to exploration through writing, rather than simply using print as a means to return to a traditional form of assessment (e.g., "Provide evidence that you have learned X"). This is what is happening in online remix chat-rooms, which might be models for talking or writing about music in the classroom in ways that ideally are communal, democratic, honest and open-minded. Pedagogical interventions based on full participation have a better chance of helping students discover and develop their own hermeneutics than lectures on the meaning of *Troilus and Cressida*. For some students, music remix might be the best way into this kind of discussion and learning.

Conclusion

The advent of new types of technology has begun to shift the way that educators and others talk about the work in which students are engaged. Indeed, students have to negotiate a semiosphere that is more explicitly interactive and communal than ever. They are expected to respond to and use the diverse contents of the "cultural reservoir." Taking music remix seriously offers one potential way (of many) for us to recognize how students add to and draw on that cultural reservoir. Although we cannot assume all young-people have access to and expertise with the kind of technology described in this chapter, many do, and we can only benefit from talking to them about how this technology offers the chance for old-fashioned pleasures like making music or mucking about with something that somebody else took hours to create. For many people, irreverence is fun in and of itself, but realized in the form of a discussion about how meaning is created, challenged, dissembled, and recreated, it can also be a rich opportunity for learning. However, any time educators think about ways to draw on what their students are doing outside of the classroom they run the risk of leaching the pleasure out of the activity, and thus making it into just another schoolish assignment (see examples of how disinterested students are in "sanctioned" graffiti spaces, for example). Music remix should not be reduced to being a gateway to traditional print work, or used as nothing more than a useful analogy for other academic work. It should first and foremost be recognized as a valuable activity in its own right. Once it has been established that what is at stake in music remix does not have to be justified by calling on other already accepted academic goals, moving the discussion into those other arenas will feel much more organic, and thus is much more likely to be productive for teachers and students alike.

References

Audacity (2008). *Online help reference*. Retrieved August 22, 2008, from http://audac ity.sourceforge.net/onlinehelp-1.2/reference.html

Ayers, M. (2006). The cyberactivism of a Dangermouse. In M. Ayers (Ed.), *Cybersounds*, (pp. 127–136). New York: Peter Lang.

ccMixter.org (2008). *ccMixter.org*. Retrieved August 20, 2008, from http://www.ccmixter .org

Creech, S. (2001). *Love that dog*. New York: Harper Trophy.

Haupt, A. (2006). The technology of subversion: From digital sampling in hip-hop to the MP3 revolution. In M. Ayers (Ed.), *Cybersounds*, (pp. 107–125). New York: Peter Lang.

Jenkins, H. (2006). *Confronting the challenges of participatory culture: Media education for the 21ˢᵗ Century*. John D. and Catherine T. MacArthur Foundation. Retrieved

August 22, 2008 from http://www.projectnml.org/files/working/NMLWhitePa
per.pdf

Knobel, M. & Lankshear, C. (2008). Remix: The art and craft of endless hybridization. *Journal of Adolescent & Adult Literacy, 51*(2), 22–33.

Kress, G. (2003). *Literacy in the new media age.* New York: Routledge.

Lenhardt, A., & Madden, M. (2005). *Teen content creators and consumers.* Washington, DC.: Pew Internet & American Life Project. Retrieved August 22, 2008, from http://www.pewinternet.org/PPF/r/166/report_display.asp

Lessig, L. (2008). *Remix: Making art and commerce thrive in the hybrid economy.* New York: Penguin.

Navas, E. (2007a). The three basic forms of remix: A point of entry. Retrieved August 22, 2008 from http://remixtheory.net/?=174.

Navas, E. (2007b). Regressive and reflexive mashups in sampling culture. Retrieved August 22, 2008 from http://remixtheory.net/?p=235

Negativland (1995). *Fair use: The story of the letter U and the numeral 2.* Concord, CA: Seeland.

Opsound.org (2008). *Opsound.org.* Retrieved August 20, 2008, from http://www.opsound.org

Remix Fight (2008). Frequently asked questions. *Remix Fight.* Retrieved August 20, 2008, from http://www.remixfight.org/faq

Chapter 3

DIY *podcasting in education*

CHRISTOPHER SHAMBURG

SECTION ONE

Roots of a podcaster

What initially attracted me to podcasting was the power of audio to entertain, inform, and persuade. Although I was a child during broadcast television of the 1970s and 1980s, my father's nostalgia for radio puzzled and fascinated me. I did sense a lost magic when I saw portrayals of radio dramatizations on TV and in movies—the wonders of meek actors transformed into super-heroes, sacks of flour into fist fights, and kitchen knives into duels. As an adult I became an avid listener to audio books and to the National Public Radio (NPR) station that is broadcast across the U.S. This began with long commutes to work and weekly four-hour drives between New York and Washington, D.C., which I did for two years in a long-distance romance with my future wife; I knew the layout of every rest stop and the schedules of every NPR station along the New York/D.C. corridor. So when I became aware of podcasting in 2004, I was excited to learn more about it, with only a vague and distant hope of becoming a podcaster myself.

Podcasting refers to the practice of creating and distributing audio and, increasingly, video for people to access in a variety of convenient ways, most notably, via a computer or portable media device. What distinguishes a podcast from any other media file on the internet is that it is "subscribe-able." A user can use an intermediary service to automatically locate new episodes of a given podcast series or show and make them available for downloading. The term "podcast" refers to the syndicated show as a whole as well as to individual episodes. Nevertheless, it really is the syndication and resulting "subscribe-ability" that characterize podcasting. Moreover, the ease of subscribing to a podcast show and the increasing file storage capacity of computers and portable media devices encourage consumers to subscribe to numerous podcasts simultaneously. The simplicity of accessing, searching, and continually revising subscriptions encourages a broad and diverse pool of podcasts and a fascinating array of individual podcasters.

The medium and the diversity

The process and practice of how podcasting is consumed are crucial to considering the medium itself as generative, just as the process of sitting in a large and dark theater with a group of people viewing moving images was crucial to moviemakers through most of the 20th century. The term "podcast" is a combination of the words "iPod" and "broadcast." That being said, neither an iPod nor iTunes nor any other proprietary Apple software is required to create or consume podcasts. It's possible to listen to podcasts on a variety of portable media devices (e.g., portable mp3 players), simply listen using a computer and audio software or via a CD player once the podcasts have been burned to a CD disk. There are dozens of "podcatchers"—intermediary software or online services that enable listeners to subscribe to and download a podcast. For example, Microsoft's Zune software enables users to subscribe to podcasts and load them automatically each time they "sync" their Zune player with their computer. The same holds for Creative's Zen portable media player, too. Nonetheless, it would be naïve not to acknowledge that the most popular way to access podcasts at the time of writing is through iTunes software on a computer and then to transfer the podcasts to an iPod portable media player (cf., Brown & Green, 2007). Apple was the first company to build podcatching capabilities into its portable media player interface software, and "being first" with respect to launching new technological developments certainly directly impacts the extent to which a particular medium comes to dominate the field. Thus, any potential podcaster needs to consider the popularity of the iTunes interface and file format early in the production process, regardless of their own preferred software and portable media players. Thus, in what follows, I will refer to the common technologies of iPods and iTunes, while recognizing at the same time there are numerous other options.

It is nothing unusual for a person to subscribe to 2 to 3 *dozen* podcasts at the same time and to have 5 to 10 episodes from each of those podcasts loaded to an iPod. Subscriptions can be set to download and refresh the most recent episodes from every podcast. Plugging the iPod into the computer "synchronizes" the iPod with the downloaded podcasts and automatically transfers the most recent episodes to the iPod (this function can be set to manual transfer, too, for greater control over what is transferred and what isn't). Below are three examples of podcasts that could be found on a typical iPod.

Podrunner

Begun as music mixes for his wife's exercise programs, Los Angeles DJ Steve Boyett's Podrunner is one of the most popular podcast downloads on iTunes, with an average of over 600,000 downloads per month and sponsorship of the series including the U.S. Navy and Timex. These weekly podcasts are intense musical mixes, each about an hour long, and correlated to different target heart rates for running, cycling, and aerobic exercise (e.g., "Relayered" at 158 bpm or "Dawntreader" at 168 bpm). A subscriber has a continually changing set of mixes on an iPod to run, spin, or walk to.

The Brian Lehrer Show

Brian Lehrer is a radio talk show host on New York Public Radio, WNYC. His Peabody Award-winning show broadcasts from 10am to noon each day, attracts a widespread and loyal listenership, and usually contains 5 different segments of interviews, call-ins, and conversations each day. Every segment of every show can be downloaded from the WNYC website or via podcatcher software such as iTunes. A listener who might be at work during the time of the show's broadcast can now access each segment of each show. After listening to a segment, synchronization with the computer can be set-up to delete the shows that were listened to and replace them with new ones.

Although an example of repurposed media—where an already in-place show is converted to a podcast, rather than being produced in the first place as a podcast—it is an excellent example of the power of podcasting. In fact, in 2005 the *Annenberg Online Journalism Review* titled an article "Will NPR's Podcasts Birth a New Business Model for Public Radio?" (Glaser, 2005). In July 2008, repurposed public radio programs account for seven of the top 25 most-downloaded podcasts on iTunes.

Millennium Influence

> Daren and Katie Sutton work in the Christian youth ministry field. According to their website, Millennial Influence (http://www.minfluence.com), their show Millennium Influence Podcast (MI Podcast), "strives to help encourage parents through an open discussion of topics relevant to raising teenagers." The show offers engaging and accessible advice for parent on topics such as talking to your kids about a parent's remarriage, dealing with summer boredom, and what to do if you think your child is gay. Capitalizing on the medium, MI Podcast's description on iTunes reads, "the MI Weekly Podcast is no longer than a short commute (10–15 min)." Their podcast promotes and extends their work in training youth ministers.

Though diverse in their resources, rationales and target audiences, it would not be unusual to find such diverse podcasts as these (each with 5–10 episodes) on a person's computer or iPod along with a few dozen others. Not only do all of these podcasts share free and simple distribution networks—such as iTunes—on a relatively equal footing, but it would not be difficult to rival the production value of any of them using free software and an eight-dollar microphone. To me, this is the equivalent of having a fully functioning radio station in your garage in 1993. The popularity of do-it-yourself podcast production also means there is easy access to countless how-to manuals and intuitive production and distribution technologies online as well. Furthermore, the amateur podcaster today has a potential global reach that was unattainable—perhaps even unimaginable—for the majority of radio stations prior to the internet.

Getting hooked

The potential power to reach a large audience using technologies to create audio shows that rivaled those of professionals was about half the enticement for me. I spent the first ten years of my career as a high school English teacher (and my wife is a high school English teacher), and I tend to look at the world through that lens. What really lit the fire under me about podcasting were three key events in my own life. First was a trip to Disney World that I took with my wife and two kids in 2004. One of the exhibits there focused on Foley artists (the people who recreate the in-the-moment, everyday sound effects heard on movies and television shows). The exhibit comprised a demonstration of how ordinary items are used to make everyday, often taken-for-granted sound effects like footsteps, doors opening and closing, ice clinking in a glass, and so on. It was mesmerizing. I suddenly realized that the ability to convey entire worlds of spaceships, armies, and jungles using ordinary objects such as mop buckets and paperclips held the kernel of a powerful idea that could thoroughly engage students (and, from the sight of parents jumping to their feet in their eagerness to participate in the demonstration, adults, too!).

Second, I long had been a fan of Youth Radio (http://www.youthradio.org), a non-profit initiative to empower youth by engaging them in using audio technologies to broadcast their own ideas and reporting. U.S. National Public Radio would occasionally play segments from Youth Radio, and it was about the same time as my trip to Disney World that I found the Youth Radio podcast. The reports in this podcast are a mix of interviews, reporting, and commentaries, with titles such as "Children as Medical Interpreters" about kids who act as interpreters between doctors and parents who do not speak English, and "Return of the Girlie Girl" about femininity and *Sesame Street* Muppets. These reports integrated adolescent experiences with a range of social and cultural phenomena in compelling ways. I listened to dozens of segments and over time created step-by-step guidelines and templates for students to use to create similar segments (Shamburg, 2008).

Third, I came across the two particular podcasts which simultaneously provided entertainment for me as a listener and inspiration for me as a teacher: ArtMobs and Dramapod.

ArtMobs

David Gilbert and his students at Marymount Manhattan College created alternatives to the standard museum tours with their ArtMobs podcast (http://mod.blogs.com/art_mobs). In producing their podcast shows, Gilbert asks his students to consider such things as what the characters in paintings would say and to create a soundtrack for a particular piece of art. These podcasts promise subscribers who visit the Museum of Modern Art (MoMA) that "you'll hear things you'll never hear through MoMA's headphones."

Dramapod

Dramapod (http://www.thedramapod.com) is a collection of new and old audio dramas; from old time radio shows, to author readings of self-published books, to current fanfiction. A listener can subscribe to individual shows and vote and comment on individual episodes. Dramapod offers content to listeners with tastes that lie in old radio serials or who have unquenchable appetites for Star Trek fan-written stories.

These three sets of experiences coalesced in 2005, when I was working as a consultant for an online high school. I suggested, developed, and later taught "Podcourse" (http://podcourse.blogspot.com), an online high school English class based on student-created podcasts and which continues to run each year. The course approaches literacies and new literacies by focusing on culture and digital technologies within the context of authentically producing podcasts rather than on reproducing traditional English classroom activities (e.g., round-robin play reading, teacher-directed poetry analysis). In Podcourse, students conduct interviews (like Brian Lehrer does in his radio show podcast, or Daren and Katie Sutton do in their IM Podcast), create audio tours (like ArtMobs) and audio plays (like Dramapod), and remix music and poetry for walking or running (like Podrunner). They produce this content for real audiences and for real purposes.

Communities and resources

My shift from listener of podcasts to creator of podcasts would only have been a dream if it were not for some very special communities and resources. First, as a teacher who wanted students to have access to this software at home, expensive professional audio editing software was not an option. After some searching, I came across the SourceForge Project (http://www.sourceforge.net), a community of open source software developers and open source software projects. One of SourceForge's projects is Audacity (http://audacity.sourceforge.net); a free and powerful multitrack audio editing software package (see Chapter 2 in this volume for more about Audacity). David Murphy (2005) of *PC Magazine* writes that "the program mimics its more expensive brethren—Adobe *Audition* and [Sonic Foundry's] *Sound Forge*—in providing recording and audio file-editing tools, and it's easy enough for beginners while including plenty of advanced features for audiophiles." *PC World* voted it one of the top 100 products of 2008 (Sullivan, 2008). The Audacity website (http://audacity.sourceforge.net) also has tutorials and a dedicated support wiki for users.

Many potential podcasters are stymied by a fear of unintentionally violating copyright law. Copyright and fair use laws are ambiguous, and media industries—especially in the U.S.—have reacted to the relative ease of creating and sharing digital copies of media in often highly restrictive and punitive ways that can have a chilling effect on amateur new media creators. In the next section I give some advice on the legal and ethical use of copyrighted material. Suffice it to say for now that my podcasting work (and the work of my students) would have been thwarted if not for the help I received from the Creative Commons Mixter service (http://www.ccmixter.org) and the Free Sound Project (http://www.freesound.org). These spaces provide music and sound effects that have a "sliding scale" of copyright restrictions (e.g., free to use for commercial and non-commercial purposes through to the resource must be attributed to the original author or creator, cannot be remixed, must remain intact and cannot be used for commercial purposes).

Both services also provide extremely helpful communities of audio editors and audiophiles who are happy to help novices navigate the ethical appropriation of other people's material.

Audio lives

I would like to conclude this section with a note about video podcasting. One of the inevitable requests I get from teachers and students is to work with video podcasts (also known as vodcasts). While I'm not opposed to video podcasts, I strongly favor working with audio. Audio is here to stay. There is a physical reason why audio is a medium that will not go away. The Romantic poets attributed the physical attributes of aural communication—the phenomenon that sounds need to physically penetrate the body through the ear to be perceived—to its hold on our emotions and imaginations. There is also another, more practical reason for the timelessness of audio as a medium. People will want content that they can experience while they are still able to see what they are doing at the time. Driving a car, working on a computer, running a marathon, or walking down the street are all experiences that we can do as we listen to an audio podcast. Regardless of the sophistication of a video device, it is hard to imagine doing any of these activities safely or productively while watching video. Indeed, some audio podcasts even work harmoniously with these physical acts to actually improve performance. Thus, for me, the creative and imaginative powers of audio hold me spellbound.

SECTION TWO

Doing your own podcasting

There are two main features of a podcast: the medium itself and its "subscribe-ability." For this tutorial we will focus on a particular audio file type—the mp3 file—which is an extremely space-efficient audio file that runs in a large number of software programs and on a wide range of audio players (much of what follows applies equally to vodcasts or video podcasts, too). Subscribe-ability refers to audio content that has an RSS file (also known as an RSS feed) associated with it. "RSS" stands for "Really Simple Syndication" and is a combination of programming code inserted into a file and a syndicating service that enables users to subscribe to this file (or set of files) in much the same way that analogue newspapers are subscribed to in the physical world and appear on one's doorstep without you having to do anything more than pay your annual dues. RSS is what gives a podcast its "legs."

To begin, we will first create an mp3 file using Audacity, the free multi-track audio editing program created at SourceForge. Audacity is available for for PC, Mac, and Linux platforms. It is a small but powerful program. If you prefer to use a different piece of software (e.g., GarageBand, Sony Acid Xpress), you can still follow the general steps of this tutorial. Audio editing software is like word processing software—the majority of the skills are transferable among programs. Also, if you already know how to use a word processor and a tape recorder, you already have about 90% of the skills needed for audio editing (e.g., hitting a record button, copying and pasting). In terms of hardware, all you need is a computer and a microphone. You can buy a good microphone for under $20 at a computer or office supply store. Access to the internet while creating your podcast is also optimal with respect to being able to locate audio files you'd like to use but isn't absolutely necessary as long as you have a range of audio files to hand on a harddrive or CD-ROM.

Podcast tutorial: Goals and procedures

There are technical and educational skills that this tutorial addresses. On the technical side, the overall goal is to create an mp3 file using multitrack audio editing software. You will do this by mixing original audio that you record with existing audio files that you (legally and ethically) download from the internet. You will then edit and manipulate the individual tracks to create a single new audio file. Finally, you will use free podcast hosting and RSS subscription services. The technical procedures of this tutorial are based on the principles of effective procedural instruction identified by Black, Carroll and McGuigan (1987) in their article, "What Kind of Minimal Instruction Manual Is the Most Effective?"

Along with technical instructions, there are some broader, educational ideas embedded in this tutorial. You will get a chance to examine the role of context with respect to situations and language use, explore unique aspects of audio in terms of mediums, and practice ethically using the intellectual property of others to create original content. These goals will be of interest to you if you want to use or build upon this tutorial with students.

Keep in mind that your own podcast show can be a variety of—or even a mix of—formats (e.g., interviews, dramatizations, commentary). For this particular podcast tutorial, you will create a short audio dramatization because it teaches a broad set of technical and educational skills related to podcasting. Here are the steps that you will complete:

1. Download the software and accompanying encoding and media files (see below)

2. Record original dialogue and narration (you will play two characters and the narrator in an audio play)

3. Mix in existing music and sound effects—freely and legally

4. Shift and manipulate audio tracks

5. Export your project as an mp3 file

6. Submit your file to a free podcast hosting service

Getting set up

So, to begin, download the following three files:

(1) The software: Audacity (For beginners or "newbies," avoid "beta" versions of the software because these often tend to be unstable and can contain glitches that can cause unnecessary frustration for someone not familiar with how the software should work.) Available free of charge from: http://auda city.sourceforge.net

(2) The file: Lame_enc.dll (You will only have to access this file one time, when you create your first mp3. It comes in a zipped folder with documentation.) Available from: http://lame.buanzo.com.ar/

(3) The zipped folder: cs272_-_Free_and_Legal_Podcaster.zip (A collection of songs and sound effects that you can use freely and legally if you cite them). Available from: http://ccmixter.org/files/cs272/15557

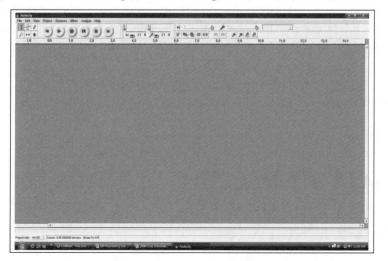

Figure 3.1: Audacity project workspace (version 1.2.6)

Getting Started with the Software

After you download and install Audacity, open it and you will see a screen like that in Figure 3.1.

The controls in the top left-hand corner are the ones you will use the most (see Figure 3.2 for a close-up). The selection tool will let you choose segments or clips from tracks, and the shift tool will let you move tracks along the timeline.

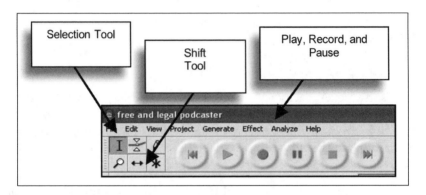

Figure 3.2: Common Audacity tools

Recording voices

The audio play you will record for your podcast will be the dialogue below. You will choose a set of characters, write a brief narrative to introduce your scene (no more that 15 words total to be recorded before the dialogue begins), enact the five lines of dialogue below, and add music and sound effects. Begin by choosing one pair of characters from the following list:

• Pet Store Clerks

• Gangsters

• Spies

• Boxers

<<Add Narration Here>>

Person 1: I missed you.

Person 2: It's been a long time.

Person 1: I forgot to give you something.

Person 2: What is it?

Person 1: This.

Plug your microphone into your computer (there should be a jack for the plug in the front or back of your desktop computer or on the side of your laptop) and record your opening narration text. You record by pressing the record and stop buttons on the Audacity control panel (see Figure 3.3). After you've recorded your narration, you should have a voice track displayed in the Audacity project window (see Figure 3.3). If you decide you'd like to try your recording again, simply remove the voice track by clicking the "x" by the track name and rerecord.

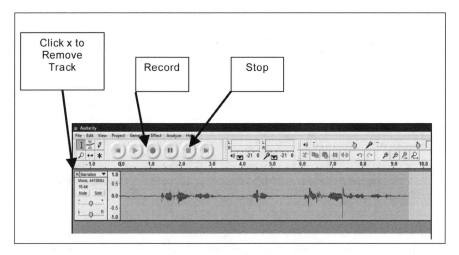

Figure 3.3: Recording the narration

Now record your audio play dialogue the same way. When you press record, a second track will automatically display in the Audacity project window. You might want to mute the first track so it does not distract from your new recording (see Figure 3.4). After you record the second track of dialogue, you use the Shift Tool to move this second track and align with the end of your narration track (see Figure 3.4)

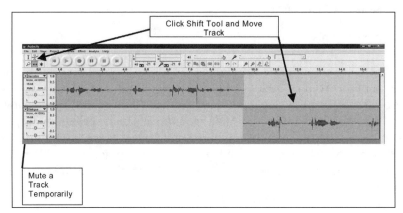

Figure 3.4: Moving and muting a track

If you have extra recording space before or after a track (fumbling for words, forgot to stop the recording, etc.), you can remove it by selecting it and deleting it (Figure 3.5).

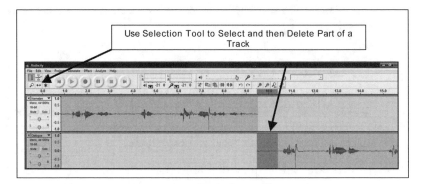

Figure 3.5: Selecting and deleting part of a track

Importing existing audio

Now you will add music and sound effects to your audio drama. After you import these additional audio clips, you will use the same skills of moving and selecting as you did in working with your spoken audio files. At this point, you should unzip the folder cs272_-_free_and_legal_podcaster.zip if you haven't already done so. You will import the tracks yourself by going to the menu bar at the top of the audacity project window and clicking on "Project" and selecting "Import Audio." You'll be prompted to open a file; this is where you select the folder containing your unzipped sound files (see Figure 3.6). You'll find a variety of music and sound effects in this folder.

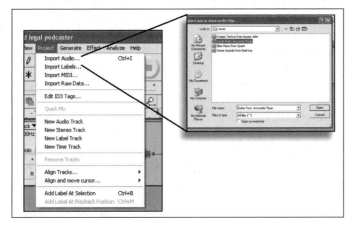

Figure 3.6: Importing an existing audio track

You should begin your audio dramatization with one of the music clips in this unzipped folder and end your audio play with one of the sound effects. The sound effect should correspond with the "This" of the audio play dialogue. Playing and experimenting with each of the files in your unzipped folder will help with your selection.

By now, your project should look something like Figure 3.7.

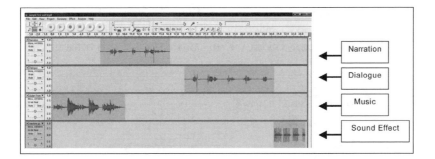

Figure 3.7: Four audio tracks inside an Audacity project

You might want to have the music and narration play at the same time. You can lower the volume of the music track by adjusting the volume of that track, or you can select a portion of the track and go to "Effects" in the menu bar and select, say, "Fade out" if you want the volume of the music to trail off (see Chapter 2 in this volume for additional instructions on adding effects to audio tracks).

Citing sources

Before you export your Audacity project file as an mp3 file, you need to cite the sources of your audio. Although the files you used in addition to the ones you created were in one of my collections on ccMixter.org, I originally took them from other sources. While you do have some flexibility to use copyrighted resources under fair use parameters, I like nonetheless to stick with "copyleft" resources, just to be on the safe side. "Copyleft" is a term used to describe intellectual property that has fewer restrictions for unauthorized use than copyrighted material *per se*. An excellent system of copyleft registration is Creative Commons (http://www.creativecommons.org), and—as mentioned earlier—two good sources of Creative Commons audio material are ccMixter (http://www.ccmixter.org) for music and the Free Sound Project (http://www.freesound.org) for sounds and sound effects. Creative Commons material comes with a sliding scale of permissions and restrictions relating to attribution, profit, and modifying the work. The one requirement found across most files, however, is that you have to attribute your sources. Thus, at the end of your podcast, you should record an attribution clip using the following script, or your own version of it:

> The music for this project came from Creative Commons Mixter <<Say Original File Nam(e)>> with a <<Say Type of License>>. The Sound Effects for this project came from the Free Sound Project <<Say Original File Name(s)>>. All sound effects have a Creative Commons Sampling 1.0 Plus license <<or whichever license applies>>.

To help with your attribution script, Table 3.1 presents a summary of the original file names and copyleft licenses for the set of zipped files (i.e., cs272_-_Free_and_Legal_Podcaster.zip) at the start of this tutorial.

Music				
Mp3 Name	Original File Name from ccMixter.org	Artist	Original Source	Creative Commons License Type
Creepy Techno from Aussie John	AussieJohn_-_Around_Dusk.mp3	Aussie John	http://ccmixter.org/media/files/AussieJohn/13476	Attribution 3.0
Guitar from Accoustic Ryan	accousticRyan_-_Acoustic_sunrise_guitar_background.mp3	Accoustic Ryan	http://ccmixter.org/media/files/accousticRyan/5248	Attribution 2.5 Generic
Slow Piano from Quest	oscarx_-_Quest.mp3	Oscarx	http://ccmixter.org/media/files/oscarx/1638	Sampling Plus 1.0

Tense Sounds from Noel Kay	noelkay_-_Fourmi_2.mp3	Noelkay	http://ccmixter.org/media/files/noelkay/12926	Attribution 3.0
Sound Effects				
Cat	cat2.wav	noisecollector	http://www.freesound.org/samplesViewSingle.php?id=4914	
Growl	dog.wav	ljudman	http://www.freesound.org/samplesViewSingle.php?id=23387	
Machine Gun	m240.wav	Matt_G	http://www.freesound.org/samplesViewSingle.php?id=30749	All sound effects from the Free Sound
Punch	Stomp That.wav	JCambs1990	http://www.freesound.org/samplesViewSingle.php?id=38156	Project come with Attribution 1.0
Single Gun	Shot.wav	mastafx	http://www.freesound.org/samplesViewSingle.php?id=33276	
Ticking Sound	SmallCarriageClockTicking.wav	acclivity	http://www.freesound.org/samplesViewSingle.php?id=30608	

Table 3.1. Sources for Music and Sound Effects in Tutorial

Exporting your audio project as an mp3 file

Finally, you will export your entire audio project as an mp3 file. Doing so makes your project transportable as a file that will play using a range of software programs and on a range of media players. Omitting this final step means your project will only ever play inside the Audacity program and won't be upload-able to the internet. I would recommend saving your work as an Audacity project as you go along—this keeps all of the individual pieces together in the one folder in case you want to revise it later (you won't be able to work "under the hood" of your audio file once it's saved as an mp3). Exporting your project file as an mp3 is simple. However, there is one important, extra step that you need to take the first time that you export any project file as an mp3.

The first time you export an mp3 from within Audacity, you will need to tell the program where the lame_enc.dll file is; this is the encoder file that you downloaded earlier. This small program will interface with Audacity and enable it to produce mp3 files (see Chapter 2 for an explanation of why this extra step has to be done manually). When you click on "File" in the menu bar, then "Export," the program will prompt you to find the location of the lame_enc.dll file. Click the "Browse" button and locate this file on your computer harddrive (see Figure 3.8).

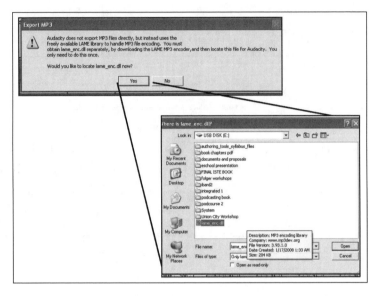

Figure 3.8: Locating the mp3 Encoder File

Syndication

As I previously mentioned, an mp3 file is not a podcast unless it is syndicated, even if it is posted to the internet. You need to give it the power of "sub-scribe-ability" so that listeners can retrieve your podcast automatically using a podcatcher service such as iTunes. There is a long and ever-changing list of options for adding subscribe-ability to your mp3 file, and no single one will fit everyone's needs. Four popular services that offer free hosting and syndi-cation services are Podomatic (http://www.podomatic.com), OurMedia (http://www.ourmedia.org), Blip.tv (http://www.blip.tv), and Liberated Syndication (http://www.libsyn.com).

The specific procedures followed for uploading your podcast vary from serv-ice to service (and are modified by individual services over time). However, if you can add an attachment to an email message, you should easily be able to visit a hosting and syndication web site, register with their service, and submit your audio files. You can submit the audio play that you created in the tuto-rial above or develop new material.

All of these hosting and syndication services will allocate you a dedicated webpage that will archive your shows. In this way, a listener can access your work simply through a web browser without having to subscribe. In addi-tion, each service will also allocate you an RSS address for your new podcast show (it will look something like this: http://www.mugglenet.com/muggl ecast/mugglecast.rss). You can use this RSS address to register your podcast with iTunes.

Advice on copyright

In the tutorial above we used copyleft material that has Creative Commons licenses. By far the most frequent question I'm asked when working with digital media is about copyright. It has been my experience that most educators have an overly restrictive perception of copyright and digital media. This correlates with a report by The Center for Social Media, *The Cost of Copyright Confusion for Media Literacy* (Hobbs, Jaszi, & Aufderheide, 2007). Hobbs, Jaszi and Aufderheide found that confusion about copyright laws within education has debilitating consequences for educators. In particular, they found that "[t]eachers use less effective teaching techniques, teach and transmit erroneous copyright information, fail to share innovative instructional approaches, and do not take advantage of new digital platforms" (p. 1).

Educators in the United States should know that U.S. Copyright Law does allow for fair use (U.S. Copyright Office, 2006). Fair use allows people to use other people's material (print, music, images) without obtaining or paying for their permission—within reason. To be able to use another person's work under fair use guidelines, there are four interrelated factors to consider.

- The purpose and character of the use (How are you going to use the work? Fair use favors criticism, commentary, satire, and educational purposes)

- The nature of the copyrighted work (What kind of work is it? It is much easier to claim fair use for facts like the weather or scientific information)

- The amount and substantiality of the portion taken (What parts are you taking? Fair use favors small amounts, unimportant sections or parts)

- The effect of the use upon the potential market (Will anyone lose money if you copy and play this? Fair use favors copying in which no one loses money)

This process of reflecting on and applying the four fair use factors to working with digital media should be a welcomed "teachable moment" in classrooms. Students and teachers *have* to be able to navigate the ambiguous legal guidelines for media use with their own well-developed ethical compass. I would strongly recommend avoiding strict rules about the amount or types of material that you can use without permission. Guidelines offering such advice typically represent the most conservative interpretations of fair use.

The most salient example here is the "Guidelines for the Fair Use of Multimedia" document developed in 1996 by the Conference on Fair Use. These guidelines specify limits for the educational use of video, audio, and images that do not require obtaining permission from the rightsholder (e.g., 3 minutes of a movie, 3 seconds of a song) (University of Texas, 2001). These guidelines are replicated within numerous policies in school districts and universities, despite the fact that they are hotly opposed by organizations such as the Association of Research Libraries, the American Library Association, the National Association of School Administrators, the National Education Association, the U.S. Catholic Conference, and the National Association of Independent Schools (Association of Research Libraries, 1997). Indeed, in response to these guidelines, the Association of Research Libraries called on its members to "resist relying on any proposed code of conduct which may substantially or artificially constrain the full and appropriate application of fair use" (Association of Research Libraries, 2007).

SECTION THREE

Educational applications

Podcasting offers a powerful tool that can engage students in learning and prepare them for lives in the 21st century. The key for using podcasting successfully in education is, I believe, to abandon the model of simply enhancing the existing curriculum and to deeply reflect on the types of skills we want students to have in the kind of world in which they are living now. Podcasting offers an inexpensive way to create and share compelling media that correlates to authentic activities outside of classrooms. With podcasting, students can create original content as they ethically and effectively collect and remix the work of others and become participants in culture, politics, and society.

Educators need to believe that podcasting can be a vehicle for teaching powerful ideas. Applying the term "powerful ideas" to educational technology was pioneered by Seymour Papert in his groundbreaking book *Mindstorms: Children, Computers and Powerful Ideas* (1980). Papert saw technology as a catalyst and incubator for powerful ideas, as opposed to a means to simply improve the teaching of existing curriculum. Papert writes that "one comes to appreciate how certain ideas can be used as tools to think with over a lifetime. One learns to enjoy and respect the power of powerful ideas" (1980, p. 76). My observations and my hopes encourage me to think that student podcasting can promote several powerful ideas that students can use as tools in their thinking. For example, the hands-on and reflective approach to copyright, fair, use, and digital media that students employ in their podcasting becomes a tool for them to think further about the balance of individual rights and community benefits. The powerful idea of creating something for a particular audience becomes a tool for students to use to anticipate audience needs and to empathize with others. Here, issues of fair use and audience are not disembodied lessons but fundamental to the "doing" of podcasting.

Using podcasts can be a bad idea for teachers if doing so does not come with a deep concern for doing things differently. Podcasting—the medium and associated technologies—just as easily can lead to bored students, vacuous classrooms, and tedious teaching as any rote learning activity can. Imagine this scenario—a projection of my own mistakes early in my career teaching high school English. A tech-savvy teacher listens to a variety of podcasts, continually searching and culling his subscriptions on iTunes, and is eager to bring some of this compelling content into the classroom. He hears a great feature about the history of an indigenous tribe along the Amazon basin that ties in perfectly with a unit he's teaching on the Amazon Rain Forest. A few days later, he schedules some time to share this podcast episode with his students. It will be just the perfect enhancement of and exposure to the topic that will motivate his kids: compelling content with high production value that brings the outside world into his classroom.

He brings in his iPod and Bose speakers and sets them up at the front of the room. The students sit in their seats; the teacher goes to the back of the classroom and hits play on his remote control. The kids sit and listen. Some kids sit attentively, genuinely interested and following along. Other kids surreptitiously work on homework for other classes; they will not be quizzed on the content of this podcast and it really isn't that interesting to them. The remaining students put their heads down on their desks, giggle, whisper, or play with rubber bands.

Podcasting can be a powerful medium, but unless we use it within a broader context of educational reform it can be misapplied easily and reinforce an increasingly irrelevant educational model. It is like the Professor in *Gilligan's Island* using his genius to make a bicycle-powered washing machine from bamboo, instead of getting the castaways off the island.

Podcasting and curriculum reform: Guiding principles

My use of educational podcasting began in earnest in 2005 when I was working with the NJeSchool (http://www.njeschool.org), the largest online public high school in New Jersey. I had conducted some research for the school on successful and unsuccessful online courses and noticed that much of the online content that was commercially available was designed around students reading reams of pdf files of textbooks. We started to think about the types of content that would work well online as well as about broader questions to do with the types of skills that students would like to or need to have. We came up with what we called the Podcasting and Creative Audio course, known more colloquially as "Podcourse" (http://podcourse.blogspot.com). This was a high school English class focused on student-centered podcasting (Shamburg, 2009).

Podcasting became a vehicle for exploring authentic activities that truly engaged students. Instead of looking at trends in education, we looked at how people used digital technologies to create, produce, and communicate via podcasts. There are a number of detailed studies of new literacies that informed the direction of this work. Prominent among them were Lankshear and Knobel's *New Literacies* (2003), William Kist's *New Literacies in Action* (2004), and Henry Jenkins' *Convergence Culture* (2006b) along with *Confronting the Challenges of Participatory Culture: Media Education in the 21ᵗ Century* (Jenkins, 2006a). Below are common, key ideas that informed the direction of this work (Shamburg, 2009).

> *Participation:* Digital technologies have given us unprecedented abilities to create media and content with which to express ourselves to varied and distributed audiences. Media creation tools—which 20 years ago were only available to a handful of media conglomerates—now come preloaded on even the least expensive computers. Relatively low-cost, high-speed internet access also affords participation in networks of content distribution that have never before been possible for amateurs and hobbyists.

> *Appropriation:* Remixes, mashups, copy-and-paste practices are part of the constitution of our digital environment. Students need the skills and mindsets to effectively and ethically synthesize the work of others into original and compelling work.

> *Media:* Students need to understand that different media—audio, video, text—and different technologies—podcasting, online video archives, blogging—have different properties, advantages and weaknesses. They need to learn how to identify, choose, innovate with, and capitalize on these media and technologies.

> *Ethical Behavior:* Students need to understand that with the opportunities made possible by networked and digital technologies, there are also risks and responsibilities. We cannot teach this to students by blocking out the changing world but must develop techniques to guide them in developing their own ethical compasses and responsible behaviors. They need to be able to identify ethical boundaries and existing abuses of new media as well as to conduct themselves responsibly with respect to what they do with other people's work.

> *Personal Interests:* Schools need to take a more dialectic approach to balancing educative goals with the experiences and learning goals of students. This not only correlates with the last three decades of research on cognitive science, inter-

est and learning. This idea also pays attention to the fact that what is happening in schools with respect to skills and content doesn't always match what's being used and is needed in life outside school.

Along with these common themes found in studies of new literacies, one major guiding principle for my own work with students is the connection between the worlds of bits and atoms. In *New Literacies*, Lankshear and Knobel (2006) describe the dual worlds of bits and atoms. Building on this distinction, I explored those areas where bits and atoms intersect. When we come to rely on the internet for driving directions, when we hop across different online dating sites looking for companionship, and when we debate global warming via video responses posted to YouTube, it becomes imperative that students see the connections between our digital lives and physical worlds and avoid the solipsism of cyberspace (Shamburg, 2009). Podcasting can do this. When students interview a parent, create a walking tour, or record a recipe, they are making this crucial connection almost by default.

Student projects

The process of developing the units for Podcourse can be a model for curriculum development or at least offer points for consideration. The curriculum for the course deliberately cultivated the place where authentic podcasting activities intersected with student interests. When such activities were found or developed, I tried to uncover and nurture the powerful ideas (Papert, 1980) embedded in these activities. These ideas were used in turn to develop materials and resources that would carefully scaffold student learning. Seymour Papert, one of the earliest advocates of children using digital technologies at very young ages, saw digital technology as a way to incubate and liberate powerful ideas. While the concept of "powerful ideas" will differ among teachers, the term can be a rallying point and reminder of the important and noble work that we should aspire to as teachers.

Once the Podcourse activities were developed, they were placed in a sequence in such a way that demand on students' cognitive and creative skills was noticeably increased. Primarily, the demand for collecting and organizing material created by other people—including research findings and reports, music, quotes from texts online, sound effect files, among others—and then synthesizing this material into an original product (i.e., a powerful idea) grew as each project progressed. For example, students begin the Podcourse with an activity similar to the tutorial in the preceding section of this chapter. They have to search, select, and use other people's music and sound effects to produce their unique visions of a few simple lines of dialogue. The fascinating part of this activity is the way in which the resources they find and ultimately select not only advances, but also modifies the students' original conception of how their audio project should sound. This process is analogous to designing and conducting good research. Working on the audio play easily lays foundations for students to learn how to ethically and effectively quote from interviews, how to conduct supporting research for a podcast, and how to synthesize and comment respectfully upon the opinions of others.

Podcourse activities or projects are organized into units of work. These units traverse a range of purposes or audio text types. Some of these include:

1. *Media Reviews.* This unit focuses on students' consideration of audience. Students review a work of media of their choice—such as a television show, video game, comic book, movie, or novel—and pay close attention to the purpose of their review and its target audience. Students are given scaffolding materials that prompt them to choose an audience, consider the prior knowledge of their audience, and to anticipate certain questions from their audience.

2. *Fictional Dramatizations.* Students create an audio dramatization of segments of a novel or play, complete with music and sound effects. They are guided in the transformation of written prose or a play script into an audio drama. Here they get to reflect on, explore, and capitalize upon the unique attributes and effects of the podcasting medium.

3. *Audio Tours of Important Sites.* Students develop a walking tour of a public place that has significance to them. The main goal is that the audio tour is to be informative and interesting. Students can pick an audience (e.g., a general audience, teenagers, young children, runners) and develop appropriate podcasts. Each student is encouraged to and supported in their efforts to broaden the perspective of his or her tour by including social or historical research in their podcast as well as clips from interviews with people who are closely familiar with the site being toured.

4. *Historic Interviews.* Students interview a friend, family, or community member about a particularly interesting time period or event. The interviewee can have participated in a single historic event or there can be a focus on social history such as life during a particular time period (the home front of WWII, the 1960s, the Cold War). Students connect the experiences of the interviewee with research on larger social and historical trends.

5. *DVD Commentary.* Students can cue a movie to a particular point and then write and record commentary that runs while the movie does. They can collaborate with friends, family, or community members in developing their commentary. The project can be modified to be a sports commentary (e.g., play-by-play descriptions and what is referred to as "color commentary" in the U.S.—commentary that adds context, humor and random player or game

facts to the sports commentary), or to be a more substantive version of *Mystery Science Theater 3000* (a now-defunct U.S. television show in which a small cast of characters watched scifi movies and added in their own, usually hilarious, comments about the movie itself). This project works especially well when an interview format is used to comment on a movie clip, especially when the interviewees are family members or friends who have some experience with the subject or time period being presented in the movie.

You can see commentary and student examples at: http://podcourse.blogspo t.com.

In summary, a very real aim in my work with student podcasting—taught in Podcourse and shared in teacher education classes and in books like this— is to help students and teachers to better look outside to the world and inside to student interests.

Beyond podcasting: Teaching and reflection

Getting students comfortable with skillfully navigating the places where authentic activities mix with their interests is one of the most worthwhile things we can do as educators and goes well beyond the scope of a single technology practice such as podcasting. My argument is that this type of curriculum can help students to become self-actualized individuals within a global community. Educators and labor experts see this kind of skillful volition as an important component in the new digital economy (cf. Gee, 2004; Rifken, 2004). Joseph Campbell's (Apostrophe S Productions & Public Affairs Television, 1988) famous call to "follow your bliss" even gives a spiritual connotation to this pursuit. Podcasting facilitates this larger goal of productively participating in communities and networks as each participant hones and expands individual interests.

Looking outside to the world and reflecting deeply on what we do (and why we do it) inside the classroom can be more difficult than we appreciate as educators. There is a stifling cache of unwritten traditions and formal rules and standards that inhibit the type of deep questioning that should happen in schools. Podcasting offers a very real means for encouraging students to ask *real* questions about their world, to follow their intuitions about the relationship between history, people and now, to really think about things, rather than to memorize dates and facts. It's not that Shakespeare, American history, or rainforests should not be taught. It's that they should be taught in tandem with purposes that teachers and students can believe in and commit to; that is, powerful ideas as intellectual tools.

I would like to conclude with some thoughts on education from Ken Ronkowitz, a former language arts teacher, and currently an educational technology guru and writer of the blog *Serendipity 35* (http://www.serendip

ity35.net). Ken reflects on a virtual field trip a group of English teachers were taken on within Second Life. It is a virtual tour of the house that was the model for Nathaniel Hawthorne's *House of the Seven Gables.* Ken writes that, "the English teacher in me would immediately wonder what value it would be to walk through the home anyway. What does an actual field trip offer students?" (Ronkowitz, no date). I am not dismissing this virtual project, but I hope that it comes with important reasons for studying that novel in the first place and that the virtual world is not a spoonful of high-tech sugar for doing obligatory work. In that same blogpost, Ken goes on to write a poignant passage about his successes teaching S.E. Hinton's *The Outsiders* and concludes, "It saddens me to see that there are Cliff and Spark Notes for *The Outsiders.* What might a teacher do to that book that would send a reader there instead of [to] the book itself?" (Ronkowitz, no date). My guess is that such a teacher would treat it in the same way many teachers have been treating literature for the last 50 years, focusing on "rising actions" and arcane symbolism instead of treating it like a great story that kids can enjoy and engage in, and which is closer to the authentic reasons why we read books outside of school anyway (for a fascinating description of the contrast between reading inside of school and reading outside of school, see Atwell, 1998). Podcasting—like helping kids to be active readers—begins by looking at ways we engage with the world outside school.

For podcasting and for teaching beyond podcasting, one of the noblest things we can do as educators is to teach the powerful ideas that live in authentic activities outside of school while validating who our students are and who they want to be in that outside world.

References

Association of Research Libraries (1997). Association of Research Libraries: CCUMC multi-media fair use guidelines letter. Retrieved July 17, 2008, from http://www.arl .org/pp/ppcopyright/copyresources/ccumc.shtml

Association of Research Libraries (2007). Association of Research Libraries: Conference on fair use joint statement. Retrieved July 17, 2008 from http://www.arl.org/pp/ppc opyright/copyresources/confu.shtml

Atwell, N. (1998). *In the middle: New understanding about writing, reading, and learning* (2nd ed.). Portsmouth, NH: Boynton/Cook.

Black, J. B., Carroll, J. M., & McGuigan, S. M. (1987). What kind of minimal instruction manual is the most effective? In P. Tanner & J. M. Carroll (Eds.), *Human factors in computing systems and graphic interface* (pp. 159–162). Amsterdam: North Holland.

Brown, A. & Green, T. (2007). Podcasting and video podcasting: How it works and how it's used for instruction. In C. Crawford et al. (Eds.), *Proceedings of Society for Information Technology and Teacher Education International Conference* (pp. 1915–1921). Chesapeake, VA: AACE.

Apostrophe S Productions & Public Affairs Television (Producers). (1988). Joseph Campbell and the power of myth [VHS tape]. New York: Mystic Fire Video.

Gee, J. P. (2004). *Situated language and learning: A critique of traditional schooling.* New York: Routledge.

Glaser, M. (November 29, 2005). Will NPR's podcasts birth a new business model for public radio? *Annenberg Online Journalism Review.* Retrieved August 3, 2008, from http://www.ojr.org/ojr/stories/051129glaser/

Hobbs, R., Jaszi, P., & Aufderheide, P. (2007, September). The cost of copyright confusion for media literacy. *The Center for Social Media.* Retrieved July 29, 2008, from http://www.centerforsocialmedia.org/resources/publications/the_cost_of_copyright_confusion_for_media_literacy.

Jenkins, H. (2006a). *Confronting the challenges of participatory culture: Media education for the 21st century.* Boston: MacArthur Foundation. Retrieved July 7, 2008 from http://www.projectnml.org/files/working/NMLWhitePaper.pdf

Jenkins, H. (2006b). *Convergence culture: Where old and new media collide.* New York: New York University Press.

Kist, W. (2004). *New Literacies in action: Teaching and learning in multiple media* (Language and Literacy Series). New York: Teachers College Press.

Lankshear, C., & Knobel, M. (2003). *New literacies.* London: Open University Press.

Lankshear, C., & Knobel, M. (2006). *New literacies* (2nd ed.). London: Open University Press.

Murphy, D. (April 5, 2005). Music utilities. Retrieved July 23, 2008 from PC Magazine [online] at http://www.pcmag.com/article2/0,2817,1814231,00.asp

Papert, S. (1980). *Mindstorms: Children, computers, and powerful ideas.* New York: Basic Books.

Rifkin, J. (2004). *The end of work* (2nd Edition). New York: Penguin.

Ronkowitz, K. (no date). Virtual paths into literature. Retrieved July 25, 2008 [online] from Serendipity 35 [blog] from http://smsdesign.org/index.php?/archives/459-Virtual-Paths-Into-Literature.html

Shamburg, C. (2008). *National educational technology standards for students: English language arts units for grades 9–12.* Eugene, OR: International Society for Technology in Education.

Shamburg, C. (2009, in process). *Student-powered podcasting: Teaching for 21st century literacy.* [manuscript]. Eugene, OR: International Society for Technology in Education.

Sullivan, M. (May 27, 2008). The 100 best products of 2008. Retrieved July 28, 2008 from PC World [online] http://www.pcworld.com/article/146161–12/the_100_best_products_of_2008.html

U.S. Copyright Office (2006). Copyright office basics. Retrieved July 29, 2008, from http://www.copyright.gov/circs/circ1.pdf

University of Texas (2001). Multimedia fair use guidelines. Retrieved July 29, 2008, from http://www.utsystem.edu/ogc/INTELLECTUALPROPERTY/ccmcguid.htm

Part 2: Still Media

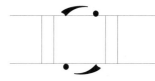

Chapter 4

Visual networks: Learning and photosharing

GUY MERCHANT

SECTION ONE

Introduction

Last summer I was invited down to a Graffiti Jam held in the old tennis courts on the edge of an urban park near where I live. I had become interested in graffiti a while back. As a professional educator with an interest in literacy practices—and particularly in the ways in which some of these practices are formalized and held in high esteem while others are marginalized, or even, as in the case of most graffiti, simply made illegal—I'd been photographing the tags, slogans and wall-art in my neighborhood for a year or so. I used these images in my work, as examples of forms and mark-making processes that normally are overlooked as a literacy practice.

I had also been using Flickr (http://www.flickr.com), the photosharing site for a number of years, and here I gradually built up a set of pictures on graffiti. These pictures had received some comments from others but had never really created a stir except in one instance when a colleague was rather vociferous about how graffiti defaced the environment. Little did I know that some graffiti artists actually used Flickr to store images of their own work, and, over time, had come across some of my pictures on that same site. As a result I received some illuminating comments—translations and footnotes to some of the work I had photographed—and then an invite to the Graffiti Jam. I almost decided not to go, but in the end my curiosity won out.

The air was thick with the smell of spraypaint and the sound of R&B music when I arrived. Some of the artists worked freehand; others from sketches or manga strips. I was acknowledged by some and ignored by others as I took my pictures. One of the organizers talked to me and told me how there was no place for some of these people to work and how they were forced to do "illegals" on warehouse buildings and railway bridges, always keeping an eye out for the police and so on. This was writing on the run indeed! But the organizer also explained how across England, the graffiti, the music and the related dance styles were part of a shared culture that united this diverse social group of mostly young people. The graffiti artists had a shared sense of identity. Traveling from other cities to this abandoned tennis court, the site of the Graffiti Jam, was an important social occasion, an act of group affiliation.

My favorite photograph from that day shows a paint-spattered ghetto-blaster, a discarded hoodie, and a stack of cans, both spray paint and extra strong lager beer cans. Later on, when I uploaded my photographs to Flickr (see Figure 4.1), I received a range of comments in response. Some appreciated the pictures themselves and some heaped praise on the graffiti itself. One commenter politely suggested that I remove a picture that showed someone's face. Only the week before there had been some prosecutions targeting graffiti artists; I duly obliged, removing that shot from my photostream.

Figure 4.1: Graffiti collection (from: http://www.flickr.com/photos/on-the-run/)
Reproduced with permission of Yahoo! Inc. (c)2009 Yahoo! Inc. FLICKR
and the FLICKR logo are registered trademarks of Yahoo! Inc.

It would be easy to make grand claims about photosharing. Sites like Flickr are used in many different ways, but most of the time the people using it show ordinary, everyday events: their children growing up, their parties, their holiday snaps, and things in their neighborhood that interest them. And that's really the way I use Flickr. Flickr (perhaps it would be more accurate to say Flickrites) constitutes an online community. It's a community just like any other but one which is constructed at least partly in an online space. You can find professional photography, gifted amateurs, the arty, the quirky and of course, in the twilight zone, hidden from view, there are the less salubrious images and the outright pornographic pictures (offensive images are reported, flagged and hidden from "normal" or public view as we shall see later).

In what follows, I want to tease out some important themes that show how social networking around photographs illustrates some of the central features of Web 2.0, the attraction of user-generated content, and how new practices are emerging which present exciting opportunities for learners and teachers. In doing this I will focus almost exclusively on Flickr, arguing that it is not only a hugely popular photosharing site but that its design illustrates and supports social networking. To introduce these themes I want to spend a short while thinking back over the events that led to the Graffiti Jam, described above, and some of the issues that this raises for me and for educators and researchers interested in new media.

Picturing social networks

By uploading my own pictures of graffiti on to the Flickr site, labeling them, and putting them on public view, I had in some ways "gone public" about my own interest in graffiti as a literacy practice. Although it could be argued that the public is in this case limited to people who might be motivated to search the internet for images of graffiti and further limited by the rather slim possibility that they might come across my modest collection within this particular site, there is certainly no restriction on the viewing of a Flickr image that has been flagged as public. Flickr, with some 6 million accounts, is undoubtedly a very popular photosharing site (Guinness Book of Flickr Statistics, 2007), but more than this, its functionality allows for social networking. So visitors can comment on photographs, add tags to photos, and send each other messages through Flickr mail. In short, Flickr presents a context for social affiliation. In his studies of videogaming, Gee (2004a; 2004b) introduces the concept of *affinity spaces* as a way of describing these kinds of contexts for social affiliation: social contexts that are guided by purpose, interest or content. Here we can see how Flickr provides a context for multiple affinity groups, such as the graffiti affinity group and spaces I've described above.

Studies of Web 2.0 repeatedly refer to the concept of social networking as a way of describing one of its key characteristics (Davies & Merchant, 2009; Lankshear & Knobel, 2006), and, laying aside for the moment more complex accounts, most Web 2.0 applications can be defined by their dependence on user-generated content and the opportunities they provide for interaction between users. In this way, interaction takes place around a "social object" (Engestrom, 2007). In the case of Flickr, the social object is the digital photograph; for Amazon it is the book, and for YouTube, the video. These social objects are the focus of user-generated content and the resulting interaction that takes place. As objects become of particular interest to individuals, a social network often develops around them. This is not particularly different to the formation of traditional interest groups, save for two aspects. First, because the interaction is online, social networks are often dispersed (time and location are no obstacles to communication), and second, because social networking sites allow for varying degrees of engagement, they lend themselves to lightweight engagement and multiple group membership (see Benkler, 2006, for a fuller discussion of the implications of this phenomenon).

Concerns over the threat posed to the established social order through the growth of virtual communities begin to seem rather alarmist when we consider how Web 2.0 networking merely extends existing social interactions. In my own engagement with Flickr, something like three quarters of my interactions are, in fact, with people I already know and see face-to-face on a regular basis. So, rather than undermining social interaction, photosharing can be a form of social enrichment. Displaying pictures online can, on the one hand, add another dimension to relationships with friends and family. They may well comment on what you have uploaded when you next meet in person or view and comment on your photographs when you are traveling. On the other hand, as the graffiti example illustrates, photosharing also can lead to the development of brand new relationships. In this way we can see how sharing online can both thicken existing social ties and help to establish new ones. More complex patterns arise as offline friends begin to interact online, and online friends arrange face-to-face meetings. Of course, some online friends remain just that and have no particular interest in anything more (see Merchant, 2007a). This new pattern of social interaction has been described by Wellman (2002) as "networked individualism," and it signals the potential of Web 2.0 applications to organize social relations to suit the individual.

Pleasing yourself

The popular misconception that online communities (like MySpace or Facebook, for example) present some sort of danger, as we have seen, clearly does not hold then for Flickr. In fact, to the contrary, it does seem to be the case that social networking sites such as Flickr create new social possibilities. As mentioned earlier, Wellman (2002) introduces the concept of "networked individualism" to describe the way in which individuals can begin to exert more control over their levels of social participation by making informed choices about who they interact with and when. In this way, "user-generated content systems" like YouTube, and social networking sites like Facebook allow for more fluid social engagement. Decisions about levels of participation in photosharing communities are placed firmly in the hands of the user, as we shall see in the following section. At the most basic entry level, you can simply use Flickr as a private online archive of photographs. You then have the opportunity to view, download or upload your images directly from the Flickr server on any networked computer, wherever you are, and at any time. There is no pressure or obligation to do any more than this.

Many users are keen to make slightly more of photosharing though, by allowing contacts (classed either as friends, family, or both) to view and comment on particular photographs. This level of use gives the individual the choice of restricting viewing to existing networks or to personalized networks created as a friends list. This is entirely consistent with the notion of networked individualism, since the control lies in the hands of the user. At the next level, a more adventurous use is to make some, or all, of your images public, thereby entering more fully into the photosharing community. As we shall see, this can lead to wider involvement and networking (see Davies & Merchant, 2007), although the extent of this engagement and networking, still, remains largely controlled by the user. In this way, you "please yourself" in the Flickr environment, and it is precisely this that makes it a high quality Web 2.0 site and service. Joining groups and making new contacts and friends are achieved by invitation and consent. Flickr is designed so that sophisticated social networking tools—such as privacy controls, comment displays, photo sequencing, and category labels—are placed at the disposal of the individual.

My own use of photosharing can be seen as a way of sustaining and enriching communication within a dispersed network of friends and contacts; for me, it's an additional way of keeping in touch. As well as this, invitations to join online groups or to submit pictures to topical or thematic "image pools" can add a further attraction to using Flickr. As with blogging, there is an interesting and motivating "recognition effect" when someone comments on an image you have uploaded (Davies & Merchant, 2007). Such comments may be humorous, or simply appreciative of the object or the photographic merits of one's image. Flickr offers multiple opportunities for social interaction and so communication is both densely layered and fluid. Davies (2006, p. 219) describes how this works, as Flickr members add:

contributions such as digital images, comments about photographs (comments on photo content, composition, format, source and meanings) and technological solutions and suggestions; as well as all kinds of information. These contributions are brought to the Flickr space, thus constituting the fabric of the Flickr space. The space is therefore in a state of constant affirmation and renewal, for contributions can be seen to both sustain the existing values as well as develop them.

In this way, joining Flickr is about becoming part of a much wider community. But the architecture of the online space allows the individual to control the level and frequency of involvement and to use photosharing in ways that are most pleasing or useful to the individual.

SECTION TWO

Getting started with Flickr

All you need to get started with Flickr is a digital camera and an internet connection; in fact, you can even begin to explore the site before you decide to upload any of your own photographs. On the home page of Flickr (http://www.flickr.com) you can take the official tour (see the hyperlink labeled "Take the Tour") and this will take you through a 7-stage orientation process. If you have read the previous section of the chapter, this is probably not necessary; you could simply sign up for a Flickr account. The initial sign-up process is straightforward and free of charge. You just go to http://www.flickr.com, click on the "Create Your Account" button, and follow the instructions.

This requires you to create a Yahoo ID (if you don't already have one), enter your email address, and confirm some basic details. Once you are signed up it is well worth spending some time simply exploring the site. What follows is a straightforward guide to doing this. Individuals will want to explore the site in their own ways, according to their own interests and ways of learning. Below I suggest some ways in which you might get to know Flickr—they are not in any particular sequence but point to some of the features that you may find interesting. Alternatively you can locate a Flickr tutorial on YouTube (e.g., search for "Flickr" + "tutorial") or go to orangejack's tutorial, which is a more advanced guide that is linked to his own examples in Flickr (at: http://rob.orangejack.com/2006/01/25/get-flicker).

Searching using tags

Once you are in the Flickr environment it is well worth becoming familiar with the social tagging system. Tags are the descriptors (technically referred to as "metadata") that people use when sharing their pictures online. Tagging operates like a key-word system. For example, the graffiti photographs I referred to above show tags like "street art," "graffiti," "writing," "Sheffield." These labels were chosen and added by me to help categorize my photographs and to help other people find my photographs. To see how this works, go to the Flickr "Explore" page (at: http://flickr.com/explore). Scrolling down this page you'll see the Flickr *tagcloud* (see Figure 4.2). This tagcloud is a summary of the most commonly used tags in Flickr, with the larger-sized words representing the most popular tags. The aggregation of tags is sometimes referred to as a *folksonomy* (see Marlow et al., 2006). The idea behind a folksonomy is that a body of knowledge can be built democratically through participant-users without recourse to the traditional authority of a discipline, a body of experts, or an established tradition of practice.

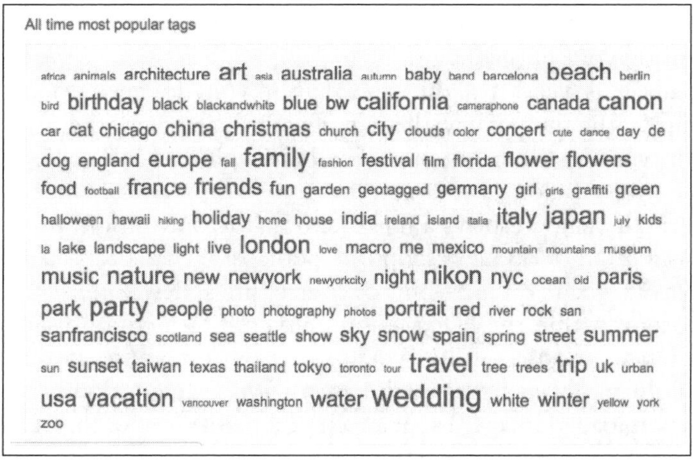

Figure 4.2: The Flickr tagcloud. Reproduced with permission of Yahoo! Inc. (c)2009 Yahoo! Inc. FLICKR and the FLICKR logo are registered trademarks of Yahoo! Inc.

The tagcloud is only one of several ways of exploring photos on Flickr. The main Flickr tagcloud will show you popular tags but, of course, you might not be interested in any of these. Let's suppose, for example, that you are interested in images of Canada. Although Canada does not feature on the tagcloud you can still search for photos people have tagged with the word "Canada." A simple tag search will take you straight through to the most recently uploaded photographs that have been given the "Canada" tag. Results of this tag-based search will be displayed as a grid of thumbnail images. Clicking on a specific picture will take you directly to a larger view of this image, whereas clicking on the photographer's Flickr name (underlined as a blue hyperlink) will take you through to that person's page or photostream.

Uploading your pictures

Flickr offers a number of different tools for uploading your own photographs. Figure 4.3 shows the basic image upload interface. Here you need to click on "You" on the navigation bar at the top of the Flickr page (it's near the Flickr icon and opens a drop-down menu). Choose the "Upload Photos and Videos" option. If this isn't showing, then you need to check that you are signed in, since this option is always available when you are. From here on, you just need to follow the onscreen instructions. You can upload directly from your camera, from images on your desktop, or images stored on a smart card or flash drive plugged into your computer. I find it quite useful to edit and label my images *before* I start uploading—otherwise they just have an obscure numeric filename and you end up with images you might not particularly want on your photostream.

Uploading is very straightforward, but you do need to be patient. Depending on the time of day, the size of your images, and the speed of your machine it will take a few minutes. The basic uploader interface or window shows you how far along you are in the uploading process. Once uploading is complete, the page displays a message near the bottom of the screen that says "Finished! Next: add a description, perhaps?" That's all you need to do to display your image online—but, of course, titles, descriptions and tags are very important within the Flickr community, not to mention useful for personal reference purposes, so it's worth spending some time on this by clicking on the hyperlinked text "Click here to add a description" that appears below each uploaded image. From a technical point of view, this is how Flickr prompts you to add metadata about your images (Marlow et al., 2006).

Because Flickr searches take into account image titles as well as tags and member screen names, choosing a suitable title for your photograph is helpful. In the example displayed in Figure 4.3, I have chosen "Footprint in the Snow" for the title of the image, which is about as accurate as you can get. You have a little more leeway with tags, because you can describe your image in a number of different ways. Here, I've used "boot," "snow," "footprint," and "print" as my tags for this image. Finally you can add your description. Descriptions vary enormously in the Flickr environment. Some Flickrites use the description to provide further information about the context or about camera settings used to take the photo; some use this option to evaluate or comment on their image, and many simply don't use this function at all.

Any of the above operations can be left to a later date, and they can all be easily modified. If you want to change a description or add or remove a tag, simply click on the image with which you want to work and the options will be available on the new page that appears after you click through. This is also one of the ways by which you can create a set of pictures, grouped, for example, around a theme, an event or an interest.

Figure 4.3: Titles, descriptions and tags
Reproduced with permission of Yahoo! Inc. (c)2009 Yahoo! Inc. FLICKR and the FLICKR logo are registered trademarks of Yahoo! Inc.

At this point it might be interesting to look at how experienced users of the Flickr site operate and how they use these and other features of photosharing (see also Chapter 5 in this volume). Here are some examples:

- *Nancy Waldman* (onscreen: nuanc) runs a webzine called The Practical Creative Quarter (http://practicallycreative.net). She takes a whole range of interesting images. They are titled, tagged and organized into myriad sets. Search for "Barry's grandfather's fiddle" to see how Nancy uses notes on her images (you need to roll your cursor over the picture to activate and read the notes). See: http://www.flickr.com/photos/nuanc

- *Thomas Williams* (screen name: thw05) is a professional photographer who concentrates on industrial photography. He uses precise titles, and his descriptions that are usually about the image and why he took it. His photographs are carefully tagged and grouped in to sets. See: http://flickr .com/photos/thwphotos

- *Julia Davies* (screen name: DrJoolz) is a friend and colleague. She is an academic who enjoys photography and writes about Flickr and other new literacy practices. DrJoolz uses titles, contextual descriptions, and tags. She enjoys the interactivity of Flickr and responds quickly to comments on her pictures. For example, look at the image "swoon and man with bag" for a good example of the kind of social interaction that takes place within her photostream. See: http://www.flickr.com/photos/drjoolz
- *Craig Robertson* (screen name: craigrobertson), based in Scotland, takes some amazing landscapes. He uses titles, has a lot of tags and submits his photographs to a number of image pools. His images attract a lot of attention. For example if you search his photostream for "Stairway to heaven" you can read the many comments made about this particular image (currently at 66, which is a large number of comments within the Flickr universe). See: http://www.flickr.com/photos/craigrobertson

These are examples of some of the ways in which photosharing and social networking intersect, but it is worth recalling how I previously outlined ways in which members are in control of their level of participation in Flickr communities and can "please themselves" with respect to how they choose to use Flickr. How you choose to participate is entirely up to you. In addition, it's also very much worth noting that you don't have to be a skilled photographer (I'm certainly not one) to enjoy what photosharing has to offer. Likewise, many people—again, like me—are quite content to display quite ordinary "snaps" from their everyday life rather than limit their displays to serious artistic images.

Creating your Flickr identity

Venturing out into online social networking spaces is a personal choice. For some people this is a daunting experience, whilst others find it exhilarating and even mildly addictive! The first obvious step is to establish a Flickr identity by working on your profile page. You can access this by clicking on "Your Profile" on the drop-down menu at the top of your "home" screen. You'll find it alongside the "You" hyperlink. Editing your profile page allows you to say a bit about yourself and your interests. You can also upload a photograph or image to represent you (this is referred to as your "buddy icon" and appears on your personal pages, on comments you leave on photos, and on messages that you send to other Flickrites). Like many people I use a photograph of myself, but others maintain anonymity by choosing a symbol or graphic image instead.

By clicking on "Your contacts" at the top of the profile page, you can find out how to invite friends to view your photostream. As you begin to participate more in Flickr you will increase your number of friends, and they will be listed on your profile page. Most of my Flickr friends I know quite well already; some I meet face-to-face on a regular basis, and others, usually because they are geographically remote, I only see from time to time. Contacts who are not existing friends, but people I simply have contact with through Flickr and shared interests, are also displayed here. This is a good illustration of how online social networking can both strengthen existing social ties with friends and family and help to establish new relationships.

Images that are marked as "public" on your photostream will soon begin to attract some attention, particularly if they are seen as interesting by others and even more so if they are carefully titled and tagged. Others who are photosharing may leave a comment or invite you to be a contact. Of course, you are free to accept or decline, but in this way you can begin to build up a list of contacts. This means that new photographs you upload will appear on their Flickr home page, and similarly, their new images will appear on your home page. Over time you can build up quite a complex web of interactions through photosharing.

Participating in the Flickr community

Full participation in photosharing depends upon responding to approaches from others who visit your photostream as well as active engagement with the images uploaded by your friends, contacts, and the wider community. New content and regular interaction play a central role in the affirmation and renewal that are necessary to maintaining online social networks. As Davies (2006, p. 222) observes, "the organisation of content and the interactivity of [Flickr] work in unison, each fostering the other, keeping the site viable and dynamic."

So, regular uploading of images is enhanced by the notes people attach to your actual images, comments they leave in response to an image, and Flickr mail that is exchanged between friends and other contacts. It is as if this written, verbal interaction is the lifeblood of the social network. As the examples of different people's photostreams described above show, this creates a dense and sometimes nuanced web of meanings. In Figure 4.4 we can see how some of these richer meanings are created. The image has a title, description, and a tag list, which provide the wider communicative context. Superimposed on the photograph is a note, which reads: "You must be crazy if you think we could get away with that!" This message is revealed as you run your cursor over the image. In this case the note has been used to function as a speech bubble. In the text box below, titled "Add your comment," you can see an interactive comment in the process of being composed.

Figure 4.4: Comments and notes add meanings to images

In this way, some images can become the focal point for a whole range of interactions between a number of people. This is a good example of multi-modality (Kress, 2003) at work—the visual and verbal modes work together to establish and develop meanings.

The architecture of Flickr also provides other opportunities to create affinity spaces through the use of image pools or groups. These can be either public or private and are "owned" by a group administrator. Public groups can opt to be either invitation only or they can allow anyone to join. Private groups are hidden from view and you join by invitation only. There are groups on just about every conceivable topic area. For example, a quick search for image pools on insects showed 4,281 groups at the time of writing, with the largest group having 9,473 members. If you want to increase your participation in Flickr, then the message is clear: join groups you are invited to join, find groups to join that share a photographic interest of yours, or even set up a group of your own.

Using Flickr as a resource

Many popular uses of Flickr extend out of the photosharing site itself. My account of the Graffiti Jam at the beginning of this chapter illustrates one way in which this can happen. As I have explained, visual and verbal exchanges around posted images serve to enrich social contact between friends and family, as well as with those within the Flickr community. It is also not unusual for some of these virtual friendships to become "real" friendships. One of the ways in which this happens is through Flickr meets. Here, groups who are interested in photographing similar subjects, or those with members living in the same area, will arrange to meet up in person with the intention of taking photographs together. So, for example, the Flickr Blog—a companion to Flickr itself that's used to alert users to things of interest (see: http://blog.flickr.net)—advertised a Street Art Photowalk on June 14, 2008, organized by members of the Tate "Street or Studio" Group (see also: http://upcoming.yahoo.com/event/734886). Figure 4.5 shows Trois Tetes (camera held up to face)—a real-life friend of mine—on one such Flickr meet.

Figure 4.5: Flickrites on a photowalk

The ways in which Flickr can become a resource for wider social networking are augmented by its capacity to work alongside, and integrate with, other online spaces. The interoperability of Flickr and a number of blogging services allow users to post images directly from their photostream to their personal blog. This encourages two-way traffic between bloggers and the photosharing community. Flickr members can direct visitors to their photostream on to their blog (for instance, by including their blog address in their Flickr profile), while readers of their blog can be directed to Flickr, by clicking on images embedded within blog posts, or via a click-through Flickr "badge" on the blog's sidebar.

Other Web 2.0 applications also integrate well with Flickr. It is possible, for example, to subscribe to photostream syndication (RSS) feeds from Flickr to keep track of friends' updates. I use Netvibes (http://www.netvibes.com) to organize and share my feeds. Netvibes is a customizable web service that acts like a kind of "webtop" (i.e., like your computer's "desktop," but completely online). You link your blogs, Flickr photostream, social network spaces, and anything else you use regularly online to this one webpage that automatically updates every time you log on. In addition, Voicethread (http://www.voicethread.com)—explored in a later section—allows you to import images directly from your photostream into a multimedia environment to create a customized and interactive slideshow. This has obvious social affordances in terms of developing networks of interested others but also has considerable educational potential.

Other Flickr features

It is simply not possible in a short chapter to capture and describe all the features of this popular and sophisticated photosharing site. My choices have been guided partly by my own preferences but [partly] also by the desire to illustrate some of those Web 2.0 features that seem to have direct relevance to education. So, rather than ignore some of the aspects of Flickr that I have chosen not to focus on in detail, this section ends with a listing of applications that you're likely to find both interesting and useful.

- *Geo-tagging*. This is a facility that allows you to match images to specific locations. Using the "Organizer" menu on the navigation bar in Flickr, you simply drag and drop your chosen image on to a world, regional or local map. (There's a short screencast tutorial at: http://flickr.com/help/screencasts/vol1/)

- *Discussion forums*. This is a standard feature of many websites. Forums on Flickr are usually located within groups, and so they become useful for following up particular interests or needs. For example, the "Flickr for Education" group has an active discussion board where educators exchange ideas about using photosharing to promote learning.

- *Interestingness*. This is an idea developed by Flickr. It is a way of drawing your attention to different images in the photosharing community. If you click the "Explore" button on your Flickr navigation bar, the first page gives you a brief rationale for the "Explore" function. A further click will take you to the most recent "interesting" images. However, the algorithm used by Flickr to calculate "interestingness" remains a mystery and is hotly debated among aficionados.

- *Popularity*. Information on number of views per image can be quite a hook for some people. On your Flickr home page you will notice that Flickr automatically lists the number of views (and comments) for each photograph. But you can also get information on your whole Flickr stream. Clicking the "Popular" button on your navigation bar takes you to a page that rank orders your images. You can look at rankings for number of views, number of comments, number of times an image has been nominated by someone as a favorite . . . and a ranking in terms of interestingness. It's quite engaging to watch these data over time and to see how your photographs are doing within the Flickr community.

- *Flickr stats.* You can also request more sophisticated Flickr statistics for your photostream. It usually takes Flickr 24 hours to generate this information. This service is pretty sophisticated and probably has little relevance for the occasional user, but it does give some insight into the kind of information that can be collected. Among other things, Flickr stats provide graphic representations of views over time, more detailed information on the images most viewed, and details of where your viewers are coming from (i.e., referrals from websites outside Flickr).

SECTION THREE

Learning through photosharing

Photosharing is applicable to a wide range of educational topics and contexts. It certainly could be argued that, in a very general sense, the usefulness of any resource depends upon the vision and creativity of the teacher and the capacity of learners to experiment with, and explore, its wider potential. At a very basic level, a photosharing site like Flickr is an enormous archive of images that can be drawn upon to support and enrich almost any area of learning. After all, recent developments in the socio-semiotic field of multimodality (see Kress & Leeuven, 1996; Kress, 2003) have shown how for some kinds of learning, the visual image can be more effective than a verbal explanation. It is also widely accepted that the inter-relationship between the verbal and the visual helps to create new meanings (Duncum, 2004).

While photosharing in and of itself clearly constitutes a substantial general resource for teaching (see also Chapter 5 in this volume), this section focuses on some important and specific educational uses. In what follows I suggest five areas in which Flickr can play an important role. These are illustrated by examples from a range of educational contexts. The five areas are as follows:

- *Learning through seeing.* This is concerned with the ways in which sharing visual images can lead to a process of learning which I describe as "attentive noticing." Here, the learner, by becoming part of a specialist or expert community, is able to build on an initial interest in order to learn more about a topic.

- *Learning through reflection.* This depends on using an image or a sequence of images to frame and provide critical distance on an object or event. Part of the process of reflection involves looking again or looking more closely at phenomena, and I argue that visual images provide potent opportunities for doing so.

- *Learning about image.* This is about building an understanding of visual culture, about image composition and effect. It also involves looking at image and context, as well as at how techniques such as cropping and manipulation change the way we read the visual.

- *Learning about multimodality.* This can complement work on learning about images, but looks explicitly at how the visual image mixed with other modalities (such as sounds and music, spoken language, and the written word) creates meanings.

- *Learning about Web 2.0.* As we have seen, photosharing sites such as Flickr, incorporate key social networking features. The wide range of social interactions that are supported, the practices of tagging and aggregation, as well as features such as personalization and inter-operability make photosharing a good study in Web 2.0 orientation.

Learning through seeing

In a paper titled "Mind the Gap(s)" (Merchant, 2007a), I wrote about my own experiences in learning through social tagging. I showed how the process of categorization led to the accumulation of new information as well as a new way of seeing. I illustrated this through my own involvement in the "Padlocks" group on Flickr (see: http://www.flickr.com/groups/28363713 @N00). I described what I called the process of "attentive noticing" and knowledge building in this particular area. Although the example was of a slightly frivolous everyday topic, you only have to substitute the attentive noticing of padlocks for looking at, say, geometric shapes in the school environment and you have a familiar item in the early years mathematics curriculum. Alternatively, placing the focus on categorizing lifeforms as vertebrates or invertebrates establishes a fundamental building block for the natural sciences. In this way, social tagging and the construction of folksonomies have an important role to play in illustrating how knowledge-building practices between dispersed individuals can be achieved. It also underscores the educational relevance of photosharing (Marlow et al., 2006).

Figure 4.6 is a model of the processes involved in social tagging and suggests ways in which we can learn through seeing. In the first part of the cycle, I distinguish between the everyday experience of *seeing* the world and *attentive noticing*. Seeing can transform into attentive noticing when we begin to label things in our environment. The act of labeling is normally linguistic—it could be an oral or symbolic representation—but in the Flickr environment, this is achieved through written words or phrases. To suggest that the simple act of attentive noticing leads automatically to *knowing* is of course oversimplifying complex issues. It might be better to cautiously suggest that attentive noticing sets up the conditions for knowing. More importantly, though, I suggest that this cycle of events can transform our seeing into *informed seeing*, as we begin to look more closely at objects.

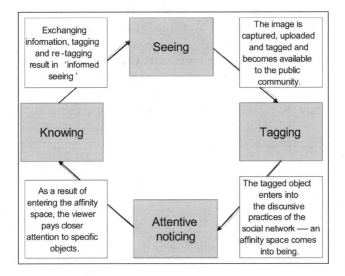

Figure 4.6: Attentive noticing and the role of category-tagging (Merchant, 2007a, p. 252)

A final and important element in this process hinges on motivation and purpose. It seems to me that the amount of energy and resources that one is prepared to invest in a particular act of knowledge-building will determine the level of social participation and the learning that takes place. In short, the degree to which one identifies with the affinity space directly affects learning outcomes.

This model shows how informal learning can take place through the meanings that develop around visual images of specific objects and events. It illustrates how a visually oriented affinity space can provide opportunities for learning by encouraging participants to "look closer" and to exchange information that can facilitate that process.

As we have seen, an important feature that Flickr shares with other social networking sites is the use of tags. Tags can be used to search items within one's own photostream or in everyone's photos. Clicking on a tag, such as "padlocks," will conjure all the images that have been tagged with that word. In this way, a tag search will change the context of individual images, showing an image alongside others that are tagged in the same way, reflecting something about the meaning of the term in this community.

Category tagging is a process by which objects or ideas can be classified *by users.* So in blogging, photo-sharing, and music-sharing sites, one can code content with keywords or tags that can then be searched for and grouped in a variety of ways. Of course, in some ways there is little difference between this activity and the established academic practice of attaching keywords to journal articles; however, there are some small but significant differences.

First, category-tags in online social networks are, as noted, primarily generated by user interest, rather than by pre-set norms and conventions. Second, category-tags can be changed, updated or added to as new relationships to other objects are realised. And third, other people can add category-tags to your objects. This allows objects to be pooled and grouped in diverse and fluid ways in a process that is controlled by the community of users, rather than by an elite group. Users' values, interests, and priorities are the ones that count in a folksonomy, and these will change over time as the nature of the people and images continue to change.

A folksonomy is responsive to change in data and interactivity. Imagine a library in which books and journals could be organized and reorganized at the click of a finger by subject, by topic, by date or by size and colour—or whatever category readers apply—and you begin to understand the magic of a folksonomy.

Learning through reflection

Sequences of visual images can be particularly useful in developing what Schön (1983) has described as reflection on action. Very often, when we are immersed in educational activities, in practical or professional learning, it can be quite challenging to untangle ourselves from the immediacy of specific incidents and to reflect more deeply on something. Whether you want young children to reflect on what they are learning through playful experimentation in block play or in the sand tray or whether you want teachers to reflect on aspects of their classroom practice, visual images can help by allowing us to see things differently, to make the familiar strange, and to capture or frame our experience in new ways. This sort of reflection can be approached in a number of ways. Here I suggest two possibilities.

The first and most simple application involves using two tools already available in the Flickr environment: the comments and the notes functions (both described earlier). As an example of this, 10-year-old children involved in a unit of work on river pollution took photographs of a waterway that runs through a nearby urban area. In class they researched the ways in which fly-tipping, industrial effluent, and non-native plant growth were threatening local wildlife habitats. Some of their photographs showed examples of these forms of pollution. Using the teacher's Flickr account, these images were uploaded to her photostream. Children used the notes function to annotate the images, having been told to concentrate on the possible outcome(s) of each pollutant. This helped to move them on from simple labeling to analysis and reflection. Other adults in the school were then encouraged to comment on the annotated images and the children in turn dialogued with these comments. Through this work, children learned to use still images as stimulus for reflection and to engage in online discussion about environmental issues.

A second example of using images to promote reflection involves the use of Voicethread (http://www.voicethread.com). Voicethread allows you to create a slideshow of still or moving images, which others can then view and upon which they can comment. Comments can be either written in a text box or recorded as a spoken comment. Flickr images can be imported into Voicethread by following simple onscreen instructions. Student teachers in my courses have been using this application to analyze and reflect on their own teaching. They are able to take photographs that highlight resource-based learning in their placement contexts and upload these to the site. The slideshow feature encourages them to look at learning sequences, and they begin by recording their own commentary on the activities they have initiated. This work can then be viewed by their peers, who add their own spoken or written reflections. Voicethread promotes reflection through interaction, with the added benefit that participants do not need to be co-present. When students are working in different locations this is an extremely useful approach.

These are just two illustrative examples. Of course there are many other possibilities. For example, many educators use their blogs to display images and to provide reflective commentary on them. Since it is now especially easy to use images in blogs—particularly if you are using a photosharing site like Flickr—the opportunity to post longer reflective pieces of writing based on images is attractive.

Learning about image

In one sense, any educational use of photosharing involves some sort of learning about the visual image. However, much of this learning can be quite incidental. Learning *about* image is very much about developing an understanding of the meanings we make when viewing images and necessarily places an explicit focus on how the selection and presentation of an image influence viewers' interpretations. This more technical approach to images is sometimes referred to as "visual literacy." Although I usually avoid the use of this term in my own work (see Merchant, 2007b, for an account of why), it usefully draws attention to the centrality of the visual in contemporary life and to the processes of encoding and decoding meaning from images that are important for full social participation (Averinou & Ericson, 1997). Advocates of media literacy regularly suggest that educational institutions should be helping students to question, analyze, and evaluate material, including visual images. Ofcom, the UK's independent regulator for the communications industry, takes a somewhat softer line and encourages an approach that helps learners to access, understand, and create media (Ofcom, 2008). In what follows I take the position that educators should encourage an approach in which students become critical and analytical producers and consumers of visual material.

Bamford (2003), in a helpful exploration of visual literacy, uses linguistic terminology in distinguishing between the syntax and semantics of the visual image. For Bamford, syntactical elements include things such as framing, scale, tone and space, whereas semantic elements refer to form and structure, cultural views and assumptions, and the relationship between producers and consumers. Although she acknowledges that these elements can be studied separately, Bamford (2003) suggests that an integrated analysis is a more useful approach. So, for example, a class of 14-year-olds explored how the use of different syntactic elements in their digital images influenced interpretations of their work. Using different kinds of framing, close-ups, and experiments with color manipulation, they produced images of their school environment which sometimes depicted it as a busy, exciting and attractive environment and, at other times, as a gray, run-down and un-inspiring place. These were then shared with a partner school using Flickr in order to collect comments and to test the effect of different images. In this work, students were able to learn how visual image choices were influential in the production of school brochures, promotional material and, of course, in advertisements.

Classroom work that involves learning about image is appropriate at all ages. Often it is planned as part of the literacy curriculum, as the examples of work in the 5–11 years age range in *More than Words* (QCA, 2004) show. Photosharing can add an extra dimension to this sort of work by making images available to a wider audience and by exploiting the learning potential of social networking.

Learning about multimodality

Over the last five years, following the groundbreaking work of Kress (1996, 2003), there has been a great deal of interest in promoting multimodality in educational settings. Kress' work not only illustrates the ways in which different modes communicate meaning, it also draws attention to the ways in which meanings are made from the inter-relationship between modes. Music videos that combine the verbal and gestural with moving image are a good example of the ways in which different modes can work together to create meanings (see also Chapter 9 in this volume). And in a similar way, Flickr images can be a useful resource in educational explorations of multimodality. Perhaps it is worth noting at this point that even the most cursory explorations of the Flickr site will reveal how the social interaction that takes place is equally dependent on visual and verbal exchanges.

It has been argued that visual images rarely function on their own; Duncum (2004, p. 252), for example, goes so far as to claim that "*[t]here are no exclusively visual sites*. All cultural sites that involve imagery include various ratios of other communicative modes and many employ more than vision."

These ideas, like the perspectives on visual literacy in the previous section, touch on some larger debates, which cannot be fully explored in this chapter. But it is important to underline that photosharing sites like Flickr are inherently multimodal and, as such, offer many possibilities for exploring the interplay between verbal and visual expression and interpretation.

Learning about Web 2.0

As I have repeatedly argued, Flickr incorporates many of the defining features of Web 2.0. In a way, you could see Flickr as a case study of social networking and Web 2.0 design. This, in fact, is the line taken in *Web 2.0 for Schools* (Davies & Merchant, 2009). Colleagues looking for a resource to use that illustrates what Web 2.0 means could introduce their students to Flickr and some of its features in much the same way as I have done in an earlier section in this chapter titled, *Getting started with Flickr*. Below I list some features that could be used to evaluate Web 2.0 sites and could be illustrated or explored through the use of Flickr. These features draw on the work of Harper (2007) but have been adapted and extended to incorporate my own views and the particular emphasis on learning that underpins this chapter.

- *Attractiveness.* What attracts users to this site? Once it has been "found," how does it encourage you to become more engaged?

- *Use value.* How clear are the benefits of this site? Can you see how it could be used for enjoyment, learning, or in conjunction with other online or offline activity?

- *Signing up.* How easy is the sign-up process? Are there any hidden catches? Does it feel safe?

- *Clarity.* Is the on-screen design helpful? Are the navigation tools intuitive? How is exploration facilitated?

- *Trust.* How can you gauge the trustworthiness of the provider and the community? How are you and your material protected? How easy is it to avoid or block inappropriate material or behavior? Does it seem fairly easy to leave the community?

- *Invitation and participation.* Does the site encourage participation and uploading of your own material? Is this relatively easy to do?

- *Interactivity.* How is interaction and communication encouraged and controlled?

- *Customization.* Does the site allow you to personalize your own page? Is this easy to do? How can you manage and update your own profile?

- *Updating.* What sorts of updates are provided and to what extent do users have control over updates?

- *User feedback.* What are the different kinds of user feedback that can be left on the site? What sorts of feedback from other users or the site operators can be expected?

- *Interoperability.* How might the site, your profile identity, or material from the site be incorporated into other online spaces?

These features and associated questions could be used as a starting point for exploring Flickr as a Web 2.0 learning tool. Alternatively, however, educators may prefer to encourage their students to discover features for themselves and to generate their own criteria and perhaps to use these to compare and contrast with other photosharing or social networking sites.

A final view

Photosharing sites like Flickr have contributed to new ways of looking at the role of the visual image in our lives. It is as if our albums of photographs can now be released from the shelves and cupboards of our domestic life and thrown open for public viewing. As I have argued earlier, this has turned our visual images into social objects that can "focalize" our online networking. As user statistics on photosharing suggest, this has considerable attraction for people who wish to develop and strengthen friendships and establish interest groups around topics that they find attractive. In this way there is plenty of evidence to suggest that online spaces like Flickr provide rich opportunities for informal learning. Whether that learning is about photography itself, whether [or not] it is considered "worthy" or frivolous, seems to me to be a secondary consideration. The most important lessons to be learned from photosharing are about the power of social participation and its relationship to learning through interaction.

Two key features of Web 2.0 technology are significant in photosharing. They are the centrality of user-generated content and the multiple opportunities afforded to distributed users to interact within any particular site. It has been my intention in this chapter to draw attention to these features, through illustrating how Flickr gets used, how those new to photosharing can investigate its potential, and how educators can explore new kinds of learning that emerge. However, in acknowledging that photosharing suggests new kinds of learning, I am also aware of the extent to which we urgently need more theoretical sophistication, more classroom research and more curriculum development in this area. The simple fact that your visual image can be generated and stored in such a way that it can be viewed by others irrespective of geographical and time constraints, that it persists and can be accessed repeatedly from multiple sites is a potent use of new technology. That the same image can draw comment and stimulate interaction (potentially on a global scale) brings an entirely new set of conditions into being. The ease in which we can engage in this sort of interaction belies the complexity and the social reconfiguration that is implied. We are only just beginning to understand the implications and opportunities that result from relatively accessible online spaces such as those that focus on photosharing. From this point of view, the ideas expressed in this chapter constitute some first steps in image-based DIY media that will continue to grow in sophistication.

References

Averinou, M. & Ericson, J. (1997). A review of the concept of visual literacy. *British Journal of Educational Technology, 28*(4), 280–291.

Bamford, A. (2003). *The visual literacy white paper.* Retrieved July 1, 2008, from http://www.adobe.com/uk/education/pdf/adobe_visual_literacy_paper.pdf

Benkler, Y. (2006). *The wealth of networks: How social production transforms markets and freedom.* New Haven, CT: Yale University Press.

Davies, J. (2006). Affinities and beyond! Developing ways of seeing in online spaces. *E-Learning, 3*(2), 217–231.

Davies, J. & Merchant, G. (2007). Looking from the inside out—academic blogging as new literacy. In M. Knobel & C. Lankshear (Eds.), *A new literacies sampler* (pp. 167–197). New York: Peter Lang.

Davies, J. & Merchant, G. (2009). *Web 2.0 for schools: Learning and social participation.* New York: Peter Lang.

Duncum, P. (2004). Visual culture isn't just visual: Multiliteracy, multimodality and meaning. *Studies in Art Education. 45*(3), 252–264.

Engestrom, J. (2007). *Microblogging: Tiny social objects.* In *On the Future of Participatory Media.* Retrieved May 31, 2008, from http://www.slideshare.net/jyri/microblogging-tiny-social-objects-on-the-future-of-participatory-media

Gee, J. P. (2004a). *What videogames have to teach us about learning and literacy.* New York: Palgrave Macmillan.

Gee, J. P. (2004b). *Situated language and learning: A critique of traditional schooling.* London: Routledge.

Guinness Book of Flickr Statistics (2007). *Fun, Achievements, News, Welcoming and Sharing.* Retrieved May 31, 2008, from http://www.flickr.com/groups/stats/discuss/72157594473501148/

Harper, L. (2007). *Heuristics analysis and redesign.* Retrieved July 1, 2008, from http://www.idesigntech.org/2008/03/30/heuristic-framework-for-evaluating-web-20-applications/

Kress, G. (2003). *Literacy in the new media age.* London: Routledge.

Kress, G. & Leeuwen, T. (1996). *Reading images: The grammar of visual design.* London: Routledge.

Lankshear, C. & Knobel, M. (2006). *New literacies: Everyday practices and classroom learning.* Buckingham: Open University Press.

Marlow, C., Naarman, M., boyd, d., & Davis, M. (2006). HT06, Tagging Paper, Taxonomy, Flickr, Academic Article, ToRead. In U. K. Wiil, P. J. Nürnberg & J. Rubart (Eds.), *Proceedings of the Seventeenth ACM Conference on Hypertext and Hypermedia* (pp. 31–40). Odense, Denmark: ACM Press.

Merchant, G. (2007a). Mind the gap(s): Discourses and discontinuity in digital literacies. *E-Learning, 4*(3), 241–255.

Merchant, G. (2007b). Writing the future. *Literacy, 41*(3), 1–19.

OfCom (2008). *Ofcom's Strategy and Priorities for the Promotion of Media Literacy—A statement.* Retrieved June3, 2008, from http://www.ofcom.org.uk/consult/condocs/strategymedialit/ml_statement/

QCA (2004). *More than words.* Retrieved May 31, 2008, from http://orderline.qca.org.uk/gempdf/1847212875.pdf

Schön, D. (1983). *The reflective practitioner: How professionals think in action.* London: Temple Smith.

Wellman, B. (2002). Little boxes, glocalization, and networked individuals. In M. Tanabe, P. Besselaar & T. Ishida (Eds.), *Digital Cities II: Computational and Sociological Approaches* (pp.10–25). Berlin: Springer.

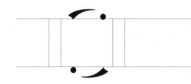

Chapter 5

Photoshopping/photosharing: New media, digital literacies and curatorship

JOHN POTTER

SECTION ONE

Photoshopping/photosharing: Understanding digital literacies and curatorship

The image in Figure 5.1 is taken from the photosharing site, Flickr (http://www.flickr.com; see also Chapter 4 in this volume). It shows some paintings on sale in bright sunlight, propped against a former colonial house in the oldest part of Monterrey in Nuevo Leon State, Mexico.

The picture was taken in March 2005, during a walk in a recess break at a seminar being held in the city. It has been uploaded to the online photosharing service and has been tagged with three words: "Monterrey," "Mexico," and "Nuevo_Leon." If you look closely you will see that you can learn even more about this image. You can see what kind of camera it was taken with (a Canon Powershot A95), and you can follow a link to locate where the photo was taken on a map. As the owner of this space on Flickr you can also edit the tags and any further description. In addition, you can see that this image has generated some engagement with other users of the space. It has been marked as a "favorite" by one user. A positive comment has also been added, alongside a gentle correction of poor spelling by a user called

Figure 5.1: An example from Flickr

"TeoSal." The Flickr software itself analyzed and presented the information about the camera and the location of the photo. This same software also recorded and posted the number of times people have viewed this image. You can also see at the top of the picture that there are tools that the owner could use which would post this very image directly into a blog, allow them to resize and edit the picture, and even, should they wish to do so, order printed copies of this image.

Of all the tools of production and sharing in new media that are capable of fulfilling the promise of closing the gap between the polarities of consumption and production, digital image making is the single most widespread, most-used form. In developed and developing countries, devices capable of taking images of varying degrees of resolution are carried, pointed and clicked; images are captured, stored, sent, saved, organized, tagged, uploaded, downloaded, shared. How many terabytes worth of pictures have just been taken in the space of time it takes to read the opening sentences of this paragraph? If there really is a global form of DIY media production that touches almost all users of the internet, it is the photoshared image.

We can make a case, of course, for the moving image, too; the YouTube/video clip phenomenon is another of these ubiquitous media forms. Yet, research shows the gap between those who consume and those who produce is very wide. Even when we arrive at video hosting websites in search of a tutorial, a clip of a band, a home video, or a holiday video, we are drawn in by the still-image thumbnails, the opening frames on display. Without the play buttons we remain in the world of the still image and the organized and tagged photo album.

This chapter is concerned with aspects of DIY media as they relate to the making, sharing and organizing of still images. Specifically, and with agentive educators in mind (from parent/caregiver through to teacher, tutor, youth worker, lecturer and others), it attempts to draw these strands into current debates about digital literacy, one of a number of emergent new literacies. I aim at working in three different ways in the chapter. In the first section, I will say a little about what is different regarding our personal production and organization of still images in the age of new media. In the second section, I will focus on generic sets of skills: image editing, image sharing and image curating, which could be developed further in a number of different directions. The premise in this second section is not just a degree of awareness of some of the techniques and possibilities but also a desire on the reader's part to find out more about what she or he needs to know and from where that information may be obtained. There will be links to places where users can be found sharing ideas, information, and advice. The third and final section comprises a series of thoughts on how all of this relates to the educational significance of this kind of activity, to the important skills and dispositions which we may expect to develop in our learners as well as alongside them as we endeavor to make meaning from not just images in isolation but images in collections.

I would like to offer some relevant and hopefully resonant vignettes throughout the chapter—in a way, communicating via memes of experience with the reader. Many of us will have been at a concert and found image-harvesting going on all around us, though perhaps not all of us will have experienced the performer engaging in a philosophical debate about reality (see below). Many of us will have received news of a family event via digital images from around the world. Many of us will have been on holiday and felt compelled to experience the places through a lens, lest we forget them or why we went there (Susan Sontag has things to say about us doing this, as we will see). Many of us will have been struck by something useful and usable on the way to work and will have snapped it using whatever device was available. All of these experiences and practices—and more—will be presented in italics, just like this one:

My brother-in-law excitedly announced the arrival of his and his partner's first child with some pictures in his web gallery. Within hours of the appearance of this gallery the link was circulating amongst friends and relatives. I produced an edited set which did not include the actual moments in the operating theatre. So two albums were online in two spaces within minutes of one another (they actually showed the caesarian itself—well he is a doctor, she was a nurse and I guess that's what medical folk do when they share such moments!). The point here is the speed with which the event in Australia reached our side of the world in England and was shared in two edited forms as online albums. And a word here too about the moving image. There was a moving image clip included in the set. And, as it happened, this presented the only problem in terms of storage and software, viewing time and viewing decisions. The still images were the most editable and sharable assets to arrive from the other side of the world.

In some ways this all no longer seems miraculous, particularly to users of photosharing spaces and social networking services (Bebo and Facebook, for example, are enormous repositories of digital images). On the other hand, to be in the situation and to have an affective relationship with events is to experience a connectedness and relatedness online, which was not possible in times gone by.

The study of still images has long attracted scholarly writing and reflection, along with critical, technical and cultural theories to explain them. This body of research pre-dates current theories of digital literacies and networked affinity spaces. Two much-cited touchstones in scholarly writing about images date from the end of the past century. They are Susan Sontag's *On Photography* (1979) and Roland Barthes's *Camera Lucida* (1993). Both texts are meditations on the meaning of meaning-making with still images. Each was written prior to major changes in photo sharing and exhibition possibilities brought about by the widespread adoption of the internet and social networking software as tools for photosharing. However, when Sontag wrote about the multiplicity of images and the human need to record lived experience, she could have been anticipating an era of near-instant recording, editing, and exhibiting. Certainly, viewing online galleries in photosharing sites, such as Flickr or Picasa, or on profile pages in Facebook and elsewhere, calls to mind passages like the following:

> It would not be wrong to speak of people having a compulsion to photograph: to turn experience itself into a way of seeing. Ultimately, having an experience becomes identical with taking a photograph of it, and participating in a public event comes more and more to be equivalent to looking at it in photographed form (Sontag, 1979, p. 24).

When was the last time you attended a concert and did not either take a picture yourself or watch as others fiddled with their cameras to record videos or take still pictures of it? At a concert in London last year, a performer debated with the audience the need to record the performance. I wrote about it afterwards in my blog . . .

> *This was the question at Mark Kozelek's concert last night at the Union Chapel. A number of notices were pinned up all over the venue requesting no taping, no photographs from phones, cameras, etc. About halfway through a typically quiet, intense, tuneful performance, Kozelek picked out a guy taping the whole thing from one of the seats down to his right, saying something like "What is it with you with your red light recording devices and your MySpace? Is it more real because you go home and stick it on your computer? Isn't this enough? I remember a time before all this MySpace, phones with cameras, iPods, I'm forty years old, man," etc., etc. And the guy in front of us was also obsessively trying to photograph on his little camera in very low light, giving up and leaving about two thirds of the way through. He wasn't "press," but he couldn't get it down and so he left. So where does this leave us with "live" performance? And do you need a record of it for it to be real to you?*

> *If you have no idea who Mark Kozelek is, have never heard of the Red House Painters or Sun Kil Moon you can learn more at http://www.markkozelek.com*

Kozelek's point seemed to be about paying attention to the moment as being more real than capturing it with a device. Perhaps he was echoing Barthes (1993, p. 15), and asserting his " . . . *political* right to be a subject . . . ," not an object of someone else's making. The audience response would undoubtedly be that they wished to somehow make the moment live again elsewhere at another time for their own reasons (some of which could include publication within their own social networks, thus reflecting their wish to be identified with a particular sort of musical knowledge. This point is discussed later in this chapter).

Networked images

At another concert a year later, another singer was photographed, not by me, but with me in the frame from the balcony. Searching for reviews the next day I found the picture on Flickr. The experience was reported visually and it had been edited, either in-camera or using photo-editing software, into black and white which gave it the look of an old, newspaper-reported, lived experience. I could have selected this image and added it to my blog with an accompanying written description of the concert, or added it to one of my online social network profiles. The relationship with image and text can be so strong, with one validating the other perhaps.

Of course, many bloggers feel a compulsion to record as much of their lived experiences as possible and posting a daily photograph online is a way of saying something, even if no words accompany it. An example would be

Heather Armstrong's "Dooce" blog (http://www.dooce.com), an early successful example of the form containing personal journal accounts of her life, her family, and a daily photograph. Throughout the site the images go hand in hand with the writing. The "About" page is dominated by an image and the banner announces the existence of a daily photo (see Figure 5.2).

Figure 5.2: The "About" page of Heather Armstrong's blog at www.dooce.com

Seemingly limitless choices of where to go and what to do with an image is the essential difference between hardcopy or analog images and new media affordances and photosharing practices. At the very least, digital images can become part of a collection—an exhibition of the self. Experiences are recorded and added to an online gallery—like Flickr, Picasa, and Photobucket—which becomes a repository for images of holidays, parties, concerts, exhibitions, family events and on and on. And the accumulated images, when exhibited, stand for that person when they are not there. They say to a viewer: "Look who I know. Look whose concerts I have seen. Look where I've been in the world." In the case of certain sites and certain ways of presenting images, they may also say: "Look at the way I've recorded this, how I've taken the picture." In a site of civic action—like Witness.org, for example—they may also claim: "Look where I was when the police broke up the demonstration." Or: "Look at the state of this street. When is my local authority going to do something?"

Users of social networking sites are amongst the most numerous examples of this kind of online curatorship, endlessly shifting photographs around to represent a moment or collection of moments that represents aspects of the self at a particular point in time. We could look to Goffman (1990) and the notion of the "performed self" to see how different images are selected as part of the whole presentation, how they are representative of the different ways of playing at being "you" in the world: "I am serious. I am playful. I am cultured. I have friends. I am well traveled. I am all of these things." And for ways of thinking about how this is entirely an aspect of living in late modernity—to be fluid, hybrid and multi-purposeful—Giddens provides an account of the "fractured, brittle, fragmented" self (1991, p.169), which is readily identified in some social networking sites. Facebook profiles provide good examples of what Goffman is getting at: where the owners belong to professional and personal networks simultaneously and sometimes struggle to contain them both within the same space. But, at the same time, online images can also represent attempts to fix these aspects of self at a particular moment for a particular purpose—the "latest exhibition"—drawn from the collection, shared and curated and announced. Examples of this include image assets assembled in MobileMe galleries (http://www.apple.com/mobileme) following major life events, holidays, or professional travel of one sort or another, and employed as a holistic, representative collection.

Shared image production or quotation—and here I am referring to the practice of quoting from other people's collections by linking to, or appropriating, images which are integrated into that person's own site—sits alongside online gaming, social networking sites and the emerging semantic web (which, among other things, uses tags that people add to their online texts and images to organize information) at the leading edge of a new set of skills and dispositions within media literacy. Indeed the explosion of interest in what people do with images online, within all fields of cultural studies and media studies, and the re-invigoration of semiotic theories, suggests that theories, as well as media, are converging on a range of phenomena that have absorbed the connected, mainly (but not exclusively) technology-rich regions of the world.

Souvenir images

Away from online spaces, our own use of images begins to resemble the museum world in the production of artifacts *around* photographs. Our own digital images can be the raw material for hardcopy versions printed on photographic quality paper, as well as on tea towels, calendars, mugs and more. In art museums, we visit the museum shop for these sorts of souvenirs of the paintings and other works we've just seen, and now we have a perfect corollary in our own DIY media: souvenir production.

At a basic level this can simply be achieved by printing hardcopy images at home. Consider the rise of the home color printer and sales of photographic paper. Consider also the implications of the following advertisement for a color printer:

> *As the television advertisement opens, a small child is seen bouncing on a bed. From the ceiling rain down hundreds of printed digital photographs. The child catches them as they fall and announces to viewers, "I've had a wonderful life so far." The implication is that the ownership of the images as well as the means of displaying them is a way of holding on to the experience, of owning it.*

At a more commercial level, this can include turning one's photographs into souvenirs or commodities for others to buy. Commercial interfaces like Zazzle.com (for selling t-shirts with your photos printed on them) or Cafe-Press.com (for selling everything from mugs to knickers with your photos printed on them) are just some of the services made possible by the transportability of images (and money) across the internet.

Daily life images

Practices and concepts from the physical world of printed photographs proliferate in digital image management software both online and offline. In iPhoto (an offline image management application located on a Mac user's harddrive) or in Flickr (an online digital image management application located entirely on the internet) the language refers to the "album," "set," and "batch." Our photographic practices don't always fit the assumptions underlying these terms and program features, however. Sometimes, when retrieving images from your camera phone, you realize what you have is a series of isolated, orphaned images that nonetheless make it possible to trace your experiences over the past few days. Or sometimes these isolated images really are just that, random pictures on your phone that are difficult to account for in any logical way. Here, for example, is a series of subjects I took with my camera phone on a single day with every intention of blogging them at some stage . . .

- A mobile exhibition of "extinct technology" in a London market (later used in a presentation)
- A missing pet sign in a local park
- An uprooted tree
- The pattern of light on the window blind in the morning

None of these images is connected to the others in any logical way, and neither are these images a reliable map of my past week. Thus, the very portability and ease of use of digital cameras—in all their forms (e.g., camera, mobile phone camera, SLR digital camera) makes it possible to step outside "albums" and "sets," and record images as part of the daily act of moving around and experiencing life wherever you are. This fluidity of recording and documenting everyday life contrasts markedly with how things were in the previous century . . .

> *The boy stands at about the same height as the small snowman. Aged about 18 months in the coldest winter in London in living memory at the time, in the second half of the twentieth century. He is wearing a red all-in-one winter suit. He extends an unsteady hand to the snowman's head and draws it back to his mouth. The ice is melting on the mitten and he sticks it in his mouth to taste it. His mother calls to him to look at the camera; his father has now adjusted the light according to the meter he carries in a small leather bag with the camera. Smile, snap, it's gone . . .*

I don't know if this represents my earliest memory, or if I've remembered it because I have seen the picture my father took many times. It is a thing of wonder and puzzlement, which possibly goes back to simultaneous strong emotions alongside those notions of ownership of the "original" object and its "aura." And now, many years later, this image is an infinitesimally small particle in a universe of visually sustained memories. I can hold the only copy of this moment captured by my father, now torn at the edges, and think about how to integrate it with the act of exhibiting and remembering and perhaps tag it "Archaeology" once it is digitally scanned and added to the photoshopped and the photoshared.

SECTION TWO

Photoshopping/photosharing: Tutorials and affinity spaces

The intention of this section is to provide some practical pointers in each of the categories under exploration: photoshopping and photosharing. For photoshopping we will look at ways of working with individual images to change them in simple ways, or in more complex operations to achieve certain effects for an arts project or similar task. For photosharing, we will look at ways of uploading the results of this work, how photos may work as groups of images, and how they may be added to the sum of human images on a particular theme (as well as thinking about how you might access other people's work in the same field). We will also think about the next step, curatorship, which is very close to sharing as an activity but subtly different, since it need not involve sharing at all. There will also be sections on copyright and ownership within educational contexts, followed by a series of suggestions for how all this fits with educational practice that involves new media.

Photoshopping: Editing images, starting points and some places to go

When I worked as an Information, Communication and Technology (ICT) advisor and, later, when I worked in ICT in Education as a tutor for student teachers, I sometimes had to produce guides which were known as "Getting started . . ." guides. These offered guidelines for using the basics of common Microsoft Office software applications, graphics programs and, later on, video editing software. I quickly came to realize that "Getting started . . ." almost always meant " . . . and moving on . . ." since mastery of the first few steps in anything inevitably led to greater engagement and increased ambition. The guides, I felt, trod a very fine line between accessibility and patronization. The end result, with varying degrees of success, was to take nothing for granted and to assume certain starting points for all.

Some years later, we find that the internet itself is teeming with such guides. Some of them can be located within product sites, others within educational sites, or within other affinity spaces of like-minded individuals offering support for one another. Many of these guides offer a starting point and a set of "moving on" ideas, including pointers to advanced features for users. There is simply too much to know and too much to learn about most tools now, especially in an era of continuous upgrades and newly invented feature sets. The kinds of "handing down" of "craft" skills from experts to learners that used to accompany "mastery" cannot take place in a definitive and comprehensive way in environments where the craft itself is changing moment to moment. As a result, one of the prerequisites to learning successfully how to edit images, or indeed work in any DIY media, is to know where to access "just-in-time" learning and advice.

The "photoshopping" part of working with images begins long before you get to the computer. An account of the technicalities of digital cameras—whether inside a phone or standalone—is beyond the space available to me here. However, it is worth noting that the in-camera decisions and adjustments which you make amount to the earliest editing decisions: from deleting an unsuccessful image altogether, to adjusting exposure, filters, coloring, or contrast at the point of image capture, and the like.

Advice at the point of pressing the camera's button to take the picture is available in any number of self-help books and resources online and offline. One beautifully illustrated offline example, by Tom Ang, is *How to Photograph Absolutely Everything* (2007). Ang addresses the reader as a colleague, a co-conspirator, a willing-to-learn non-expert but also as one who does not wish to be patronized. Some sample constructions used by Ang that are positive and affirm the potential for skill development include ones like the following:

To refine your exposure technique, use the centre weighted or spot metering mode to determine exposure. These read only a limited part of the scene, and you will learn by evaluating the results and making adjustments (Ang, 2007, p. 23).

Note the "you will learn by evaluating the results": the encouragement, the exhortation, to continue to experiment. In addition to texts like this, you will find fellow users at all levels willing to post solutions to technical and artistic problems or issues in many online forums. One site—http://photo.net/community—gathers these forums into one place, listing, at the time of writing, some 33 forums across a wide range of abilities and interests in digital photography.

Your camera, whether a separate device or attached to a phone, takes digital images of varying sizes and types. Professional photographers work with very large files containing the most amount of information possible about a single image. Those of us who are not selling work but still wish to take good quality images will work at the highest resolution our storage or sharing systems—online or offline—allow. There are some compromises to be made here, with compression being the key (see Table 5.1) to successfully moving images around the internet, via email, or uploading them to photosharing sites. Fully uncompressed files are very large and contain vast amounts of information about the picture. These image files are known as "lossless" files. Other, smaller sorts of filetypes are known as "lossy," although the loss of definition may not be visible to the eye at normal display sizes for photographs. So, if you are planning to use simple screen-viewable images, or small printed photograph sizes, as opposed to making a poster from them, then "lossy" files should suffice. Four very common image file types are shown in Table 5.1.

You will also encounter various other formats, which are proprietary and not easily shared due to size or lack of interoperability (e.g., file types that will only be viewable inside a particular commercial photo editing application). These are to be avoided as they are not especially portable. It is quite useful to have a file conversion program that changes your images between the different file types. "Preview," an application that ships free on Mac computers, allows you to do this easily. The disk that came with your digital camera will also almost certainly have a software title (in "lite" or full version), which also will enable you to change file types. One way to work is to take images in the highest resolution possible and then edit at this resolution before saving the final image in a smaller, lighter format for sharing online.

File type	Typical compression	Notes
TIFF or TIF	From uncompressed, completely lossless, through to fairly compressed.	Very flexible format which is used professionally in its highest, most uncompressed form.
RAW	Another large lossless file type which is output from some high-end digital cameras.	There are different kinds of RAW files from different makes of camera, so you may need proprietary software to view them.
JPG	A compressed, lossy file type which nevertheless gives very good results due to the way its compression works by discarding information invisible to the eye.	Used by large numbers of digital cameras because of its range and versatility. Used extensively on the internet because of its relatively small size for such high quality.
GIF	Another common kind of compressed file type which analyzes images of 16 million colors or more and produces a 256-color image.	Less common than JPG but still used widely on the internet. More successfully used with diagrams and line art than photographs.

Table: 5.1: Four Common Image File Types

Photoshopping with and without "Photoshop": Some common image editing programs

To be hard and fast about specific software titles or even specific photosharing sites is to run the risk of being rapidly outdated. Things are changing all the time—software is continually upgraded or developed into something distinctively new. It is even possible now to consider doing away with photo editing software on your own computer altogether and work with an online editing service (see below).

The most ubiquitous image editing software is Adobe's Photoshop. It is so ubiquitous as to have passed into the language as a verb (as shown in the title of this very chapter). To "photoshop" something is to change an image in some way, to crop it, to resize it, to remove red-eye and blemishes, to change lighting, to adjust color, lighting, or contrast, to apply finishing effects to regions or to the whole image, to amplify details in pursuit of an aesthetic effect, or to change its meaning-making properties.

Manovich (2001) discusses the ways in which the tools of new media contain affordances within their screens, icons, and language from, or based on, the worlds of old media. Thus, Photoshop, with its filters, retouching, brushes and erasers, resembles a photo-retouching lab; although, of course, Photoshop adds even more functionality than is typically available in labs. Playing with the notion of photography as truthful and "realistic" (see Sontag, 1979, p. 24), Photoshop gives the editor power to play with juxtapositions which could not have occurred in "reality," to add people to events which took place before they were born, or to allow a politician to look like she or he was at an event when they were not, as in the row which erupted in the United Kingdom over the photoshopping of a government minister into a picture of a meeting at a hospital for which he actually arrived too late to attend (Pierce, 2007).

Tricks of light they have always been, but digital photographic images are also tricks of information. Each image file contains multiple pieces of information, and each of these pieces tells the computer how to display the image and to what extent the picture can be manipulated and altered. Pictures can be changed in intensity, color, hue, and tone. They can have effects added, too (e.g., watercolor or charcoal effects). At an even more simple level, the user can engage with altering the framing of the picture to prioritize elements in ways that alter the original picture's meaning (e.g., a family portrait originally incorporating a sunset is reframed by cropping closely to the figures, giving the family unit salience over the time and the location; the relation of the family members to each other becomes a more central part of the meaning-making of the image). Kress and van Leeuwen—both social semioticians—identify framing as one of the key elements of composition (Kress & Van Leeuwen, 2006, p. 206). Cropping tools allow for the exploration of parts of images, and for playing with the frame and the "meaning potentials" of any image. In digital image editing, the frame itself and everything in it are malleable and adjustable. Editing processes thus become part of each image's final composition.

Vast numbers of image editing software tools are available to users. They all have similar names and are easily confused: "Serif Photo Plus," "Ulead Photo Editor," "Arcsoft Photo Impression" (some of these will be familiar to readers). There are others which are open source and completely free to download and use (e.g., Gimp, Inkscape). Many of these low-cost or free applications have interfaces that are very close in appearance and functionality to their high-cost, commercial equivalents. Some, like "Irfan View," concentrate on image viewing and file-type converting with simple editing facilities included as extras. These and many other such titles are available to download through freeware sites, such as Sourceforge.net or TuCows.com.

Some image editing programs are serious high-end tools for graphics-focused workplaces. These programs include functions designed for professional image editing and support private collaboration on large-scale commercial image editing projects. Luckily, however, many of these high-end editing programs have spawned less-complicated versions for amateurs and hobbyists, which are much more affordable.

For example, if your school budget does not extend to multiple licenses for Adobe Photoshop, then consider the cut-down alternative: Adobe Photoshop Elements (like its parent program—Adobe Photoshop—which is available for PC or Mac). There are very significant savings to be made with Photoshop Elements. It includes the majority of useful-to-amateurs-and-hobbyists functions found in its parent program but at a fraction of the price. Surprisingly, perhaps, there are common tasks that Photoshop Elements allows you to perform that are not actually available in Photoshop (or else are hidden under layer after layer of arcane professional tools in its vast and complex menus).

Also available online for you or your students to use free of charge (up to a limit—check the small print accompanying each service) are a growing number of photo editing sites. Some of these are aligned directly with photosharing facilities (discussed later in this chapter). Here, for example, are seven popular examples of online image editors with their accompanying slogans:

- http://www.picnik.com: "Photo editing made fun"
- http://www.splashup.com: "Jump right in—image editing made easy"
- http://fotoflexer.com: "The world's most advanced online image editor"
- http://snipshot.com: "Edit pictures online"
- http://webresizer.com: "Making photos faster"
- http://www.creatingonline.com: "Creating online—including online image and photo editing"
- http://www.flauntr.com: "Professional photo editing. Easy and free"

Typically images are uploaded to the site, and effects are applied remotely with the results downloadable soon afterwards, if not immediately. How-to guides for using these and other image editing programs can be found via internet searches. For example:

- Picnik photo editing tutorial: http://www.brilliantprints.com.au/blog/2 008/01/15/picnik-photo-editing-tutorial-part-1-beginners-guide/
- Another Picnik tutorial: http://anapronaday.blogspot.com/2008/06/tu torial-super-duper-easy-photo-editing.html
- SplashUp video tutorial: http://www.youtube.com/watch?v=Bh7_FQV OL-4

If you are reading this as both a hobbyist and as someone seeking to use image editing for and with students in an educational setting, some questions worth asking are:

- What kinds of editing will I be doing?
- Will it be for print publication in a parents' or caregivers' newsletter?
- Am I working entirely in new media, looking for images for a static web-site or for a more dynamic environment such as a blog or a wiki?
- Am I working with art students looking for particular effects?

So, what should one look for in the basic toolkit? Assuming that you wish to alter the basic properties of your image, such as its shape and size, then some kind of cropping tool is the most straightforward to use. This tool is sometimes available as part of an image viewer (such as "Preview" on Mac computers). Figure 5.3 shows a basic set of icons for image editing applications provided for software developers by GoSquared.com. It is a useful illustration of the most basic set of operations on any single image that you or your students would need to perform.

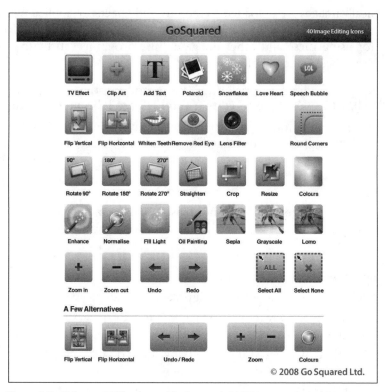

Figure 5.3: 40 Image Editing icons (GoSquared, 2008; image used with permission)

The sorts of tools represented by such icons can be grouped according to function.

The icons for rotation and straightening, for example, represent image orientation. At the very least you would expect to be able to re-orient an image you had taken in portrait mode to, say, landscape mode. Such tools represent functions which would allow you to work on the image at a basic level, either making corrections or additions, exploring and being playful with color or tone, or altering meaning or mood by adding effects (e.g., a grainy TV "look" for your image).

Image editing is often available as part of toolsets in applications not devoted directly to image editing, too. For example, office software packages, including Microsoft Office, often have image editing capabilities of increasing range and sophistication. Many of the basic functions represented by the GoSquared's basic icon set (see Figure 5.3), and more, are available simply by clicking on an image inserted into a word-processed text. The most recent Office toolset for image editing inside a document on Mac computers includes common tasks, such as adjusting color, contrast, hue, and saturation. This same editing toolset also enables users to be playful with images by digitally mimicking the effects of a range of non-photographic art media, such as pastels, spray paints, and so on.

An example of image editing in Photoshop Elements

My own image editing software of choice is Photoshop Elements. I'm not in any way affiliated with the program or company that makes it; I just find the software meets my image editing needs really effectively. It is also close to impossible to really talk about the practicalities of image editing without homing in on a specific application. Photoshop Elements has a vast toolset and easy-to-use image management system (see later in this chapter for more on this). There are many places on the internet where it is possible to discover support for getting to know the basic functions and concepts of how to use Photoshop Elements or any image software for that matter. Some such sites are official, company-affiliated sites, and others are support sites developed by schools, colleges or universities providing guidance for students or staff. Examples include:

- http://www.photoshopelementsuser.com (company-developed tutorials and samples)
- http://www.ischool.utexas.edu/technology/tutorials/index.php (a free guide to using Photoshop Elements developed by a university)

What do students make of (and with) Photoshop Elements? As with many people facing deadlines and working under pressure, there is not always the time to learn the "right way" of using any piece of software. Having someone demonstrate just the basic functions is often the best method for learning or performing a series of simple edits on a practice image. Watching a YouTube clip of this kind of demonstration (use the search function to find introductory tutorials) and knowing where to go for additional online support are other ways of quickly learning how to edit an image. It could take years to develop the knowledge necessary to use every part of the "feature set" of Adobe Elements. However, beyond some basic starting points, the concept of "just in time" learning applies well in this context, provided that the user shows some persistence in the face of adversity and keeps backup copies of everything they might need along the way. Photoshop Elements was designed with this in mind and is generally supportive of fallibility in the way it saves work as a project unfolds.

Talking with my daughter about how she produced a set of images for a school project revealed the intuitive way she was using Photoshop Elements at home while working on a relatively low-resolution image taken on a camera phone on London's South Bank near the Tate Modern Art Gallery.

Her photograph was the starting point, and, here, Alice explains how she moved through a series of tools drawn from various menus to arrive at her end result. In the first edit (Figure 5.4a) she has already blackened the legs of Louise Bourgeois' spider ("Maman"), an enormous sculpture positioned in front of the gallery itself.

Figure 5.4a: Edit 1

Figure 5.4b: Edit 2

Figure 5.4c: Edit 3

Figure 5.4d: Edit 4

Figures 5.4a–5.4d: Four example edits for a series of pictures from a series featuring St Paul's seen through Louise Bourgeois's Spider ("Maman") on the South Bank in London.
©Alice Potter 2008 (used with permission)

Alice explains:

I opened it into Photoshop (edit 1), chose Photo Enhancer . . . then I just did "filter", then "sketch", then "photocopy"—I did black and white—except that's a negative and it had the white in the front and then I got this image (edit 2) . . . then I decided I didn't like the dottiness in the background (edit 3) and I got the fill tool and picked a color here and there . . . then literally did that and that's my favorite one (edit 4) . . . and that's with the edited dottiness (back in). . . . occasionally you would get a fill that would do something that you didn't want it to do then I'd use the drawing tool and make sure that all the lines were connected (by zooming in) . . .

The idea of "filters" in Photoshop Elements and similar software tools is extended into "layers," where images can be manipulated on top of one another, producing montage and collage-like effects. This allows the addition or removal of sections of the image, people from within the frame, and events from the storyline.

Photosharing

Having edited individual images and gathered them together, the next step is to share them and connect with others (see also Chapter 4 in this volume). We have seen in the first section in this chapter how photosharing is an example of the new paradigm in internet function and form. Since the earliest days of graphic-interface internet browsers, it has been possible to place images into webpages in the form of "galleries." More recently, online social networking functions have enabled interactive connections to be made between the images themselves and the people uploading or viewing them.

Perhaps the most famous example of socially-networked photosharing is Flickr (http://www.flickr.com). Historically speaking, Flickr's origins lie in an attempt to develop a multiplayer online game. The photo gallery feature developed for this game—the Flickr bit—was actually an offshoot of this larger project. Its founders—Katerina Fake and Stewart Butterfield—saw the potential of this gallery feature and launched Flickr in 2004. In the space of just a few years, Flickr became the largest photosharing site online. Flickr was sold to Yahoo! a year later for approximately $35 million USD—further attesting to this photosharing site's rapid and large-scale success. Flickr was designed from the very outset to exploit the Web 2.0 properties of the internet. As Fake and Butterfield explained in an interview with Ian Katz in a feature on social software in *The Guardian* (2006),

> The photo-sharing sites that existed [prior to Flickr] had as their paradigm photo albums. Flickr came along and had the idea you no longer had an album, you had a photo stream. (Katz, 2006, p. 29)

This idea of a fluid, ever-changing stream of images is the essence of new ways of being digitally literate with images. Flickr's founders predicted in 2006 that the mobility of the end-user would be the driving force behind innovation in the field: users carrying cameras as phones and phones as cameras. The latest versions of these have high-resolution cameras, which compete successfully with the quality of purpose-built digital cameras of only a few years ago. From the same interview:

> You're going to start seeing much more of the web off the web. Things that are not intended to be consumed on the web but work on your mobile devices, on

your PDAs [personal digital assistants], transportable with you everywhere. The web will be something you return to do the heavy lifting of your computation, but for the most part you're going to have very light devices. (Katz, 2006, p. 29)

By their own account, Flickr passed the milestone of their two-billionth user-uploaded image in November 2007.

Flickr is not the only photo-hosting site online. Other popular services include:

- Snapfish: http://www.snapfish.com
- Webshots: http://www.webshots.com
- Imeem: http://www.imeem.com
- Piczo: http://www.piczo.com
- Shutterfly: http://www.shutterfly.com
- Zooomr: http://www.zooomr.com
- Ovi: http://share.ovi.com or http://www.twango.com
- Picasa: http://www.picasa.com
- Photobucket: http://www.photobucket.com

Not all of these are free to use. Some will expect you to pay for additional facilities and storage. Some, like Imeem and Piczo, are built around more than just images and provide music and video sharing options. They explicitly provide social networking services for users, too. Again, because information changes so rapidly I am not going to attempt to cost any of these or to recommend one over another. By the time this appears in print, the terms, ownership and, possibly, existence of these services will have changed. The best way to learn more is to log in and see if the tools are intuitive, non-invasive, powerful, low cost and whether they open up the possibilities inherent in Web 2.0 applications for participation, sharing, and discovery.

Conversely, the largest social networking sites—like Bebo, MySpace, Facebook—all offer varying services having to do with organizing and displaying images alongside their social interaction tools and resources. This is, in fact, now where the majority of shared images on the internet reside: in people's personalized web pages and spaces. Facebook, for example, currently hosts *more* photographs than does Flickr. Here, social networking is the primary function for people's photosharing, and photographs are simply one way among many for sharing experiences and marking out identity. In short, you have decisions to make about the sorts of activity you are engaging in and if organizing, sharing and cataloguing images is your starting point, rather than music or social networks, then a bespoke photosharing space might be the best place to start.

Some photosharing sites are the photo-arm of much bigger concerns. Picasa, for example, makes available a tool for tagging and organizing your pictures, which is, in turn, a subset of a whole series of applications from Google. For example, the geo-tagging function available in Google Maps syncs with Picasa to enable users to display maps of where their photos were taken. Likewise, if you are a Mac user with a MobileMe account, you also have automatic access to a set of free online services that include photo album spaces, photo sharing functions, image publication features, and the like. Finally, Ovi is an example of a photosharing site which has been built by a mobile phone company—in this case, Nokia—as the main way of rapidly archiving and easily displaying photos taken on-the-go using Nokia's very powerful phone cameras.

As an educator and as a co-learner with your students, you will, perhaps, need to apply the principle of "affinity spaces"—derived from Gee (2004)—to your selection of photosharing sites or forums to use for your own learning, or for that of the students with whom you work. James Paul Gee defines such spaces as "specially designed spaces (physical and virtual) constructed to resource people who are tied together . . . by a shared interest or endeavor" (2004, p. 4). Michele Knobel and Colin Lankshear add to this account that "affinity spaces instantiate participation, collaboration, distribution and dispersion of expertise, and relatedness" (2007, p. 207). A key question to ask yourself, then, is whether or not the photosharing site you choose has the qualities of an "affinity space." Do you need also to consider working with people online who are in the same "space" as you are, who are working in education or who are in the early stages of using digital photography in their work? Is the site purely for photo display and comments of a technical nature, or are one or more areas of affinity engendered? (See also Merchant's discussion of "Flickr Groups" in Chapter 4 in this volume.) In addition, Photo.net was mentioned earlier as a source of useful photography-focused discussion forums. Any number of these forums may represent affinity spaces for you or for your students and colleagues. Yet another useful space for amateur and professional photographers to exchange information about photography and image editing and to support each other's work is Open Photography Forums (http://openphotographyforums.com).

Curating your images online

You will see as soon as you have uploaded a set of photographs to your chosen photosharing service that labeling and curating your collection is a key aspect of these sites. The incalculable number of sources from which images can be drawn by you, or any students with whom you work, demands some way of organizing and cataloguing them in order to retrieve and view them readily. Your digital images could have any number of destinations and serve a range of purposes online, and so the choice of how to organize them goes beyond the simple hierarchical arrangement of folders and file names on your computer's harddrive. Flickr, for example, makes it possible to add your own descriptors to each photograph once it is uploaded. Here we are immersed in the world of "folksonomies" or non-hierarchically organized labeling. You may reveal as little or as much as you like about each photo or yourself when adding tags, but the most effective tags are those that enable you to find your image again and to find other images uploaded by other users who applied the same tags (this also means that they will be able to find your images, too).

A quote from an example of an album used in this way demonstrates the consequences of same (see also Figure 5.5):

> *We drove a really long way from the coastal area where we were staying over the Tuscan hills inland from the coast, round hairpin bends and through the alabaster city of Volterra and out the other side in to the great medieval centre of Siena. With two cameras snapping away, a great many terracotta rooftops, misty hills and pale English tourist faces were encoded that day. In keeping with a habit that frustrates my family I spent some time also snapping away at pavements and details such as lampposts and walls. Once home I edited them into a set for Flickr and spent some time uploading the images. I left the settings on public and my images just happened to include a street lamp which featured a porcupine. There is a race every year on horseback through Siena which draws in huge crowds from all over the surrounding areas and much further afield. The families which take part are each represented by an animal and their animal appears on street furniture in their specific districts. That year the winning family was the Porcupine and I was contacted through Flickr by more than one person with connections to Siena for permission to use the picture*
> . . .

In the example shown on page 126, the tags included "Siena" and "Italy." Other users clearly were able to make use of these tags in searching out photographs of interest or relevance to them. Users with similar images thus can experience connectedness and relatedness by using the same tags, making use of the full functionality of the online galleries and albums. It allows you to search for and visit the work of other users who have tagged their images with some or all of the same tags you yourself have used, or for which you go searching. My advice is to explore as many of the "interconnective" functions of photosharing sites as you can, and decide how these functions might be applied to your own teaching contexts.

Figure 5.5: Flickr and connection to cultures outside of your own experience. Reproduced with permission of Yahoo! Inc. (c)2009 Yahoo! Inc. FLICKR and the FLICKR logo are registered trademarks of Yahoo! Inc.

Sharing and working with other people's images: Attribution, safety and copyright issues

It is possible to locate images for educational purposes all over Flickr and other photosharing sites. However, despite this proliferation of images and the ease of downloading them, it is sensible to be aware of safety issues and ethical considerations. Sharing photographs in such spaces with tags that name your own educational institution means that children and young people, some of whom could be vulnerable, are more easily identifiable. If you do not have permission to publish their images, then you need to obtain it. Many schools ask caregivers for permission to use digital images (and video) alongside other official agreements at the point of entry to the institution. It is important for you to be familiar with the reach of such agreements.

Likewise, finding the perfect image for use in a resource or publication for school on a photosharing site does not always imply permission to use it. The principle of "fair dealing" is often invoked for education, in the sense that the owner of the image will grant a "not for profit" use of their images. Attribution and credit are usually all that is required in return and should always be given. Further information about these issues is usually given by the photosharing sites themselves, with the terms of the copyright license typically stated next to the image. Other sources of images that are free to use for non-profit purposes (with attribution to the creator of the image) can be found here:

- http://creativecommons.org/image/
- http://wiki.creativecommons.org/Image

Photoshopping/sharing, education and new literacies

The editing, organizing, and curating of exhibitions of photographed assets in new media forms, and within Web 2.0 environments in particular, represent a key set of skills and dispositions in learning to work with new literacies. From their early years children are aware that their experiences often are documented for displays on walls, in books, and online (with the necessary permissions obtained and posted as well). At the same time, they easily can make choices themselves about which images to capture and to use to stand in for themselves when they are not there and which to use to make meaning from their experiences.

Skills and dispositions for a new century, for a new way of being literate, will need to take learners—young and old—beyond simply capturing images to engage them actively in decision-making about editing an image and in managing collections of images. The practice of creating cataloging systems by using tags—some self-generated, others suggested by existing content—is a potential key skill for becoming proficient users of new media and digital literacies. The distinction between "folksonomy" (user-generated words that organize content) and "taxonomy" (specialist resource-manager generated indices) is an important one; how to create and curate collections from user-generated tags and how to use them to navigate and locate information and resources is fast becoming a central dimension of photosharing. The potential in opening up searches to include experiences and resources discovered by others in a folksonomic system is too great an opportunity to miss with respect to learning about one's world, and an important skill to develop in learners.

The situation in schools is, of course, complicated by the fact that access to photosharing sites is frequently made difficult and sometimes actually blocked by internet filters. Social networking sites like MySpace and Facebook are widely assumed by many adults to be places of great moral danger, rife with all kinds of inappropriate activity. Photosharing sites tend to be included in bans that seek to protect children from danger. Unfortunately, however, the end result is more often than not an impoverishment of experience and missed opportunities for learning. Approved search engines may find usable images in the classroom, but these stand-alone, decontexualized images *will not* enable children to become productive end-users and sharers of images in the twenty-first century.

Children are often engaged in school settings in making their own photographic images. In preschool settings, photography has long been used to document daily events, to retell stories, and to develop an awareness of history. Baby photographs, for example, often are used in school to help develop a meta-awareness of a past and the sense of a life story being told across time. Digital photography has simply multiplied by a huge factor the possible number of images that can be produced cheaply by students themselves. A key consideration is the management of digital photography in meeting educational goals. Digital photography and online photosharing can be used to:

- leverage the immediacy and ubiquity of digital photography in order to learn more generally about folksonomies, affinity spaces and memes; that is, the terminology, skills and dispositions arising from the uses of new media

- participate in collective visual story telling projects. A good example of this kind of project is the "Tell a Story in Five Frames" group on Flickr: http://www.flickr.com/groups/visualstory/

- develop imaginative visual stories about non-human objects. For example, the "Secret Life of Toys" group on Flickr: http://www.flickr.com/groups/secretlifeoftoys/

- connect home and school in shared, secure areas with younger children during literacy activities that involve photosharing (as in the work of Lynn Roberts [2008] in her "digital shoeboxes" project)

- develop interactive history or social studies projects using Picasa.com and geotags

- document and publicize local issues

- generate work around "identity" in new media spaces which explores the issues of self-representation and self-preservation from the earliest ages to the oldest students, using, for example, scans and digital camera images of the self over time

- work offline in projects which involve communities in developing countries not connected in the same way as those in the developed world, such as photosharing using physical media and postal services.

Many writers have identified some of these new skill sets and dispositions as directly pertinent to new literacies generally, from the familiarity with and manipulation of memes or "contagious patterns of thought" (Lankshear & Knobel, 2006), to school-based digital and media literacy debates (Buckingham, 2003; Marsh, 2004; Burn & Durran, 2007), and wider engagement with visual literacies and multimodal meaning-making as part of a subset of new literacies (Cope & Kalantzis, 2000; Kress, 2003; Kress & Van Leeuwen, 2006). Connections can also be made with the consumption and production continuum described by Jenkins as arising out of popular culture and fandom as well as the convergence of devices, spaces and cultures (Jenkins, 1992).

The vast numbers of easily edited, collected and exhibited images made for, by, and with children in settings of formal and informal education represent a sizable repository of meaning-making about experience. Integrating children's experiences of the world around them, their inner worlds, and these experiences' relationship to the curriculum and to their learning creates new challenges to educators today. For example, those issues that arise concerning learners and those who work with them, such as access, safety, ownership of digital images, human rights, potential abuses of trust and more. The benefits are often claimed to far outweigh the risks, but learning how to deal with safety and ownership of images is arguably one of the skills of new media literacy and should be of serious concern to those involved in making decisions about pedagogy in photosharing. Rather than being closed off from both the curricular potential and the lived culture of photosharing, students of all ages can learn and share their own learned strategies, ways of living and being safe in such spaces.

The relationship between digital photography and photosharing sites is more complex than that of hardcopy photographs displayed in paper-based albums. The concept of "audience," for example, no longer holds for photosharing sites, where more active concepts like "user" hold sway and where photographs themselves are no longer static objects. Digital image media are "not done to" or "performed at" an audience. Image viewers can actively comment on the content or quality of an image posted to a photosharing site and can even participate in producing their own images by editing, remixing, and reassembling other people's work (with permission, of course). Visual memes are a good example of this kind of phenomenon (see, for example, Lostfrog.org). Photosharing sites are important spaces for learning about curatorship and exhibition. How many times in their lives and for how many different purposes will young people have to learn the skills of assembling both media that they have discovered and media that they have produced? These texts and assets will sit side by side in a variety of spaces: in their e-portfolios for school and college, in their personal social networking spaces, in online storage environments such as Flickr, and so forth.

Indeed, this notion of curatorship posits a new skill set that is beyond the duality of the consumer-producer model. Assembling collections that locate users in time and space and make it possible to create a narrative which suggests that childhood was happy and varied in its pursuits, that life in college is good, with work and social activity playing a big part in it, is just one such approach to using curating as an expressive tool. Similarly, students can tinker with these same images to tell not such a rosy story as they explore the meaning potential or affordances of different sequences of images, cropping and resizing, and visual effects. I am suggesting that curatorship in this sense is a hybrid skill which merges the ability to make meaning from resources which have been collected at a particular point in time and assembling them for exhibition at any given moment for any given purpose. It is the interrelationship between and across the images that creates overall meaning. This is just as true of a collection of photographs juxtaposed and assembled for an online space as it is for anything else that gets made and presented to others.

It has been suggested that new media presuppose new relationships between artifacts, social practices, and the arrangements which shape them (Lievrouw & Livingstone, 2006). Engaging in practices which shape meaning in this way is to take part in—and advantage of—the representational aspects of popular culture at a ubiquitous level. We could be involving our students in becoming aware of these practices and what they mean to others who visit their exhibition spaces and make meaning from them.

Whether the perspective is of performance through the image, the idea that there is a "backstage" self somewhere behind the curtain and these images are part of the performed self (Goffman, 1990), or whether these collections of images represent the hybrid and multiple aspects of identity in "late modernity" (Giddens, 1991), the assemblages and juxtapositions of the images in photosharing spaces also contribute to the representation of self online, too. This is a key aspect of photosharing that is overlooked in "educational" applications of digital image-making and sharing in classroom contexts (all too often, images posted to online school sites, or school-sanctioned photosharing sites, have been taken by teachers or other adults and not by students themselves, for example).

Why should editing, collecting, organizing and displaying digital images be a part of educational experiences for young people? It is not simply the reductive argument about "relevance" that is important here; the suggestion that simply by engaging with a contemporary cultural phenomenon you are engaging children with something that is directly relevant to them. Relevance is not a given that is conferred by the educator in any setting. The learner has to agree to that proposition. The fact is that the digital image is simply a part of daily, lived culture for so many young learners. If the moving image is the thing that grabs them the most—the popularity of "YouTube" suggests moving images are an attractive medium—the still image represents the cornerstone, the foundation of how they are seen online by their peers: their profile picture on their social networking space, their discussion board icon, their marker of identity on an educational Virtual Learning Environment (possibly).

That being said, it is the combination of the images on the page, the visual statements they make, and the overall effect of the exhibition of images that need to be taken into account by viewers in photosharing spaces. This presupposes an awareness of how a folksonomy operates, as well as the re-usability and re-mixability of images. Learning to see images as arrange-able and re-purpose-able assets in different contexts means that students can use an image in a presentation, a piece of writing, a journal, a blog, a photo album—every destination is possible. A shift in purpose and destination establishes a new meaning for the image because the context in which the picture is viewed alters the reading of it. Being able to use, read, and (re)present images in such ways is an important life skill, one that is applicable across all contexts of media production, consumption, and curatorship.

References

Ang, T. (2007). *How to photograph absolutely everything: Successful pictures from your digital camera.* London: Dorling Kindersley.

Barthes, R. (1993). *Camera lucida.* London: Vintage Classics.

Buckingham, D. (2003). *Media education: Literacy, learning and contemporary culture.* Cambridge: Polity.

Burn, A. & Durran, J. (2007). *Media literacy in schools.* London: Paul Chapman.

Cope, B. & Kalantzis, M. (Eds.). (2000). *Multiliteracies: Literacy learning and the design of social futures.* New York: Routledge.

Gee, J. P. (2004). *Situated language and learning: A critique of traditional schooling.* New York: Routledge.

Giddens, A. (1991). *Modernity and self-identity: Self and society in the late modern age.* Cambridge: Polity.

Goffman, E. (1990). *The presentation of self in everyday life* (New edition). London: Penguin.

GoSquared. (2008). *40 image editing icons.* Retrieved July 1, 2008, from http://www.gosquared.com/liquidicity/archives/384

Jenkins, H. (1992). *Textual poachers: Television fans and participatory culture.* New York: Routledge.

Katz, I. (2006, November 4). 'Flickr, Caterina Fake and Stewart Butterfield'. *The Guardian Weekend Magazine.* Nov. 1, 2009, at: http://www.guardian.co.uk/technology/2006/nov/04/news.weekendmagazine8

Knobel, M. & Lankshear, C. (Eds.). (2007). *A new literacies sampler.* New York: Peter Lang.

Kress, G. (2003). *Literacy in the new media age.* London: Routledge.

Kress, G. & Van Leeuwen, T. (2006). *Reading images: The grammar of visual design* (2nd ed.). London: Routledge.

Lankshear, C. & Knobel, M. (2006). *New literacies: Everyday practices and classroom learning.* Maidenhead, UK: McGraw-Hill Education/Open University Press.

Lievrouw, L. H. & Livingstone, S. (Eds.). (2006). *The handbook of new media* (Updated student edition). London: Sage.

Manovich, L. (2001). *The language of new media.* Cambridge, MA: MIT Press.

Marsh, J. (Ed.). (2004). *Popular culture, new media and digital literacy in early childhood.* London: Routledge.

Pierce, A. (2007, January 10). James Purnell in fake photo row. *Daily Telegraph*. Available Nov. 1, 2009, at: http://www.telegraph.co.uk/news/uknews/1564465/James-Purnell-in-fake-photo-row.html

Roberts, L. (2008). *Digital shoeboxes: Online photosharing in a cross-contextual literacy project*. Unpublished Masters Dissertation, Institute of Education, University of London, London.

Sontag, S. (1979). *On photography*. London: Penguin Classics.

Part 3: Moving Media

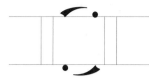

Chapter 6

Machinima: Why think "games" when thinking "film"?

Susan Luckman and Robin Potanin

While to non-games players the world of video gameplay may seem a weird and irrelevant one (something best left to children at leisure), the rapid and global growth of the games industry clearly speaks of a more complex story. So, too, does the emergence of games studies as a serious area of university study, alongside literary, film and television studies. Ultimately what we can see going on here is the emergence of digital games as a key communications and entertainment medium in the twenty-first century. Many people—at least, within developed countries that is—who are themselves now parents grew up with platform video games. Given the powerful capacities of video games to enthrall an audience (a quality frequently giving rise to moral panics about addiction and other health issues, especially in children) and as a technology already ahead of the curve in terms of a narrative experience based on interactivity and immersion (a clear hallmark of the future of filmic storytelling in a post-Web 2.0 age), it's hardly surprising that games technology is now being used to do everything from:

- leading us through a yoga routine (e.g., WiiFit yoga games)
- helping us cook a meal (e.g., Nintendo DS *Personal Trainer: Cooking*)
- training emergency services workers (e.g., NFPA's *Virtual Terrorism Response Academy: 'Ops Plus for WMD Hazmat.'*)

- and, more controversially, recruiting and training military soldiers (e.g., the U.S. Army's *America's Army* series of games).

Significantly too, especially for this chapter, games offer a cheap, entry-level tool for creating animated films known as "machinima."

SECTION ONE

First, what is machinima?

Machinima was initially referred to as "Quake movies" because *Quake* (the enormously successful and groundbreaking massively multiplayer online game from the second half of the 1990s) was the first game players hacked in order to create and edit recordings of game play (Hancock & Ingram, 2007, p. 12). In simple terms, machinima is animated filmmaking which uses 3D game engines as the source of the video material to be edited together. Three-dimensional games are those games that have characters which can be moved somewhat like puppets (e.g., Tetris is not a 3D game, and neither is Solitaire or Minesweeper). The term "machinima" (pronounced "muh-shin-i-mah") is an amalgam of: "machine" + "cinema." As intimated earlier, today's machinima scene grew out of the demos created by online game playing communities which were circulated to show off an individual player's prowess or to brag about a game clan's superiority. It is also in many ways an extension of practices implicitly embedded within the games production and marketing process itself; namely, the creation of in-game cut scenes, along with promotional video clips featuring characters and gameplay (cut scenes are filmic stretches within a game—typically occurring between an old level and a new one—that carry important narrative information about the next set of quests or problems to be solved in the game). Machinima utilizes the inbuilt capacity within some games' programs—single player and massively multiplayer online role-playing games, or MMORPGs, alike—which allows you to record game play action for sharing with others or for privately reliving game glory. For example, a game-play video that took the internet by storm in 2005 was recorded using the in-game video recording functions built into *World of Warcraft*. A guild—a group of players who agree to play collaboratively in order to complete quests—was about to storm a formidable bunch of enemies, and the video—clearly meant to be a trophy video recording the guild's resounding victory—begins with the group meticulously planning their attack and choreographing themselves for full-on battle. But before they can complete their planning, one of the players suddenly screams out his onscreen name—"Leerooooooy Jenkins!"—and dashes into the room where the enemies are waiting for them; the rest of the guild can only follow suit as they rush to try and stop him, and the video records the utter carnage that takes place and the guild's humiliating defeat. This video clip also records Leeroy Jenkins' explanation that he'd missed the planning bit because he'd been in the kitchen eating some chicken his mother had prepared and had only just returned to the computer before launching into attack mode. Leeroy is, of course, roundly berated for his actions in very strong language by all of his guild members. This video clip became enormously popular within *World of Warcraft* discussion forums, and in wider online circles, not least because it was often read as an inadvertent spoof of "nerd guilds that meticulously and statistically plan out raids with all the seriousness of actual military tactics" (Wikipedia, 2009, p. 1).

From here, it's a relatively small step to thinking about the gameworld as a "stage" upon which other narratives beyond the expectations of the pre-programmed game structure can be played out and recorded. As Paul Marino (2004) explains in his extended discussion of machinima production, looking at a role-play video game this way meant that "the viewpoint of the player became the viewpoint of a director" (p. 4). Machinima, like remixes and mash-ups, is about creating derivative new works, which use existing material in new ways. Machinima also relies on online distribution networks for its growth and development as a medium of expression. As we'll see shortly in the case of the famous machinima series *Red vs. Blue*, the ironic juxtaposition of pre-defined game characters in new and unfamiliar narrative structures is a significant source of the pleasure to be derived from creating and viewing machinima texts.

Machinima: A short history

Machinimists are evolving into a dedicated creative community of their own, but in the early days of the medium, machinima-making was associated largely with fan communities that grew up around particular video games. Even now, many machinima sites remain tied to particular games (e.g., http://halomovies.org, http://sim-movies.com, http://warcraftmovies.com) This phenomenon is due both to love of the game, and to people coming together with a shared interest in discussing and experimenting with the possibilities of the particular scene-capturing environment afforded by a given game. Machinima is best produced in a team in order to allow—among other things—for manipulation ("acting") of multiple characters within the gamespace. Interestingly, the machinima community today is less self-contained and intersects increasingly with other online digital film production communities, especially via sites like YouTube.

The development of machinima as a DIY medium is an interesting one, and is best discussed by means of key machinima texts. Most of these are available online for viewing, and we recommend reading the remainder of this section in tandem with viewing these machinima.

Coming as it did out of a fan demo background, by today's standards early machinima was relatively unsophisticated and relied heavily upon simply recording gameplay as it unfolded with minimal scripting and editing. This is clear in the early pioneering machinima: *Diary of a Camper* (1996, United Rangers Films, http://www.machinima.com/film/view&id=15043). This machinima plays on the dismissive name given to players who "camp" their characters at key points in the story-world rather than moving around the gamespace (which means being more actively engaged in the game, but by doing so, taking greater risks). *Diary of a Camper* may look simple but is an object lesson for the beginner in terms of how much thought and planning needs to go into even the most basic of machinima, especially if it's a joint project with multiple characters. In 1996, *Diary of a Camper* broke ground as the first machinima to include an explicit storyline. Filmed within the gameworld of *Quake I*, members of the Rangers clan added a story element to one of their demos. The complexity here lay in the choreographing of their player characters' movements, while yet another player acted as the "camera" and initially recorded the action—from their own character's point of view—as a program script that could be replayed within the game. But ultimately, in retrospect, it still pretty much looks like a straight recording of gameplay, rather than a "film" as we typically recognize them. As we will see shortly, however, later machinimas have added further narrative and better production values, turning machinima into a sophisticated filmmaking medium.

After *Diary of a Camper*, machinimists started to develop richer narratives that engaged stories from worlds beyond that of the game, and to draw on genres not typically found in role-playing games at the time, such as comedy. In the late 1990s, you still got a strong dose of "characters walking around game space" on the screen, but the story told began to offer new takes on the game world, and, as we will see shortly with the famous *Red vs. Blue* machinima series, this storytelling strategy became a source of much of the humor in machinima comedy pieces. This is evident in the ILL Clan's *Apartment Huntin'* (1998, http://www.illclan.com/video/apthunt-qt.mov) made using *Quake I*. In it, Larry and Henry—who are lumberjacks—are looking for a new home, and much of the humor lies in the banality of the task, a disco dancing scene, Larry's habit of smashing things, and the dramatic, industrial *Quake* settings. The machinima utilizes the basic *modus operandi* of many first-person shooter, role-play computer games—that is, running around exploring space—to support this alternative narrative. Early in the piece, one of the key limitations of much machinima—the difficulty in controlling the film's *mise-en-scène* (the staging and design aspects) when you're confined to the character models and limitations offered by the game—emerges. For example, while looking for their apartment our fearless heroes are holding giant axes, all the while trying to hide their lumberjack day job behind their trademark jeans and plaid shirts. Meanwhile the erstwhile landlord appears with a giant gun, which is accounted for within the narrative as he leaves Larry and Henry to look around while he "goes hunting." The makers deal head-on with not being able to remove weapons from the characters' hands by making it the source of humor, which is an excellent tactic but one which probably wouldn't work if you were making a more serious dramatic piece.

Hot on the award winning heels of their success with *Apartment Huntin'*, the ILL Clan continued the adventures of Larry and Henry in *Hardly Workin'* (2000, http://www.illclan.com/video/hw-grindomatic.mov) and have since gone on to make a number of machinima that further develop these two characters. The ILL Clan, through their ILL Clan Animation Studios, have gone on to significantly develop the sophistication of machinima as a communication medium, as demonstrated by the corporate machinima shorts showcased on their website portfolio (see: http://www.illclan.com/our -videos).

Returning to the early days of machinima as an evolving animation medium, it's impossible to overlook the impact the success of Rooster Teeth's increasingly sophisticated *Red vs. Blue: The Blood Gulch Chronicles* and now *Red vs. Blue: Relocated* (beginning in 2003, and now into its sixth season; http://redvsblue.com) has had on the world of machinima. A parody of first-person shooter games, *Red vs. Blue* is a "comedy series, featuring two squads of hapless *Halo* heroes locked in an endless civil war prolonged mostly by their own ineptitude" (Kohler, 2007, p. 1), or, if you prefer, sensitive New Age soldiers having existential crises. Therefore, in this instance, the humor comes from placing the overall storyline in an unexpected context— into the "wrong" genre. It's a classic example of using the limited characterizations offered by the game environment to "play against type" to generate ironic comedy. As such, *Red vs. Blue* offers a model of how to circumvent the limits of characterization and "casting" in machinima (especially in first-person shooter games) for a range of genres by showing how such limitations can be a real source of humor. Rooster Teeth, the team that produces the series, "film" their scenes inside *Halo* using four Xbox consoles rigged together to allow up to 12 players to interact together, with one of them working the inbuilt camera controls to record the action (Cefrey, 2008). The team then edits the video footage using Adobe Premiere (Cefrey, 2008). Today, the quality of these episodes and the ongoing, self-contained soap-opera-like narrative make them enjoyable in and of themselves. However, familiarity with playing Halo itself allows for a whole new level of appreciation of the story.

Other key texts to emerge out of the "early" years of the machinima community include:

- *Rebel vs. Thug* (Dir. Ken Thain, 2002), made using *Quake 2,* is an early example of machinima being used to produce music video visuals (see: http://www.machinima.com:80/film/view&id=232)

- *Eschaton* (Strange Company, 2002), this series, inspired by the work of H. P. Lovecraft, was Strange Company's first machinima project (see: http://www.strangecompany.org/strangeco/eschaton). Among their other work is *Tum Raider* (2001, http://www.strangecompany.org/strangeco/tum raider).Commissioned by the BBC, this (surprise, surprise) parody of the *Tomb Raider* game features not the svelte, yet strangely buxom Lara Croft but rather her less athletic brother, Larry.

- The *Cantina Crawl* Series, is an exemplar of the "machinima as music video clip" genre. It has been an innovator in getting large numbers of players to come together and act out a rehearsed script (or in this case, choreographed dance sequences) *en masse* for a "shoot." *Cantina Crawl* is filmed in the *Star Wars Galaxies* gameworld, which allows for some fanciful characters and (especially) bar scenes (see for example *Cantina Crawl VII,* set to Chumbawumba's song "Tubthumping," (http//www.machinima.com/film/view&id=722#). In addition to the music video mode, the *Cantina Crawl* machinima also explore other genres such as parody—as in the form of movie opening sequences *Cantina Crawl XVI* http://profile.myspace.com/index.cfm?fuseaction=vids.individual&VideoID=1798126)—which clearly parallels non-machinima mash-up culture.

- *The Strangerhood* (Rooster Teeth, 2004–2006) sees the blokes behind *Red vs. Blue* expanding beyond the world of first-person shooter games and into more domestic drama settings, using *The Sims* to reveal the dark side of suburbia in a parody of sitcoms and reality TV (see, for example, http://sh.roosterteeth.com/archive/).

- Paul Marino is a key figure in the machinima world (his credits include being co-founder of the ILL Clan and Executive Director, Academy of Machinima Arts and Sciences, as well as being on the production team for many of the films listed above). His machinima music video, *Still Seeing Breen* (2005), showcases his skill in synching audio and visual tracks (for example, this music video has highly accomplished lip-synching). Indeed, this is the first truly successful lip-synched machinima music video. Its online success prompted MTV to host a machinima music video competition in 2007. To really "get" the sophistication of this particular machinima music video, however, it helps to be familiar with the character, G-Man, who features in the clip and whose "day job" in the game *Half Life* doesn't usually involve singing!

More recent machinima engages with developments in games platforms, and mirrors wider shifts in game genres and away from violent gaming (especially as gender levels among players balance out with the introduction of more "girl-friendly" platforms such as the Wii with its cute Japanese-inspired graphic mode). We're also seeing in more recent machinima, evidence of greater crossover with remix culture in general and its predilection for using digital media tools to offer social commentary. For example, *An Exercise in Futilitii* (2008, USCmachinima) blends live-action action footage and machinima clips from the Wii Fit game. The main character is a Wii Fit character (and the lad who controls him), and the machinima is told from his point-of-view (see: http://www.youtube.com/watch?v=Jj_Y3UPoR6Q&feature=channel). For examples of machinima as political commentary, check out offerings that drew on the 2008 U.S. election campaign, including John Brennan's *McCain and Obama: A Half Life 2 modification you can believe in* (2008, http://www.gamepolitics.com/category/topics/machinima); along with *Palin Dances* (2008, http://www.machinima.com/film/view&id=30736), and the response to it: *McCain Loses* (2008, http://www.youtube.com/watch?v=RTFZSwOrW7I)

Serious machinima

Well, this might all sound well and good as a fan activity, but why might you wish to pursue machinima as a creative option if your students are serious about a career in filmmaking? At a basic level, as a cheap filmmaking tool, machinima can be used to quickly develop portfolio items that showcase your filmmaking and story-telling capacities. Knowing how to make a film using basic filmmaking techniques—*mise-en-scène* considerations, camera angles, shot/reverse-shot, the power of lighting and music to convey information to the audience, and more—are present in machinima production, and underscore how quickly machinima is fast emerging as a serious format, especially when compared to the early days where game players simply cobbled together brag videos. There are a range of machinima festivals held around the world each year, and it even has a formal place at the table at prestigious indie film events such as the Sundance Film Festival. Machinima is being used to make commercial films, as already seen in relation to the ILL Clan's portfolio of films. Award-winning "serious" films have also followed in the wake of success stories such as *Anna* (Fountainhead, 2003, http://www.youtube.com/watch?v=bKEr5RRKoO4), which used Quake 3 to create "a wordless fairytale about the life and death of a single flower" (Krotoski, 2006, p. 1). Critically acclaimed, this seemingly simple story deftly employs pathos to engender an emotional relationship between the viewer and the life and death of a single flower. Short, not-your-average films such as this are finding new

and wider audiences than might otherwise be possible through online distribution networks. Indeed, serious machinima film-makers can leverage such
networks to obtain monetary returns on their work. Peter Rasmussen and
Jackie Turnure's full-length feature machinima feature *Stolen Life*
(http://www.youtube.com/watch?v=wU5DXScNJHo), for example, cost
$25,000 to make, and was distributed initially through the internet. This
movie has now been sold to the HBO television channel for distribution as
well as being available for purchase on DVD. The traditional model of distribution, based on pre-selling distribution rights to broadcast companies
and/or cinema distributors in order to finance a film or television program
gives the gatekeepers (i.e., television programmers, commissioning editors,
film distributors, financiers) ultimate power over determining which stories
will be made available to the public and which will not. In marketing, new
media and creative industries circles, much has been made of the potential
for new models of digital distribution to bypass these traditional gatekeepers
altogether (Anderson, 2006; Bruns, 2006, 2007; Jenkins, 2006). These
models—such as online distribution—enable producers to immediately and
cost-effectively distribute their product to targeted niche audiences. At the
forefront of new thinking around online distribution is Chris Anderson
(Anderson, 2007). Building on Clay Shirky's (2003) analysis of internet
power laws and Anderson's concept of the "long tail" of internet practices,
Anderson (2007, p. 52) explains:

> The theory of the long tail can be boiled down to this: Our culture and economy
> are increasingly shifting away from a focus on a relatively small number of hits
> (mainstream products and markets) at the head of the demand curve, and mov-
> ing toward a huge number of niches in the tail [of the demand curve]. In an era
> without the constraints of limited shelf space and other bottlenecks of distribu-
> tion, narrowly targeted goods and services can be as economically viable as main-
> stream fare.

Narrowly targeted films, for example, are now potentially economically
viable because the online world can operate as a low-cost shopfront for any
film title. As the theory goes, a mix of peer and word-of-mouth networks, the
sophisticated user-preference tracking system behind commercial websites
like Amazon and iTunes, and savvy niche marketing legwork collide in this
moment to provide, for some, a perfect storm of possibility for bypassing traditional gatekeepers.

Machinima: Strengths as a DIY filmmaking and storytelling medium

In summary, then, the strengths of do-it-yourself machinima include:

- The opportunity to build on a ready-made framework (characters, sets, props, etc.). In short, filming inside video games accesses a ready-made animation environment/stage

- Game platforms that enable you to "re-cam"—that is, change your camera angle, even after the action has been recorded—which creates even more choices when editing the final video

- Real-time animation. That is, you don't need to build animated action polygon by polygon, frame by frame, motion by (stop) motion—it simply unfolds and you "film" it

- The option to make use of a world and world-style familiar to emerging generations of people accustomed to games aesthetics

- Cheaper costs than would be incurred otherwise if employing actors and a crew to create a film (and definitely cheaper and easier to cater for!)

- Machinima videos' "roughness" as part of their charm

- Providing a cheap space within which to storyboard and/or beta test ideas and prepare a demo as part of a pitch for a larger-scaled, different kind of video or film project.

Machinima: Weaknesses as a DIY filmmaking and storytelling medium

There are a number of weaknesses associated with machinima that also need to be considered. These include:

- The medium being bound by the limits of the platform you're using (e.g., avatars, movement, camera angles if no "re-camming" options are available, lighting, etc.)

- A general absence of romance in many of the current role-playing games. This absence is comment-worthy because romance is a staple of the commercial film industry. That being said, role-playing games like The Sims and virtual communities like Second Life are starting to provide us with "real people" to work with. These kinds of editable, 3D environments increase opportunities for using machinima to create romance and drama machinima, and not just comedy and action films

- The danger of inadvertent irony (e.g., characters saying something serious while doing something really weird on-screen) or unintentional comedy (e.g., characters saying something strange which doesn't "fit" the "serious" actions of the characters) due to the game in which you're filming and the in-game characters, props and other resources available to you

- Copyright issues. Machinima currently exists in a legal gray zone. Technically you are breaking user agreements by using the game company's soundtracks and images, but mercifully—and assuming you're not out there making mega-bucks from your machinima—most of the companies whose games are used regularly to create machinima are willing to turn a blind eye, appreciating the whole thing as a bit of free advertising for their product. Why piss off the people who love your games when you don't really need to? That said, do be attentive to issues of copyright, especially with commercial music. Music companies are far, far less forgiving than the games companies to which they license their music

- Achieving naturalistic lip-synching when producing machinima. This lack of synchrony is fine if you're creating a comedy machinima (or your characters are wearing full-face helmets as in *Red vs. Blue*), but it's not so good if you're trying to render an extreme close-up of, say, a tender or profound moment.

Game and machinima genres

Those of you who play video and computer games will know they come in a variety of flavors. Players tend to stick with the type of game they most enjoy, whether it is role-playing (RPG), strategy, action-adventure, first-person shooter, simulation or puzzle games, just to name a few. Machinima itself can be classified into different genres and modes: music video, social/political commentary, advertisements, drama and comedy are some of the more common ones. The promotional video clips that game developers make to advertise their games are referred to as "official" machinima. Every genre of game can be showcased in this category; however, advertising can use game engines to promote more than just the game itself. Let's take a brief look at the most popular game genres used in machinima.

First-person and third-person shooter games—or "shooters" for short—have proven to be the most popular genre from which to capture gameplay in machinima. Games such as *Quake* and *Halo* offer machinima makers the opportunity to film action . . . with guns. Engaging fellow players to enact scenes online puts a wider cast of characters under the director's control. Typically, shooter games are (obviously) combat-based with military, special ops, detective, action-thriller, or science fiction settings. They have pre-set storylines, plots, characters/avatars, and missions. Suspenseful and unpredictable in terms of what enemies will do and what the environment will reveal, physically and emotionally visceral, the shooter genre demands skill and fast reactions on the part of the player. The gameplay, once mastered, is highly repetitive and goal-oriented. The game characters are often funneled down a path or through labyrinth-like spaces. Shooters best suit dramatic machinima storylines, although Rooster Teeth Productions have used irony to good effect with *Halo* characters in *Red vs. Blue*.

Racing arcade/simulation games such as *Forza* and driving action-adventures such as *Grand Theft Auto* focus the camera (and rendered polygons) on the vehicle rather than the characters. Fast-paced racing games put the player in the driver's seat, and the camera faces out the front windshield or tracks from behind the player's vehicle. Cameras are also positioned around the racetrack or city streets. Gameplay is funneled, with challenges and in-game goals unfolding as play progresses. Replays or playbacks of track action occur automatically, and the movie-maker can use these as a source of raw material for machinima videos. Free-roaming, mission-based driving games feature characters as well as the cars and play up the role of enemy non-player characters and environmental obstacles. These games lend themselves to filming dramatic vehicle chases in the spirit of *The Transporter* or James Bond movies. Players can be either highly skilled to orchestrate long stunt-packed races or be mediocre players to quickly create and film a spectacular crash.

Life simulation games such as *The Sims* franchise and 3D environments like Second Life are fast gaining popularity in the machinima world, especially among female DIY directors. They feature a host of player-adapted characters and environments that are manipulated as a group in single-player mode or individually online in multiplayer mode. Settings are familiar: shopping malls, parks, and suburban homes (although Second Life offers a rich range of fictional spaces as well). Re-enactments of (or newly written) political speeches by, for instance, Senator McCain or President Obama (who both feature in Sims 3) are possible. Creating advertisements for household products or shops and services are within the realm of the machinima-maker who plays life simulation games. These kinds of games and 3D worlds are often used to re-enact favorite music videos, although still with mixed success in terms of lip-synch, dance-synch and character and scene likeness to the original piece. New music videos are easier to develop using scenes from dancing games—such as High Street 5, a free-to-play online game—that plays the song you want to feature with characters that by default dance in time with the music. *The Movies* is a computer game that is ideal for those who want to develop and stage a new script. The game entails hiring and firing actors, keeping actors happy, earning money to buy sets and props, and the like. These resources can then be used to make "directed" machinima, with the recording software built directly into the game. Movie Storm (http://www.moviestorm.co.uk) while technically not a game is an animation engine that can be used to create machinima. Drama, comedy, social commentary, and fantasy films, along with dance clips, are all possible machinima to create using life simulations.

Role-playing games, especially massively multiplayer online role-playing games (MMORPGs), such as *World of Warcraft* and the *Final Fantasy* series, offer exotic characters in fantasy locations. The machinima-maker will have plenty of opportunity to explore scenarios in the free-roaming character-rich environments of RPGs. Activities range across run-of-the-mill foe slaying, magic spell-casting, epic battles, object searching and/or procurement, and simple conversations between different "classes" of characters. The objective is to "level up" your character or avatar to access new environments and more valuable objects/weapons while at the same time engaging in more challenging quests. MMORPGs allow the machinima maker to film many players' avatars (who often fight in groups called "guilds") in action. Animated TV series *South Park*'s "Make Love, Not Warcraft" episode is a classic example of art imitating life imitating art, as well as a superb use of machinima in a commercial context. Machinima makers will need to clock up many playing hours (or use an experienced player) to best take advantage of all that role-playing games have to offer.

SECTION TWO

Machinima: Before you start

Hopefully by now you're chomping at the bit to get started on a project that sets you up as the logical successor to Pixar's dominance of the animation market. But before you jump into it, remember that in machinima—as in any form of narrative—ultimately what matters isn't the whizzbang technology, but the quality of the story being told.

Before seriously sitting down to make a piece of machinima, it's important to plan out what it is you're going to do. Think about the game platform you're going to use and how you are going to record raw footage. Different platforms require different methods for capturing onscreen gameplay. Make a short list of games that are suitable for your purposes. What "sets," characters and camera angles does a specific game offer you? How do these fit with the storyworld of your proposed creative piece?

If you haven't already done so, check out the competition. What do other machinima clips look like in your chosen genre? What features appeal? What works and what doesn't?

Be realistic. Set short, achievable targets for your first pieces so that you can see the final result quickly, and start sharing your work with the machinima world as soon as you can. Other machinima makers' feedback on your work—whether sobering or rewarding—will be invaluable to you. Music videos (see the activities at end of this chapter) are a popular option to start with, but keep in mind music copyright laws; you don't want to have to pull your piece from public display because the artist's label is bombarding you with "cease and desist or else" letters from their lawyers.

Machinima: A basic "how to"

Step 1: Play

To make a machinima movie, you need to play a game. For avid gamers, this won't be a problem. For people who have not touched a console or computer game in the last few years, be prepared to put in some time playing a game before you start recording, or persuade an expert gamer to play the game for you. Either way, it's important to be as familiar as you can be with a game before you start capturing gameplay. You may have to try out several games before you find one that best suits your purposes. Consider it research and spend 5 to 50 hours doing it. Why play a game before recording?

- Gain expertise, points or "money" to access areas, items and characters in the gameworld that are useful to you as actors, props and filming locations.
- Find optimal paths that best show off an action sequence or a subject, especially if the camera will be fixed in certain positions.
- Become familiar with the complete range of movement under your control.

Say, for example, you want to record footage of a racing game for a music clip. You'll need to test out different racetracks and a range of vehicles within the game before you find the right combination. What camera views show off the cars and the setting? What time of day, weather or lighting is appropriate for the mood of your piece? How should you take a corner to best show off drift? At what point should you try a 360° spin or spectacular roll?

There comes a point when your playing is no longer research. It's a rehearsal, and you are ready for the next step.

Step 2: Storyboard

Movie-making buffs know the importance of storyboarding, but gamers often bypass it to record. Or they might record, then storyboard the footage they know they have to hand. Our preference is to storyboard first and, if necessary, adapt the storyboard after recording footage. This is the process game developers use to make in-game cut scenes and promotional videos or "official" machinima.

Think of a storyboard as a visual plan where you set out key scenes, POV (point of view), camera angles, shot type (distant, mid, close) and timing (see Figure 6.1).

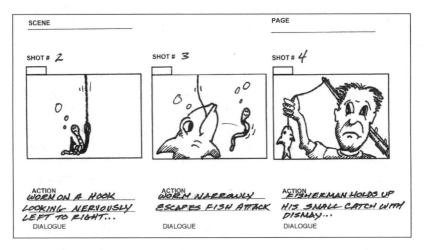

Figure 6.1: An example of a machinima storyboard (used with permission from Alexandro Nuñez, 2009)

Storyboards can take any form, from the hastily sketched to the carefully drawn-and-dialogued plan. Some machinima makers suggest using comics software—like Comic Life (Mac) or Comic Book Creator (PC)—and stills from your game footage to storyboard your machinima clip or movie.

Storyboarding can be an efficient approach to machinima making, especially if you have a time limit on your piece as well as your production, or are working with a multi-player cast. Take the music racing clip, for example. If you have a soundtrack that runs for two minutes, you need to plan for two minutes of edited visuals. Listen to the music while you sketch the key scenes. Will you cut fast-paced beats to speeding vehicles vying for the lead position on the track, the crescendo to a spectacular crash, and the denouement to crossing the winning line?

Storyboarding key scenes is like writing the visual story for your machinima clip, even if there are no words or clear-cut narrative. It allows you to put time and effort into recording the gameplay that means the most to your creative piece. This is particularly important if you have a deadline, because you focus on recording gameplay that is relevant to the storyboard, and ultimately, to the overall story itself. If, for some reason, you can't get all the shots, revisit the storyboard. It will come in handy when you edit your clip, too.

Step 3: Record

Capturing gameplay can be easy or complicated, depending on the game, the platform, the recording device and your expectations. There are a range of parameters that can steer it in either direction:

1. Scripted or non-scripted action: Scripted action is when players can manipulate the game engine to create certain actions at unique times. This, then, isn't referring to "script" as movie dialogue for actors to speak but rather to "script" as actual programming commands that tell actors where to go and what to do. This script is then "run" inside the game and the action recorded. The good thing about this kind of scripting is that tinkering with and re-playing scenes is a snap and avoids having to start each scene from scratch when a retake is required (for more on this, see, for example, Galder, no date). Game developers use scripted action and character interaction to create cut scenes. Modders—players who tinker with the game program itself to make changes or additions to the game based on their own preferences—do this to have more control over their game environment. Some games make it easy for players to manipulate the game environment (e.g., *World of Warcraft, Neverwinter Nights*). Other games don't (e.g., the Harry Potter video games). Non-scripted action utilizes whatever action is available to the player during the normal course of the game. (It is still "scripted" of course, but by the programmers in the process of actually making the game.) If you are *not* an experienced gamer, chances are you will be recording action that is *not* player-scripted. You need to make do with the in-game action and cameras available to you.

2. Camera positions: Depending on the genre of the game, there will be a limited range of camera positions at the machinima maker's disposal. A player can maintain one camera position or point of view (POV) during a recording session (e.g., through the eyes of the character they are playing, from above the action), then re-play (if it's a scripted movie) and record in another to capture the same sequence from multiple viewpoints, or switch between POVs throughout the sequence. The storyboard comes in handy for knowing which shots require which POV. Another trick is to get other players to join in, if the game allows them to do so (e.g., online), and have each of them record the sequence from their own POV. That way, each player can concentrate on their own progress and the shots are edited for continuity in post-production. If you are lucky (or particularly motivated to find an add-on application to do this) you can script camera positions to automatically occur at certain locations in an action sequence.

3. Lip-synchronization: The bane of machinima makers is to convincingly synch the movement of characters' mouths and facial expressions with the words they speak. Unless you are using in-game dialogue (in which case the dialogue lines and lip movements should already be synched), *do not* attempt to achieve lip-sync in your first efforts at machinima-making. Fudge it. Draw attention away from it. Find creative ways to overcome it, such as the previously mentioned use of full-face helmets in *Red vs. Blue*). Few character-based games support easy synchronization with player-originated dialogue. Some of you will have high expectations, however, and will aim for something that at least comes close. In the case of the latter, study the range of in-game dialogue available to your character and record voiceover that uses similar mouth movements.

4. *Sound:* Recording dialogue, whether it is a straightforward narration or character voices, can make or break the entertainment value of a machinima clip. Professionally animated scenes use the professional voiceover of hired actors. If you (and a friend) are recording the voiceover yourself, put emotion and projection into your voice. Try recording the same line spoken in several different ways so that you can pick the most suitable one in post-production. Most machinima use in-game sound effects but you may want to record a few of your own for emphasis or download sound effects from online archives (see Chapter 3 in this volume for more on this). Soundtracks, particularly for music clips, should be considered *before* recording gameplay to create the best match between visual and audio. Otherwise a professional sound engineer and composer can create original scores, or you can do-it-yourself using Garageband (ships free with Macs) or software like Cakewalk (PCs).

5. *HUD icons and interface:* Depending on the method of recording and the flexibility of the game interface in terms of "turning off" on-screen gameplay information, elements of the heads-up-display (HUD) may appear in the captured footage. This display can include player statistics regarding health, wealth, location, and the like (if you found the Leeroy Jenkins video described earlier, you'll have seen the player's HUD clearly). If you cannot remove this information from the screen, you may be able to move them out of the recording frame if you are using an external screen capture application. If not, include them in the design of your piece.

6. *Recording software*: Depending on the game's platform, there are numerous methods for capturing gameplay. PC- or Mac-based games require screen-recording software if they don't already have an in-built recording system (e.g., for replays) to which the player has access. Some recorders are free, such as CamStudio (http://www.camstudio.org), and trial versions of Fraps (http://www.fraps.com) and Debut (http://www.nchsoftware.com) all for PCs, and free trial versions of IShowU (http://www.apple.com) and Snapz Pro X (http://www.ambrosiasw.com) for Macs. However, trial versions set limitations on recording and often watermark the footage. Players of console

games can use a USB video capture card (which plugs into the console itself) to record game footage which they can then transfer from the console to their computer. Players also can make use of the more traditional method of connecting their TV to a DVD recorder or digital camcorder. Online games and environments like *The Sims* and Second Life have built-in screen recording software that saves footage directly to your computer. It is also possible to connect the video output from a console (or multiple consoles) to a computer instead of a television and record gameplay using the computer's screen capture software. Experimenting with what suits you and your technical skills best is the key to successful recording. Determine what method you use to record gameplay before, even, you decide on which game you source your machinima from.

In what follows we describe step-by-step how to create a simple machinima. This overview tutorial uses Mac software, making machinima with PCs follows very similar principles.

Sample gameplay capturing session

1. Launch your game of choice on your computer.

2. Open iShowU (see Figure 6.2).

3. Adjust recording parameters (e.g., presets, which govern size and resolution) if required, and if you want external sound as well as game sound to be recorded (see "Input selection" options). It could be useful to record your voiceover while manipulating the characters onscreen.

4. Click on "Edit Recording Area" to adjust the screen capture frame (a lightly-outlined box that by default will follow your cursor movements) to match desired field of gameplay area. Follow the instructions, or click on the corners and on the highlighted box itself to move your screen capture frame to where you want it. Press "Enter" to save your changes. Deselect "Follow mouse cursor" at the bottom of this window, unless you want to move the video recording frame during gameplay. We suggest you ensure the recording frame excludes the game control and HUD information, as well as the iShowU recording controls themselves, so that you can manipulate the game and recording session "off screen." Click on the "Record" button at the bottom of the window to start recording and start the gameplay.

5. Click on "Finish" button to stop recording. The movie file will save, by default, to your desktop (or wherever you have set your computer to save downloaded and other files automatically). If you can't find it, the file is automatically titled "iShowU_Capture.mov" and you can search for it.

6. Click on your freshly captured movie clip and it will open and play in Quicktime. Decide whether you're happy with the clip, or would like to record it again.

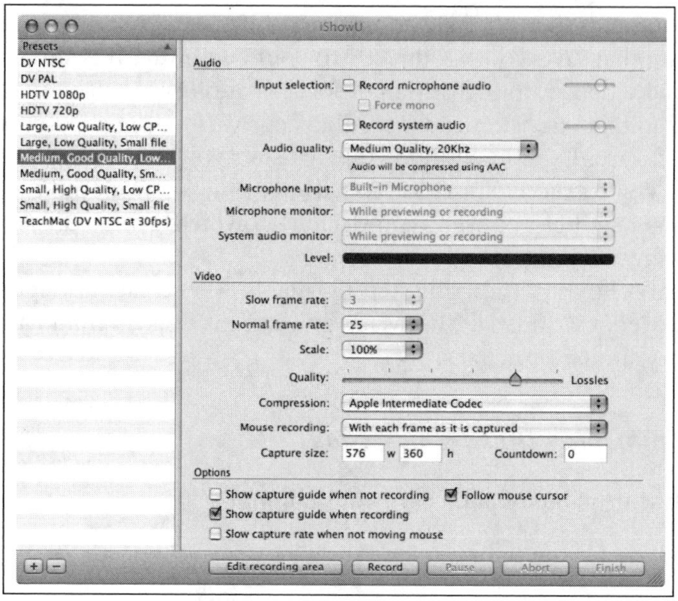

Figure 6.2: The opening screen of iShowU. (Image used with permission from Shinywhitebox.com, 2009).

Record about ten times more than what your final machinima requires. Make numerous movies of raw gameplay footage; this is definitely a case of "more is better." Again, this is where the storyboard (or shot list; see the following section) proves useful. You know which key shots are required, so you can create multiple recordings of each in order to be able to choose the best among them for your final machinima. Be flexible during the recording sessions. If the unexpected happens—and it looks great, or moves the story in a different direction—adapt the storyboard to accommodate the shot.

Step 4: Edit

The art of video editing is a process which can be learnt through training and study, but it takes skill to do it well. Teaching that skill is well beyond the scope of this chapter; however, we can provide a few pointers (see also Chapters 7 and 9 in this volume).

Make sure that the editing software you use—such as iMovie (Macs) or Windows Movie Maker (PCs)—can import and export the video file format you are using. This refers to the file format of the raw and edited game footage. Popular formats are *.avi, *.mpg and *.mov. iShowU, for example, saves onscreen video recordings as *.mov files, which play in Quicktime. Some formats are incompatible with certain software (both in terms of editing and playing), so consider your own software requirements as well as your audience's. There are also different rates of compression. Higher rates of compression result in a lower standard of visual and audio quality; however they upload and download faster (e.g., YouTube videos are highly compressed). Aspect ratio is another consideration. A width-height ratio of 4:3 is a typical landscape format. Recording in one aspect ratio and exporting in another may distort the final image. Make sure they are the same or are converted appropriately.

Choice of editing software also influences the creative direction of the edited piece. Some simple video editors have two "tracks": one for audio and one for video. This means that you need to supply a complete soundtrack (including dialogue, sound effects and music) and edit visuals to it from one video source. This type of editing software is okay if all you have is, say, a piece of music and you are making a machinima music clip from one gameplay recording session. Professional editing "suites"—like Adobe Premier Pro or Avid Express Pro—have multiple tracks which allow you to combine in-game sound, voiceover, music and multiple gameplay recordings.

Transition effects between shots can carry or interrupt the flow of the piece. You can make direct "cuts" from one shot to another, either from game footage to another sequence of game footage, or cuts to black followed by game footage. Fades and other transitions are creative decisions. Use them if they are effective. Music clips are often edited to the beat of the soundtrack. This means timing transitions to synch them with the music. Music clips are a good way for a beginner to hone his or her machinima editing skills.

Okay, you are familiar with your editing software (for more how-to advice, see Chapters 7 and 9 in this volume) and now face the prospect of picking the best shots out of twenty minutes (or twenty hours!) of raw game footage to create two minutes of machinima.

1. Using your storyboard as a guide, review the raw footage and note at which times an appropriate "shot" appears. It may help to organize a 5-column shot list (either at this point or earlier in the process). Number and describe each shot in order of their appearance in the first two columns of your shot list. Note the start and finish of the raw footage time codes in the next two columns for each shot, followed by the expected duration for each shot in the edited piece.

2. Start selecting the desired footage, concentrating on the most important scenes first (if you run out of time, you can cut or adapt the minor scenes). It

would be a shame to spend all your time on the first part of the clip and rush the finale.

3. Do a "rough edit" first without transitions or special effects or perfect timing. Use placeholders for any on-screen text (this could even be blank "slides" that will later become the movie title or credits list). Are you happy with the transition from storyboard to screen?

4. It's time to put the storyboard aside and polish the piece on its own merits. Place any on-screen text that's needed (e.g., movie title, credits). Insert the transitional effects. Fine-tune the timing of your edits.

Step 5: Disseminate

Build your portfolio online. Post your machinima clip to YouTube if you want to make it public or share it with your friends via a social networking site such as Facebook. Be aware of the technical conditions or social restrictions of certain avenues of distribution. There might be a size (megabyte) limit, a preferred file format, and audience ratings and feedback to consider. The important thing is to ensure your machinima's accessibility. Do your homework on your distribution channels before putting it "out there."

The Machinima Filmfest (http://festival.machinima.org/) held every year in New York hosts the Mackie Awards, which are given to outstanding machinima productions in numerous categories, including best long format (over 20 minutes), short format (under 20 minutes), independent producer, student work, game studio machinima produced by a developer, direction, virtual performance, voice-acting, visual design, cinematography, original music, sound design, writing, editing and machinima series. The award categories show just how "professional" machinima has become as an entertainment form. Europe followed suit with its own machinima festival, beginning in 2007. The Australian Centre for the Moving Image ran a two-day machinima festival program and series of workshops in 2008. Some film and animation festivals around the world, such as BitFilm (http://www.bitfilm.com/festival/) in Germany, now have a machinima category. The Sundance Film Festival has hosted machinima panel sessions since 2005. Some games companies—like Blizzard—host machinima competitions and screenings. There are growing opportunities for talented machinima makers—including machinima makers still in school—to be officially recognized for their work.

SECTION THREE

Suggested machinima activities

Even if you're not feeling especially skilled at or familiar with gaming, or with recording and editing software, we suggest you try your hand at the following activities to help build your students' machinima portfolio. Have them aim at making several short clips (90–120 seconds each in duration) so that their work can be created and viewed quickly. As mentioned in the first pages of this chapter, there are numerous categories that machinima falls into. Machinima has developed far beyond the boasts of gamers about their exploits to include social commentary, comedy, drama, advertisements and music videos, just to name a few. We encourage you and your students to contribute to these increasingly popular forms of entertainment.

1. The music video: Regarded as the easiest type of machinima to make, the music video requires—in its most basic form—that you select a soundtrack, play *any* game, and edit shots in sync with the music. More sophisticated efforts include "dancers" and "singers." Character-based games are best for the latter. We have seen High Street 5, an online multiplayer dancing game, used with great results.

2. Social commentary: Using either previously recorded dialogue or well-written original dialogue, record and edit gameplay footage to make a powerful social comment. Encourage your students to draw on the elements of irony, for example, to promote peace using footage from a first-person shooter game. Recreate a famous persuasive speech in front of a virtual audience of avatars in Second Life.

3. Advertisements: Whether you are promoting your own product, someone else's (beware of libel), or a fictional one, advertisements can be as spectacular as a movie trailer or as ubiquitous as a web banner animation. Search online for Volvo's "Game On" television ad, or Coca-Cola's *Grand Theft Auto*-style "Coke side of life" commercial, to use as models to show your students how machinima has been used for real-world marketing purposes. As with any marketing endeavor, be aware of your audience. Use an existing jingle or make up one of your own. Write and design on-screen text. Choose your game wisely. Do you want to shock or lure? How much of a story can you tell? How can you "sell" it without revealing too much? We have seen convincing fictional advertisements using Sims characters and sets.

4. Drama: Have students think of a scene from a favorite movie or television drama and recreate it using either the original soundtrack or by recording their own. Better still, showcase your own scriptwriting talent and make a scene, literally. *The Movies* is a game where you can write and direct your own shoots. It's also an excellent way of side-stepping copyright issues and enables students to explore and experiment with script writing, staging, lighting, music soundtrack effects, and other filmic elements in a highly accessible (and affordable) way.

5. *Comedy:* Despite being the most difficult to do and the most fun to watch, irony seems to work best in machinima comedy. Have your students record an original voiceover audio file and play it over simple exchanges between game characters. *Red vs. Blue* does this to hilarious effect using *Halo* characters that do little more than stand beside each other. The challenging part is not the gameplay; it's the storyline and the script.

To sum up, machinima-making in school encourages students to produce their *own* animated movies, rather than merely consume animations made by others (McClay, Mackey, Carbonaro, Szafron, & Schaeffer, 2007). It also engages students in thinking closely about narrative structure and "writing" with moving images. Indeed, as Lawrence Lessig, a renowned advocate for DIY remix culture, reminds us during an interview with Richard Koman (2005, no page):

> When you say the word writing, for those of us over the age of 15, our conception of writing is writing with text . . . But if you think about the ways kids under 15 using digital technology think about writing—you know, writing with text is just one way to write, and not even the most interesting way to write. The more interesting ways are increasingly to use images and sound and video to express ideas.

Thus, even if teachers themselves are not interested in creating their own machinima, knowing that it *can* be done is important.

Machinima-making also pushes teachers and students alike to move beyond digital story-telling practices and into the realm of authentic, prototypical movie making. This is not to diminish the value of digital story-telling practices in any way—studies and projects have shown time and time again how much students enjoy and learn from being able to insert still images into video editing software to create a video and then adding a voiceover track to complete the narrative (cf., Hull, 2004; Tarasiuk, 2009). What machinima offers you and your students is somewhere to go once you've explored the possibilities of digital storytelling. And, of course, a key advantage of machinima is the way in which it leverages game playing proficiencies in meaningful ways inside the classroom. Avid gamers can focus their energies on developing innovative storylines because they are familiar with what can be done in multiple game worlds. Not-so-avid gamers are provided with opportunities for looking at games in a different way—through the eyes of a movie-maker.

At the same time, teachers can work to hone students' understanding of film narrative structures and engage them in developing cinematic skills and techniques that will serve them well beyond school. DIY machinima reminds educators that narrative fiction itself is not a static form and that it is important to remain open to new ways of telling tales. As Jill McClay and her colleagues point out to teachers, in their study of Grade 10 students writing machinima scripts using the *Neverwinter Nights* game engine,

> [a]s young people increasingly become able to produce fiction in game and other digital formats, their consumption, production and understanding of fiction in such formats will likely develop in ways that we cannot now predict (McClay et al., 2007, p. 273).

We conclude this chapter with a list of resources you might find useful as you begin exploring—and creating—your own machinima, or machinima with your students.

Key websites and online archives

These websites are useful starting places, not least because they host excellent examples of the rich range of machinima that can be produced.

- Machinima.com (http://www.machinima.com)
- ILL Clan Animation Studios (http://www.illclan.com)
- The Overcast: A Machinima Podcast series (http://theovercast.com)
- Machinimag (http://www.machinimag.com)

Machinima capture and editing software

Before committing to buying a software program, explore the free and demo programs available to test on various platforms in order to obtain a better idea of the strengths and weakness of each for the kind of storytelling you want to do.

- Fraps (http://www.fraps.com)
- iShowU (http://www.apple.com)
- Gamecam (http://www.planetgamecam.com)
- ScriptEase (http://www.cs.ualberta.ca/~script/), a program that runs inside the game, *Neverwinter Nights* and enables you to script scenes without necessarily having played the game itself much
- Debut (http://www.nchsoftware.com/capture/)

- CamStudio (http://www.camstudio.org)
- FastCap (http://www.ejoystudio.com/)
- Adobe Premiere (http://www.adobe.com/products/premiere/)
- Final Cut Pro (http://www.apple.com/finalcutstudio/finalcutpro/)

Sound and music recording and editing software

- Audacity (http://audacity.sourceforge.net; see also Chapters 2 and 3 in this volume)
- Garageband (http://www.apple.com/ilife/garageband)
- Cakewalk (http://www.cakewalk.com)

Popular game engines used to create machinima

Battlefield 1942	*Quake I, II & III*
Grand Theft Auto	*Second Life*
Halo	*Neverwinter Nights*
High Street 5	*The Sims*
The Movies	*Unreal Tournament*
Half Life I & II	*World of Warcraft*

Machinima: Key "How to" Guides (books)

Hancock, H. & Ingram, J. (2007). *Machinima for dummies.* Hoboken, NJ: Wiley Publishing.

Kelland, M., Morris, D. & Lloyd, D. (2005). *Machinima: Making movies in 3D virtual environments.* Boston, MA: Thomson.

Marino, P. (2004). *3D Game-based filmmaking: The art of machinima.* Scottsdale, AZ: Paraglyph Press.

Weber, A., Rufer-Bach, K., & Platel, R. (2008). *Creating your world: The official guide to advanced content creation for Second Life.* Indianapolis, IN: Wiley Publishing (especially Chapter 13).

Machinima: Key "How To" Guides (online)

- Machinimag (http://www.machinimag.com)
- Machinima.com's Machinima 101 tutorials (http://machinima.com/machi nima101/index)

References

Anderson, C. (2007). *The long tail: How endless choice is creating unlimited demand.* London: Random House.

Bruns, A. (2006). Wikinews: The next generation of alternative online news? *Scan Journal, 3*(1). Retrieved on February 12, 2009, from http://scan.net.au/scan/journal/di splay.php?journal_id=69

Bruns, A. (2007, June). Produsage: Towards a broader framework for user-led content creation. Paper presented at the: Creativity & Cognition 6 Conference, Washington, DC.

Cefrey, H. (2008). *Career building through machinima: Using video games to make movies.* New York: Rosen Publishing Group.

Galder, D. (no date). Scripting tutorials. *Bioware.* Retrieved on February 20, 2009, from http://nwn.bioware.com/builders/sctutorial.html

Hancock, H. & Ingram, J. (2007). *Machinima for dummies.* Hoboken, NJ: Wiley Publishing.

Hull, G. (2004). Youth culture and digital media: New literacies for new times. *Research in the Teaching of English, 38*(2), 229–233.

Isbister, K. (2005). *Better game characters by design: A psychological approach.* San Francisco: Morgan Kaufmann Publishers.

Jenkins, H. (2006). *Convergence culture: Where old and new media collide.* New York: New York University Press.

Juul, J. (2001). Games telling stories? A brief note on games and narratives. *The International Journal of Computer Game Studies, 1*(1). Retrieved on February 12, 2009, from http://www.gamestudies.org/0101/juul-gts/

Kohler, C. (2007). Machinima series *Red vs. Blue* ends tour of duty. *Wired.* June 26. Retrieved February 21, 2009 from http://www.wired.com/entertainment/theweb/ news/2007/06/redversusblue

Koman, R. (2005). Remixing culture: An interview with Lawrence Lessig. Retrieved April 22, 2006,from http://www.oreillynet.com/pub/a/policy/2005/02/24/lessig.html

Krotoski, A. (2006). Lights, camera, joystick. *The Age.* Retrieved on February 12, 2009, from http://www.theage.com.au/news/film/lights-camera-joystick/2006/01/26/ 1138066913864.html?page=fullpage#contentSwap2

Lowood, H. (2006). Storyline, dance/music, or PvP?: Game movies and community players in World of Warcraft. *Games and Culture, 1*(4), 362–382.

McClay, J., Mackey, M., Carbonaro, M., Szafron, D., & Schaeffer, J. (2007). Adolescents composing fiction in digital game and written formats: Tacit, explicit and metacognitive strategies.*E-learning. 4*(3): 273–284. Retrieved February 12, 2009, from http://www.wwwords.co.uk/elea/

Neitzel, B. (2005). Narrativity in computer games. In J. Raessens and J. Goldstein (Eds.), *Handbook of Computer Game Studies,* (pp. 227–245), Cambridge, MA: MIT Press.

Shirky, C. (2003). Power laws, weblogs, and inequality. *Clay Shirky's Writings About the Internet: Economics & Culture, Media & Community, Open Source.* Retrieved February 21, 2009, from http://www.shirky.com/writings/powerlaw_weblog.html

Tarasiuk, T. (2009). Extreme reading in the middle grades. *NewLits.org Wiki.* Retrieved February 21, 2009, from http://capricorn.montclair.edu/newlits/index.php/Extreme_Reading_in_the_Middle_Grades

Wikipedia (2009). Leeroy Jenkins. Retrieved February 21, 2009, from http://en.wikipedia.org/wiki/Leeroy_Jenkins

Chapter 7

Stop Motion Animation

Angela Thomas and Nicole Tufano

This chapter contains a mix of voices of, and input from, a range of people. Writing this text was a collaborative process that spanned three countries (Australia, the U.S. and the U.K.). Given the distributed nature of this writing, we—Angela and Nicole—each took principal responsibility for particular sections in order to simplify things. Thus, in what follows, the "I" referenced in sections 1 and 3 refers to Angela, and the "I" in section 2 refers to Nicole.

SECTION ONE

An overview of stop motion animation and current DIY trends

Animation has been a significant form throughout the history of cinema, "prompting, informing and responding to each of the technical innovations in production" (Chong, 2008, p. 15). Chong labels animation as a modernist art form, a form which engages with, underpins, and changes culture and society. Animation is, according to Chong (2008, p. 1), "the technique of filming successive drawings or positions of models to create an illusion of movement when the film is shown as a sequence." Stop motion is the branch of digital animation where some form of model is used; these models can be as wide-ranging as paper doll cutouts, Lego™ blocks, clay figures, toys, and even people.

Stop motion animation is a form of filmmaking which has a long history. In fact, the first such film was recorded in 1889 and was titled *The Humpty Dumpty Circus*. This movie consisted of two filmmakers using a child's wooden circus toy set to make a silent film (The Big Cartoon Database, 2007). Now, some 120 years later, stop motion animation is highly popular with modern film makers, and has become well known through television and films such as Aardman Studios' *Wallace and Grommit*, Tim Burton's *The Nightmare Before Christmas* (directed by Henry Selick), Oscar-winning Adam Elliot's *Harvie Krumpet*, and two recently released movies, *Coraline* and *Mary and Max.*

Stop motion, like all genres of animation, is based on several important principles: (1) it uses the technique of producing a series of still images—each capturing incremental changes in the scene—before converting this series of images into a film sequence; (2) it plays on the viewer's "persistence of vision" (Webster, 2005, p. 4). That is, it creates an optical illusion whereby the viewer experiences a slight delay in vision, and the eyes naturally fill in the gaps between the still images and actually interpret them as moving images; and (3) it requires an excellent observation of reality to analyze movements and sequences of movements for any particular motion to be converted into hundreds of tiny minute steps. In short, it requires a fine-honed understanding of timing.

In his introduction to digital animation, Chong (2008) makes three highly significant observations about the use of technology to create any form of animation which in summary include: (1) new technologies come and go, but animation is more about the creativity of the animator (i.e., story and creativity before form); (2) it's not about "technical dexterity" with technology; and (3) "[e]mbracing new technology and its potential does not mean abandoning previous core skills and knowledge. The old and the new must always be brought together to achieve the most persuasive and original developments in the form" (Chong, 2008, p. 6). These core values, skills and knowledge all relate to one concept: telling a story. Creating a narrative, developing characters, and finding a visual aesthetic in which to place them are essential and central values at the heart of all filmmaking.

Chong's observations are significant because animation as a whole is considered an *art* form, a means of expression, and a form where photo-realism is not necessarily the ultimate goal. Although some studios specializing in three-dimensional computer-generated image (CGI) animation do try to achieve a level of photo-realism, there are many animators who are not interested in this at all. These animators prefer to focus on creating a whole new aesthetic and an individual voice which is both recognizable and loved by audiences as animation in its own right and for its own value. In fact, it has often been the limitations of computer graphics and technology that have forced filmmakers of animation to think beyond traditional techniques and create new ones. Certainly, the makers of the movie *Coraline* concur, with head story artist Chris Butler revealing:

> Every time I've worked on a stop motion project it pushes the technique so much further—to the point where sometimes, you can't believe they're puppets . . . there were a lot of things that were innovative that came out of the need to make this movie better, to really put us on the map. (Butler, as cited in Jones, 2009, p. 210)

and lead animator on this same movie, Travis Knight, explaining:

> I'm particularly interested in finding ways to do really avant-garde animation. Animation that is really unique and pushes the senses of what people think animation can and should be. (Knight, as cited in Jones, 2009, p. 210)

Coraline also raised a much higher level of consciousness about the production processes of a full-feature-length stop motion animation film with its clever marketing campaign. First of all, the production team released hundreds of behind-the-scene images to various mainstream media outlets (see, for example, http://photos.latimes.com/backlot/gallery/coraline/2008/9/15/Coraline_teresa_drilling).Then they made their own YouTube video channel and released 13 short video clips, mostly sharing more behind-the-scenes footage but also including audience reactions and a focus on the voice actor cast. These videos revealed such things as the painstaking work behind creating hair textures, the process of creating miniature knitted costumes, and the drawer full of tiny faces used to create a scene of dialogue for *Coraline* (seen at: http://photos.latimes.com/backlot/gallery/coraline/2008/9/15/Coraline_replacements_face).But one of the most unique pieces of marketing the production team did was to send out 50 individualized *Coraline* "mystery boxes"—boxes or suitcases that contained pieces of the set, stills and even some of the puppets inside them—to 50 very lucky, reasonably high-profile, but everyday, bloggers. This caused a sensation across the blogosphere, with bits and pieces of the movie now spread out across the world, blogged about, photographed, sent to Flickr and elsewhere. Each blogger had their own story to tell and each received a personalized letter from the film company revealing why they were chosen as a recipient of the mystery box. Some people even filmed the big reveal as they opened the boxes (seen at: http://www.animationarchive.org/2008/11/more-on-our-coraline-suitcase.html). These marketing and publicity approaches raised a significant, broad-based awareness and appreciation of stop motion animation techniques as an art form.

DIY stop motion

With the mushrooming of participatory culture and DIY media, stop motion animation has quickly become a means of expression for a much younger generation of amateur and budding filmmakers. Stop motion animation tends to be a form of choice by many animation fans because of the minimal financial outlay required. With simple tools like iStopMotion (for Macs; a free demo version is available, and the cost of basic software is only $49) and Stop Motion Pro (for PCs; for $70), and a webcam or digital camera and a tripod, the costs to make a stop motion movie are really quite affordable. Apple markets iStopMotion as a family product, using children and their toys as the hero images in their publicity campaigns. They claim that their casual user in fact is "the typical family where the parents want to have fun with the kids while providing them with a productive, creative and educational experience" (Boinx Software Ltd. 2009, no page). Stop Motion Pro (2009) for PC users also claims that young children can learn to use their software in just minutes. They offer a Stop Motion Pro Junior edition with a simplified interface for younger users and include a school showcase section on their website sidebar. There are also two free PC programs that are recommended for PC users: Monkey Jam and Stop Motion Animator.

But even if you cannot afford or do not have access to the stop motion software, the minimal requirements are a computer and a camera, as most computers come packaged with simple video editing software which can import still images and lace them together into movie format (as we describe later in this chapter). So the message is quite clear: stop motion is affordable and easy to learn. In fact, Chong claims:

> Tools such as iStopMotion represent the democratisation of computer technology and the benefits of digitisation for amateur and professional animators. The simplicity of the interface allows the user to ignore the technology and concentrate on the animation (Chong, 2008, p. 107).

This echoes the work of David Buckingham, who speaks to the development of media education as a move towards democratization and the valuing of children's out-of-school DIY experiences and practices (Buckingham, 2003). This also harks back to the core values of digital animation I highlighted earlier—the narrative and artistry of animation are more important than the technical software used to capture it. Of course, stop motion animation software does have its own unique affordances, and people are using these along with video editing programs to create magical, stunning pieces of work.

The simplicity of stop motion animation can be exemplified best by viewing the videos of Keegan, who created her first stop animation at 3 years of age, and has recently added a new animation at age four. Keegan is helped by her father, Greg, but clearly does all the animating herself while Greg does the editing and final video uploading to YouTube. This is evident because Greg included a "making of" excerpt on one video and we see Keegan moving her toys bit by bit and running back and forth to the computer to take a shot in between each movement (see Figure 7.1).

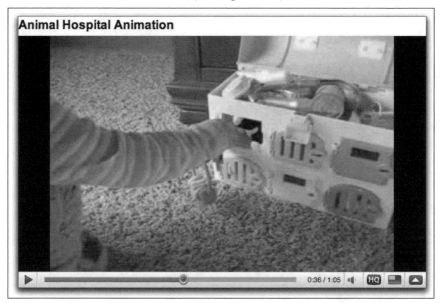

Figure 7.1: "Animal Hospital" (Keegan, at age 3) Image used with permission, 2009
(Source: http://www.youtube.com/watch?v=zKhW-Slwdr8)

By four, Keegan had developed much more sophisticated filming and storytelling techniques, using high angles and long shots to create different scenes, moods, and power relations between the audience and the text (see http://www.youtube.com/watch?v=ET4d2qeB6r8). Keegan is learning these techniques at *four years old*, and is also being encouraged to use broadcasting media such as YouTube to share her work with the world to elicit views, feedback and ratings on her work. As one of her commenters stated: "just think what she'll be capable of when she is five!" (twiggarts, 2008, no page).

The best sources of information about stop motion video are found on any number of fan and animator sites, and of course the most popular broadcast medium for DIY film makers: YouTube. Typically, an animation fan site will offer information, how-to demonstration video tutorials, a discussion forum or message board, detailed notes about stop motion techniques and a gallery or showcase of member's work. Some sites, like the Anim8 Stop Motion site (http://www.anim8stopmotion.com), also contain interviews with emerging animators who have had their work showcased or featured or popularized on YouTube. I was fortunate to meet up with Micky, the creator of the Anim8 Stop Motion site, and I asked him a few questions via email about his site and about his observations of current stop motion hits and trends. Here's what he had to say.

ANGELA: Why are you a fan of stop motion and what made you start the Anim8 Stop Motion site?

MICKY: I have always loved cartoons from being a young child to now, this included all types of animation. When I was younger I wanted to be an animator but as time passed I found myself being drawn in a different direction, namely web design.

In my final year of university I had to develop a major project around any subject matter I wanted, and having researched lots of different possibilities I was sitting on YouTube one night watching some really crude stop motion animation but enjoying it all the same while thinking, I would like to make something like this. Then I came up with this idea to do something with stop motion animation and again after a lot of research I decided to go with what is now Anim8 Stop Motion.

I think the reason I am a fan of stop motion is the whole hands on approach to it (possibly because I spend so much time on a computer), and the time and dedication many great animators devote to it, creating something, that can be moving, funny, abstract etc. It is also a really cheap and fun way to learn about animation these days.

ANGELA: What are some of your favourite stop motion videos and why?

MICKY: Well as I mentioned I was watching YouTube when I decided to do something with stop motion animation, but there was one particular video I kept watching which has now had a lot of attention over the web which is *Tony vs. Paul*: http://www.anim8stopmotion.com/play.php?vid=95; it is really well put together and fun to watch, but more than that for me it opened my eyes to a whole new perception of stop motion and how it didn't have to be clay but, could be anything you could get your hands on including yourself. Of course I have given this technique a go myself although it is not as good as *Tony vs. Paul* I still enjoyed making it. As well as me, others have also given it a go: http://www.anim8stopmotion.com/play.php?vid=346 and http://www.anim8stopmotion.com/play.php?vid=143

Another young but brilliantly talented stop motion animator and inspiration for the site goes by the name mamshmam on YouTube. He has created some great stuff with really simple clay characters. You can see all of his videos at: http://www.youtube.com/user/mamshmam. He has inspired a lot of younger people to try it and also has his own web site with a forum for people to meet and chat: http://www.mamshmam.com.

One of my favourite videos on Anim8 has to be: http://www.anim8stopm otion.com/play.php?vid=303 by James Mullins, whom I also interviewed after seeing his videos on the site. The reason I enjoyed it so much was the life he managed to give such a simple character in such a short space of time and along with that the gritty hands-on feel that I believe you only get with stop motion and which really allows the watcher to appreciate the work and life going into creating something for our enjoyment. You can see his interview at: http://www.an im8stopmotion.com/interview.php?id=10

The insight into the world of amateur stop motion animation fans and current trends provided by Micky highlights the kind of support networks and communities that are available for sharing and improving one's animation work. As I viewed all of Micky's recommendations, I was impressed by the genuine sense of learning and the level of positive critique offered by community members as feedback on each video. Just as FanFiction.net is a training ground for writers, sites like Anim8 Stop Motion provide a wonderful training ground and showcase for participants' work.

SECTION TWO

How to make your own stop motion animation: A tutorial

As we mentioned earlier, there is a wide range of software available for making your own stop motion animations, but creating stop motion movies with free software like Windows Movie Maker is not only easy but is extremely inexpensive as well once you have access to a digital camera and a computer in place. Most PCs come with the Windows Movie Maker program preinstalled, or it can be downloaded for free via any number of sites (e.g., http://tinyurl.com/cjubwb). Although we focus on PC users in this section, the general principles of stop motion animation apply equally to Mac users as well (who can use free iMovie software instead to create their animations). Aside from the materials you will use in creating your stop motion movie, the only equipment you will need is a camera and a computer. This tutorial assumes that you are familiar with the camera you will be using, that your camera is compatible with your computer, and that you know how to transfer pictures from your camera to your computer. In addition, we strongly recommend spending time watching many different stop motion videos to be found on websites such as YouTube.com, Blip.tv, and Anim8stopmotion.com. Micky's recommendations described earlier in this chapter are a good place to start. For true newbies to digital video making, it might be helpful to explore Windows Movie Maker itself and make a sample movie using still photos (see also Chapter 9 in this volume for a video-editing how-to).

Preparation tips

I like to think of a stop motion video as an old fashioned flipbook. In these flipbooks, pictures were drawn on separate pieces of paper, and on each page a subtle change was made to the picture so that when the pages were flipped or fanned quickly, it looked as though the picture was animated. These changes needed to be incremental so that the motion was smooth and believable. This holds true for photography-based stop motion, too. It's important to keep in mind that too drastic a change between photos causes the animation to look jumpy instead of transitioning smoothly from photo to photo. Therefore, it is important to keep a few things in mind before you begin your movie making.

The first thing to keep in mind is that you do *not* want your camera to move. A tripod can be very handy for stabilizing your camera. If you don't have a tripod or need to shoot a series of photos where a tripod will not work, use a table, stack some books, etc., to get the camera to the correct height. This solid, steady base will keep the camera from shifting up and down. However, it will not prevent the camera from moving forwards or backwards, or side to side. So be careful. If your camera does shift, bring up the last photo taken and try to line up the last shot with what you see on the screen in "shooting mode" before moving your movie subjects to the next position. When setting up your scenery and planning your action sequence you will also want to make sure that your background remains stable, too; otherwise it will create some unexpected and distracting effects in your final movie.

Lighting is another important aspect of movie making to keep in mind. If you will be taking all the photos with regular overhead classroom lighting, shadows should not be an issue. However, you may need to use a flash. When shooting outdoors, you will want to try to position yourself and your subjects in a manner that will avoid shadows being cast on your shots. Shadows can be a problem because your photos can be too dark. If only some of your photos have shadows and others do not, your video will not flow. If you will be taking pictures in a room with limited lighting and your photos are coming out too dark, use a small lamp with the lamp shade removed to help with the lighting. If your lamp is small enough, you easily can maneuver the lamp so that no shadows will be cast on your shot.

Finally, it is important to check the quality of the photos you are taking to be sure the lighting is the same in each photo and each photo is clearly focused. Although this process can be a little time consuming, it's important to check each photo after it has been taken, so that if a photo does not come out well you can just reshoot the photo rather than later going back and trying to adjust your scenery and subjects to match how they were originally placed in that particular sequence. An excellent way to check that your photos are transitioning smoothly is to go back to your start photo on your camera and scroll through the pictures quickly.

Photo taking process

To begin, set up your staging area or scenery (e.g., a cardboard or fabric ground and backcloth). Next, position your subjects (e.g., dolls, lumps of clay, Lego™ minifigs) according to how you'd like your movie or scene to open and take your first photo. You will then want to move your subject(s) with the slightest of changes. For example, if you'd like your subject to move its head from side to side, turn the head slightly and shoot the next photo (see Figures 7.2 and 7.3, for example). Remember that too drastic a change means your movie will not transition smoothly when it plays. Continue this process until you have moved the head completely from right to left. Then, repeat moving back in the reverse direction. Once you've returned to your starting position, you can reuse this particular sequence of photos again if you'd like the subject to move its head side-to-side more than once rather than reshooting the same scene over again. This will help save time and make the movie-making process much simpler for you. Knowing this can be done can help you plan out the action sequences in your movie.

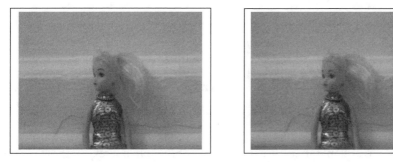

Figures 7.2 and 7.3: Animating a doll shaking its head

In this example of the doll moving her head from right to left, and then left to right, I needed to take 8 photos to make the head move completely from right to left. These 8 photos were 2 seconds of final footage. I then reused the same 8 photos in the opposite order to move the head from left to right. So, moving the doll's head from side to side is only 4 seconds of final footage. A song-length, doll-based stop motion animation I made required more than 200 individual photos for 3:46 minutes of final footage. It is also important to note that I reused many photos, included video footage and used still photos. A line-based stop motion animation I made required 100 photos for 1:13 minutes of final footage. These numbers give a sense of what's required in a stop motion animation and can help with planning the final video as well as with managing time. I strongly recommend a few practice runs at making very short stop motion animations before launching into your main project. This will help you fine-tune your techniques and sense of the incremental changes needed for creating a polished stop motion animation.

Once you have finished shooting your scene, I recommend transferring the photos to the computer and saving them in a designated folder as opposed to uploading them directly from the camera to Windows Movie Maker. This way you have a set of photos on the computer and a set on your camera so if you accidentally delete one set you have back-up copies.

Using Windows Movie Maker to create your movie

This tutorial focuses on using 3D subjects and scenery as the source materials. That being said, this same process applies to 2D stop motion animation (e.g., lines drawn on a whiteboard) and claymation, too. It is also important to mention here that I am working with Vista but that the same information applies to Windows XP, etc. (See advice for Mac users editing video in chapter 9 of this volume.)

1. Importing your photos

Once your photos have been taken and uploaded to your computer, open Windows Movie Maker, select "File" and then "New Project." Once you have your Project File open you will want to import all of your pictures. Under "Tasks/Import" on the menu bar, select "Pictures." You can do this in one of two ways. You can either import each photo individually or several at once. To import individual photos, click on the photo you would like and you will see its file name in the "File Name" box. Then click "Import." You can import several photos at once by holding the control button and clicking on each photo you will be using. You will also see a list of the file names appear in the "File Name" Box. Then click "Import" (see Figure 7.4).

In Windows Movie Maker, you can import photos that have the following file extensions: *.bmp, *.dib, *.emf, *.gif, *.jfif, *.jpe, *.jpeg, *.jpg, *.png, *.tif, *.tiff, and *.wmf. If your photo does not have one of these file extensions, I recommend using Zamzar.com to convert it. With Zamzar, you can convert files under 100 MB for free or pay a monthly fee to open an account and convert larger files.

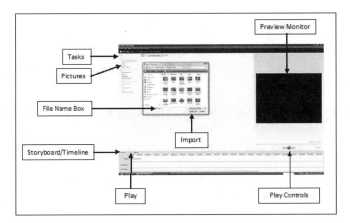

Figure 7.4: A screen grab of Windows Movie Maker in the early stages of creating a stop motion video.

It is important to mention here that you will want to save your project frequently. To save your project, click on "File" and then "Save Project As . . .." Type your project's file name in the "File Name" box and click save. If you stop working on your movie and close the program, to reopen your project, simply open Windows Movie Maker again. Your project should automatically open. If it does not, click on "File," then select "Open Project." Find your project file in the "Open Project" box, click on it and then click "Open." Your project will open and everything you have saved should appear. Once you have saved your project with a file name, to continue to save it, simply click "File" and then "Save Project."

2. Placing your photos in the storyboard

Once you import your photos into Windows Movie Maker, they will be displayed in the section under "Imported Media." If you're making a short film you will want to import all your photos at once. A longer video can use over 100 photos. In this case, you may want to break it down and import the pictures in parts or scenes. Once your photos or groups of photos are imported, drag your pictures into the storyboard at the bottom of the screen. At this point, you need to be in "Storyboard" mode. Storyboard is the default view in Windows Movie Maker. If you see the word "Timeline" in the bottom left-hand corner of the window, click on the down arrow next to it and then click "Storyboard" (see Figure 7.4 above, which shows the "Timeline" view).

Storyboard mode allows you to drop your photos into your desired sequence. This is done by dragging your photos into the initial "box" or space on the storyboard where it says "Drag Media Here" (see Figure 7.5).

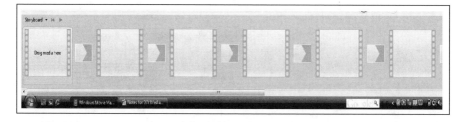

Figure 7.5: Beginning to construct stop motion animation storyboard in Windows Movie Maker

After you drop a photo into the storyboard, that photo will appear in the "Preview Monitor." This lets you check you've selected the correct photo. If you miss or forget to add a photo in a given sequence, simply drop it into the box you'd like it to be in on the storyboard and the program automatically will shift the other photos over for you to make space for the one you're adding. If you're importing your photos in scenes, repeat the previous steps until you have all your photos imported and placed on your storyboard in the sequence you want.

Storyboard mode also allows you to see and edit photo effects and transitions between photos, along with your movie's titles and credits slides. In photo effects, you can rotate your photo, adjust it to look like a watercolor painting, sharpen your photo, etc. To do this, under "Edit" click on "Effects." Select the effect you would like your photo to have and drag it to the small box with the star in it within each storyboard box. With transitions between photos, or sequences of photos, you can control whether the photo rolls in, shatters up, reveals down, etc. To select a transition, under "Edit" click "Transitions." Select the transition for your photo and then drag it to the smaller box just before your photo (see Figure 7.5). Transitions and effects are rarely used within a stop motion video, though, because they'll interfere with the overall animation, but you might want to use them for your titles and credits.

3. Timing

At this stage, you now really start to pay attention to the timing of your stop motion animation. "Timing" here refers to the duration each photo is displayed before moving on to the next. As previously mentioned, a stop motion movie is similar to that of a flip-book, which means the photos must move fast enough to make it appear as though your subjects are moving themselves. In the case of the doll moving its head from side to side described earlier, you would need to set the duration that each photo is displayed to approximately 0:00:00.13 seconds to make the sequence of photos move quickly enough for the doll to look as though she's shaking her head. To edit the timing of your photos, you need to switch back to Timeline mode (see Figure 7.4 earlier). Timeline mode allows you to trim your photo display times, adjust the duration of your transitions, and edit your soundtrack (the latter will be discussed later in this section).

Click on the photo you would like to edit. Once the photo is surrounded by a bold black box, position the cursor so that it becomes a red arrow. Next, click and drag to trim the clip and adjust the time. The time will be shown in a small box with the name of the photo and display duration. Repeat with the rest of the photos. If you accidentally change the timing on a photo that was set correctly, immediately click on "Edit" and then click on "Undo Trim Clip."

4. Previewing your movie

Once you have placed your photos into your storyboard and edited the timing to what you think will work, you will want to preview your movie. Although I find it easier to preview my movie in scenes, you do not have to. To preview your movie, begin by clicking on your first photo in your timeline or storyboard. You can also click either of the "rewind" buttons which can be found below the "monitor" or above your timeline/storyboard. You can preview your movie in either mode. Once you see the first photo on the "monitor," click "Play" in one of at least three possible places: at the top of your screen, below the "monitor," or above the timeline/storyboard. Once you click "Play" you can also stop, pause, rewind, move back, move forward, move to the previous frame or move to the next frame by clicking below the monitor, above the timeline/storyboard or under "Play" at the top of your screen. You can view your movie either on the monitor or in full screen mode. To preview your movie in full screen mode, click on "View" and then "Full Screen." To exit full screen at any time, right click on your mouse or touch pad. After previewing your movie, you may need to go back and edit display times further to make the photo sequence move more quickly or more slowly.

5. Adding music or sound

To add narration to your stop motion movie, you must be in Timeline mode. When you are in Timeline mode you will see a square with a vertical line underneath it in the area of the timeline where the time is shown. This is known as the "Playback Indicator." Move the playback indicator to a point on the timeline where the "Audio/Music" track is empty (see also Chapters 2 and 3 in this volume). Your "Audio/Music" track is located in the "Timeline" section of your screen. Click "Tools" and then "Narrate Timeline." If

"Show Options" is visible, click it. Click on the box next to mute speakers. This will prevent any noise or sound from playing over your computer's speakers while you record. Under "Audio Device" select the "audio capture" device you will be using (e.g., external microphone). Next, you will want to adjust the recording level by speaking into the audio capture device (e.g., a microphone plugged into your computer) and moving the "Input Level" slider to the place that records your voice at the volume you desire (recording with a blanket over your head and the microphone to create a "sound booth" can minimize the "tinniness" that occurs when recording in a large room). When you are ready to narrate, click on "Start Narration." Once you have completed your narration, click on "Stop Narration." When you click "Stop Narration," a "Save Windows Media File" box will pop up. Type a file name for your narration and then click "Save." You can repeat this process for another scene in your timeline if you wish. Once you have finished narrating your movie, click on "Close" to return to the main screen.

You can also set music to your movie. You import your music soundtrack the same way you imported your photos. Begin by clicking on "File," then "Import Media Files." Find the music file you would like to import and then click "Import." Your music files must have one of the following extensions to play in Windows Movie Maker: *.aif, *.aifc, *.aiff, *.asf, *.au, *.mp2, *.mp3, *.mpa, *.snd, *.wav, or *.wma. Again, if your music file does not have one of the following file names, I recommend using Zamzar.com to convert your file. Once you have imported your music, drag it to the Audio/Music section of the timeline. You can then drag it to the left or right to synchronize it with your movie. In addition, you can add narration along with a music file and have the two play at the same time.

6. Titles and credits

You can finish your stop motion movie by adding titles and credits. You can add titles at the beginning of your movie to introduce it, in the middle of your movie (before or after a clip) to introduce a character or a scene, or to create text overlays on a photo or series of photos. To add a title or credits, begin by clicking on the timeline where you would like it to be placed. Next, under "Tasks" and "Edit," click on "Titles and Credits." It will ask where you want to place the title. At this point click on either "Title at the Beginning," "Title Before the Selected Clip," "Title on the Selected Clip" or "Credits at the End." Once you have chosen where you would like the title to be, a box will pop up that asks you to enter the desired text. After you have entered the text, you can either "change the title animation" or "change the text and font color" by clicking on one of these choices below the text box. The title animation refers to whether your title "Flys in" or has an

"Exploding Outline," etc. You can change the text and font color, size and position, as well as the background. For credits, select "Credits at the End." Enter your text in the same manner as done for the title. You can also change the animation or the font and text color here, too. There are separate options for credit slide animation which include "Scroll up stacked" or "Fade in and out," to name but a few.

7. Publishing your movie

Once you have put all the finishing touches on your movie you will want to finalize your movie or *publish* it so that it will play "outside" the Windows Movie Maker software. You can publish your movie to your computer, a DVD, a recordable CD, email or to a digital video camera. To publish your movie to your computer, under "Publish to" select "This Computer" and a "Publish Movie" box will pop up. You must enter a file name and then select the location where you would like to save it. Once you have done so, click "Next." Then you must select the setting for your movie which will determine the quality and file size. After you choose the setting, click on the "Publish" button. The box will say your movie has been published and you can view your movie once you click "Finish," although you do not have to. To burn your movie to a DVD you must have a DVD burner on your computer (this is not standard on all computers). Under "Publish to" if you select "DVD" and you have a DVD burner a box will pop up telling you that Windows Movie Maker will close and save your project and then open Windows DVD Maker. A Windows DVD Maker screen will pop-up with your movie inside. Click "Next." Make sure you have inserted a blank, writable DVD disc into your computer, then click "Burn." The program will prompt and guide you through these processes, just as it will for publishing your animated movie to a CD, email or a video camera.

8. Additional online resources

• Stop Motion Animation: http://www.stopmotionanimation.com/

• Wikipedia Entry on Stop Motion: http://en.wikipedia.org/wiki/Stop_mot ion

• Clay Animation: http://www.animateclay.com

• The Art of Stop Motion Animation: http://pharosproductions.com/aosm a/smhome.html

• Brickfilms: Stop Motion Lego™: http://www.brickfilms.com/

- Clay Animation Station: http://library.thinkquest.org/22316/home.html

- Davey and Goliath: http://www.daveyandgoliath.org/

- The short films of the Quay Brothers: http://www.zeitgeistfilms.com/fil m.php?directoryname=quayretrospective&mode=filmmaker

- Gumby World: http://www.gumbyworld.com/

- King Kong Lost and Found: http://www.fullyarticulated.com/Kon gBoomer.html

- Next: The Barry Purves Film: http://www.guisarme.net/~andie

- Stop Motion Central: http://www.stopmotioncentral.com/

- Stop Motion Works: http://www.stopmotionworks.com/

SECTION THREE

Stop motion: Theory and practice

When amateurs, fans and professionals meet

One interesting trend in advertising over the past few years has been to incorporate the work of famous YouTube users—supposedly to appeal to the YouTube generation. This happened for the animators of *Tony vs. Paul* who achieved fame for their stop motion videos and were then commissioned by various advertising companies to make stop motion ads, such as their Red-Vines commercial (where they used over 10,000 pieces of red vine licorice to create a stop motion video of the red vines creating a fairytale ivy-covered balcony) seen at http://www.YouTube.com/watch?v=AUN1CfMV0PQ. Most interesting though is that Tony and Paul created a recent ad for a Belgian mobile phone company (Proximus) and called out to all of their fans to participate in the ad via the company website Proximus Generation Movie Project (http://www.generationmovieproject.be). They produced an empty shell of the ad in pencil drawings to outline each scene and invited fans to select their favorite frame from the ad and to take a photograph to fill in that frame. The final ad featured 472 fan photographs laced together within the animation (see *Proximus Commercial* directed by Tony and Paul http://ww w.YouTube.com/watch?v=z0mzG06K3fw). This clip signals just some of the creative potential to be found in large-scale collaborative stop motion animation projects.

Another interesting web trend is that of the mashup or remix. This usually consists of taking a known series of data sources (and in this chapter I am using it to particularly refer to stories, film, and other users' videos) and combining, appropriating and/or refashioning them in some way. When searching YouTube for Shakespeare remixes for another project, for example, I came across numerous examples of machinima and stop motion animation using Shakespeare, such as Jonathan Williams' *Soliloquy*, a Lego™ remix of a speech from *Hamlet*. I also came across a remix of multiple versions of this same soliloquy re-formed into a single video which combined high end commercial film productions of Hamlet with real actors and amateur versions using Lego™ characters. There are many examples of amateur animators creating fan videos or using existing texts and films as a starting point for their own storytelling. But the ease of copying any films and remixing them together allows the new and the old to be blended together visibly, and yet often times surprisingly, creating interesting juxtapositions that are both poetic and metaphoric, and for the most part, highly entertaining.

Media theory and stop motion

Stop motion animation could be argued to represent one form of the process of "remediation" (Bolter & Grusin, 1999), where the old is honored, rivaled, and transformed with the new. Stop motion videos are primary examples of remediation—where time-honored traditions and techniques are taken, used, and exploited by means of new technologies and new social practices (such as the remix) to find new expressions of meaning and identity. Many amateur stop motion animators focus on one or two elements as they learn their craft—such as focusing on making expressive characters like mamshmam does. Others use known stories or movies but focus on creating interactive stories like Patrick Boivin's *Bboy Joker*.

Two key elements are common between amateurs and professionals alike—they like to see the animator's personality come through in the final movie, and they like to see the art form showcased rather than the technology. Neda Ulaby reports in her interview with *Coraline* director Henry Selick:

> . . . Selick says he works to leave in imperfections. "Stop motion is sort of twitchy; you can feel the life in it," he says. "If we were to remove that completely, there'd be no point in it." After all, he points out, the beauty and mystery of stop motion are in those traces of the animator's hand. (Ulaby, 2009, no page)

This too supports one principle of Bolter and Grusin's (1999) theories of remediation—that of making viewers hyperaware of the media, however, not so much the technological media of the video editing or stop motion software, but the hands-on process of creating the movie one frame at a time. Viewers are at the same time enchanted by the magic of seeing clay or Lego™ or toys come to life, yet fully appreciative of the hours and hours of work that clearly were part of the production. It is the physical process of moving a model one tiny fragment of space and taking a shot—sometimes up to 26 to 30 shots or frames for every second of footage, and adding up to over 4000 shots for just five minutes of footage—that is awe inspiring. In fact, amateur animations are often more awe inspiring than anything a large production studio can turn out, precisely because we get to see more rough edges, home-made sets, and the sheer dedication of months and months of work by young creative people who create with pure passion and limited or no budget. The audience gets to glimpse into somebody else's world and indeed into somebody else's brain in a very immediate sense.

Bolter and Grusin (1999) further discuss animation in general as a perfect example of "retrograde" remediation in which "a newer medium is imitated and even absorbed by an older one" (Bolter & Grusin, 1999, p. 147). They claim that animation refashions Hollywood action films using traditional film conventions to present live action (i.e., panning, close-up shots, and so on) that are actually not possible in real live action (say a theatre with actors on a stage). Yet stop motion animation is even one step beyond this by being unashamedly and blatantly retrograde at some levels while at the same time trying to be transparent in the way it uses the new. In one way, stop motion is retrograde because it draws on techniques and conventions from live action films (using the range of known film techniques), from traditional hand-drawn animation (requiring the audience's "persistence of vision" to see the animation), puppetry performance (requiring the audience to recognize dolls or Lego™ pieces or abstract 3D objects as characters). These retrograde aspects are valued by animators. This seems to be echoed by Bolter and Grusin who state:

> The latest animated films have found new ways to pursue both the desire for transparent immediacy and the fascination with media. In being able to finally compete with the "realism" of the Hollywood style, the animated film has also become increasingly aware of and confident of its own status as mediation. (Bolter & Grusin, 1999, p. 150).

Yet these same animators strive to make the technological side of their work invisible. They don't necessarily want the audience to care or notice where you might have placed the cursor or clipped a shot. Animators would rather the audience see *them* as the mediator of the image—not the computer.

In a pure media sense, a stop motion animation can be seen within all of these media forms that came before it. But as with any text, it should also be seen within all of the cultural practices that came before it. This resonates with the Bakhtinian notion that all texts are read or understood in the context of a cultural history of textuality and the social practices in which they are embedded. In discussing the novel, Bakhtin comments:

> For the prose writer, the object [the text] is a focal point for heteroglot voices among which his own voice must also sound; these voices create the background necessary for his own voice, outside which his prose nuances cannot be perceived, and without which they "do not sound." (Bakhtin, 1981, p. 278).

This speaks to the heteroglossia or multiple voices that exist within a text. With stop motion animation and in particular the DIY stop motion that figured in section one of this chapter, the voices span multiple cultures, time, space, and generations. We are in a particular cultural moment right now where multimedia texts like stop motion animations are on the one hand magical and wondrous, but on the other hand are deconstructed and appreciated for each element and voice embedded within it almost automatically, because the boundary between spectator and creator has close to dissolved. We can all see behind the scenes of a text without really needing to see the "how we did this" extras any more.

Stop motion in the classroom

I first noticed schools becoming involved in stop motion animation creation at a digital literacies conference in 2007. One of the workshops I attended was about using claymation to enhance English and literacy in the classroom. The presenter was reporting on the work done by a group of teachers from the same school district who participated in a two-day intensive workshop with their respective classes on claymation (stop motion animation using clay models). The children were photographed as they made their claymations and then interviewed afterwards about their participation in the workshop. The children's comments in their interviews included:

> "you felt proud because it was yours" "teachers didn't do anything except walk around taking photos, we taught ourselves how to do it all–it was the power of the children!" "you felt like a professional" "we made ourselves do homework to make it better" "you have more respect for people who do this work all day long"(children's comments as reported by Camilleri, 2007, no page)

Any teacher would be thrilled with this kind of response by students to their classes. What rings through clearly from these comments is the sense of engagement and passion for learning, and the value of collaborating with both peers and expert advisors. Edson (2006) remarks that one of the values of doing stop motion animation in the classroom is the range of roles that are required for students to adopt in order to create a completed piece of work and the inherent literacy knowledge, skills and attitudes that this entails:

> The focus can also be on group collaboration. It is difficult to create an animation on your own and much easier to work in a team with various roles agreed upon. The range of team collaboration is wide and includes agreeing on a storyboard for an intended audience, understanding the underlying messages of the story, creating art works for the stage, writing a narrative, recording and editing a sound and music track. The animation process exposes students to the visual literacies inherent in multimedia and film development. For example, students can explore and experience the impact that camera angles, lighting and special effects can have in getting a message across. Understanding how to portray an emotion or evoke an audience response is part of the learning process for students. Investigating the role of music in evoking an emotion can also be part of developing an animation (Edson, 2006, p. 2).

It seems almost self-evident that having children work on creating stop motion animation would provide opportunities for them to be apprenticed in the kind of high-end digital multimedia authoring skills which would serve them well for the future. What is needed are teachers who recognize that such classroom work is not about meeting the "ICT" objectives of the curriculum. Rather, it is about developing in children a passion for being imaginative, creative, and expressing their identities—even changing their identities—through finding new ways to create and share their artwork and stories within supportive communities of learners.

One such teacher I spoke with is Martin Waller, a Grade 2 teacher from the UK. I asked him in an email exchange if he'd explain what attracted him to using stop motion animation in his classroom:

> I use stop motion animation at the end of Year [Grade] 2 because it offers different opportunities and processes for the children to engage with in comparison to our earlier work on live action film. Over the course of their time in Year 2 the children experience animated film throughout our curriculum and, in particular, the work of Studio Ghibli in Japan (who still use hand-drawn animations). In January, the children make their own live action film, with the process always being relatively short. They act in real-time and the camera records it. Since the children have only experienced the creation of live action film they do not understand the process of hand drawn and stop motion animation and, in particular, the length of time needed to achieve a quality product.

> Part of the reasoning behind the use of stop motion is the fact that it does take a long time to achieve a good quality product. Children need to understand that in the real world these things do not magically appear. As the project progresses they develop an understanding that the creative process needs to be planned, well thought out and organised effectively. It requires dedication, commitment and team work. The process they go through is a good work ethic for them to

adopt across the curriculum as they must review, adapt and finalise their work. In this sense the process is as important (if not more so) as the finished product.

Obviously another important factor is that animation allows the children to create multimodal narratives and consider how gesture, sound, language, visual and space can be brought together to create a shared meaning. We do a lot of analysis of existing texts and look at how they create meaning. The children can then use the technology to create their own world and meaning through multiple modes. Video editing also shows the children that the writing process is fluid and that texts can be changed and adapted throughout the process.

This year we are incorporating aspects of critical literacy into the project and looking at reinventing existing texts for "real world use" (Comber, 2001). We will be looking at the "Brer Rabbit" stories from America and their origins as well as reinventing them for "real world use" and a new audience. Each child in the class will have an opportunity to create and shape new Brer Rabbit stories using 2D stop motion animation [see an example of students' work in Figure 7.6]

Figure 7.6: A Walk in the Forest. A still from a stop motion animation created in Martin Waller's Year 2 Class

Martin's comments reflect a convergence of all the qualities and attitudes central to how an exemplary teacher might think about using *any* new media in the classroom—finding ways to integrate it naturally into a critical literacy program where texts are analyzed, produced, disrupted, challenged, and discussed from alternative perspectives, yet at the same time valuing and reinforcing the creativity of the process as well as the affordances of a range of technological tools through which this creativity is shaped.

Conclusion

Throughout this chapter some of the core values developed by stop motion animators, amateurs and professionals alike, have been foregrounded: namely, that animation is an art form and that perfect technical dexterity is not necessary. The strongest message was to ignore the technology and concentrate on the animation. The DIY animators featured in this chapter all see themselves as artists, and their work as a means of expressing their ideas and identities. At a theoretical level this is a really interesting characteristic that marks it differently to some of the other DIY media forms found in this book where artistry is exemplified much more visibly through the medium and what is possible *because of* the technology. The ideas expressed about stop motion provide a kind of disjunction whereby animators are trying to both de-emphasize and yet re-humanize technology at the same time. This either makes the human element of the text visible and privileged over the technological or constructs the human as blended with the technology in such a way that all that is seen is the human.

At a practical level of use in a learning context, the art of stop motion resonates closely with philosophies of arts-based education, which values imagination, creativity, story telling, performance, active participation, collaboration, and self-expression. In addition, teachers like Nicole Tufano (my co-author) and Martin Waller are also using stop motion within both a multiliteracies and critical literacy perspective and finding ways in which such an art form is valued for its capacity to teach young people not just skills but ethics and values and understandings about the world. And parents like Keegan's father, Greg, are spending time finding new ways to play with their children—integrating new media into their everyday imaginative play from age 3. In their book *A Century of Stop Motion Animation*, Ray Harryhausen and Tony Dalton state a number of beliefs about stop motion animation: "animation is to evoke life," stop motion requires "imagination, dedication and patience," and "stop motion enjoys being different" (Harryhausen & Dalton, 2008, pp. 13, 34 & 226). DIY animators—children and adults alike—featured in this chapter found stop motion animation a unique means of expression, empowerment, and enrichment in their lives.

References

Bakhtin, M. M. (1981). *The dialogic imagination: Four essays.* Trans. C. Emerson and M. Holquist. Austin: University of Texas Press.
Big Cartoon Database (2007). *The Humpty Dumpty Circus.* http://www.bcdb.com/cartoon_information/50441-Humpty_Dumpty_Circus.html
Boinx Software Ltd. (2009). Overview: Flavors. *Boinx.com* Retrieved Nov. 1, 2009, at http://www.boinx.com/istopmotion/overview/flavors/

Bolter, J. D. & Grusin, R. (1999). *Remediation: Understanding new media*. Cambridge, MA: MIT Press.

Buckingham, D. (2003). *Media education: Literacy, learning and contemporary culture*. Cambridge: Polity Press.

Camilleri, G. (2007). Claymation. Presented to the: Middle years literacy project symposium. Melbourne, November 2007.

Chong, A. (2008). *Digital animation*. London: AVA Academia Publishing.

Comber, B. (2001). Critical literacies and local action: Teacher knowledge and a 'new' research agenda. In B. Comber & A. Simpson (Eds.) *Negotiating critical literacies in classrooms*. Mahwah, NJ: Lawrence Erlbaum.

Edson, J. (2006). Clay Animation — New Approaches to Literacy. *Professional learning programme: Success for boys*. Brisbane, QLD: Curriculum Corporation of Australia.

Harryhausen, A. & Dalton, T. (2008). *A century of stop motion animation*. London: Aurum Press.

Jones, S. (2009). *Coraline: A visual companion*. New York: HarperCollins Publishers.

Twiggarts (2008). Post by gristmagazine. *YouTube*. Available at: http://www.YouTube.com/watch?v=zKhW-Slwdr8.

Ulaby, N. (2009). Henry Selick, Keeping Stop Motion Moving Ahead. In: *NPR (National Public Radio)*. Available: http://www.npr.org/templates/story/story.php?storyId=100156290

Webster, C. (2005). *Animation: The mechanics of motion*. Oxford: Elsevier.

Chapter 8

Flash fundamentals: DIY animation and interactive design

Rebecca Orlowicz

Sometimes breathtaking and beautiful, sometimes simple and rough, animation entertains the impossible, delights with the fantastic, and inspires
through technique. Animation is defined as the rapid display of still images or
graphics that creates the illusion of motion. From the early days of its history
until now, animation has amazed and impressed audiences around the world.
The collaborative art of bringing still images into life and movement has
remained a captivating medium since the first animation was seen in 1832.
The introduction of computers has continued to push the boundaries of possibility for this medium.

SECTION ONE

A brief history of flash animation

It once took a small army of artists and technicians to create a feature length
animated film or television spot. With the technology available today, it may
still require much human creativity and ingenuity, but computer micro-
processors can now handle much of the drudge work that characterizes the
production of animation. For professional animators, this means a lot less
repetition and exacting mechanics. For average consumers this means access
to the once-illusive process of animation as well as to its enormous creative
potential in this increasingly digital world.

Animation began as a very simple system. An artist would draw a character in various states of motion. Those images would be photographed and then projected at a constant rate in order to create the illusion of movement. A flip book, made up of pages of still images that are quickly thumbed through to create a "moving" image, offers a glimpse into how this illusion works. By merely flipping the pages quickly from start to finish, one can easily see the animation. If each page is viewed individually, the necessary and incremental changes in each of the images are revealed.

Not all early animation was created in this crude style. Innovations pursued by Walt Disney and other animators in the 1920s and 1930s involved whole systems of sketching, inking, and coloring (Giannetti, 1999). The efforts of these early animators turned run of the mill animation into the expression of whole artistic worlds, inhabited solely by artists' creations. This process began with multiple pencil sketches that were transferred to translucent celluloid material using ink and paint. These "cels" would then be placed on top of full color painted backgrounds and pegged in place for proper alignment. Each layered image was photographed individually, using a special fixed camera. In these early years, more progressive styles of animation required significantly more in-between steps. For example, the film *Fantasia* (Disney, 1940) was filmed using several different images painted directly on a series of glass plates that were layered and manipulated as the stills were photographed (this process was time-consuming to say the least; only 16 stills per hour could be completed). The work of many men and women was required for such a feat (Thomas & Johnston, 1981).

One modern example of innovation in animation is the use of the Imagemotion—created by Sony Imageworks—which uses motion capture technology in an effort to record the emotion and intention of live actors. Sensors are used to detect all the movement of the body and face and this digital information is then translated into the movement of a digital character in a computer. This technology was used in the film *The Polar Express* (Goetzman, Starkey, Teitler, & Zemeckis, 2004), and similar processes were used to create the highly effective facial animations of the man-beast, Gollum, in *The Lord of the Rings* film trilogy (Jackson, Osborne, Sanders, & Walsh, 2001, 2002, 2003).

Having become more and more filmic, interactive game design also now relies on much of the same digital technology as modern animation and has therefore been influenced in similar ways. Game designers can now create complex visuals as well as intricate worlds within which players navigate and interact. Interesting and unique ways are being developed to interact with the screen as more people become involved in the design and implementation of interactive features. Similar to the Imagemotion technology mentioned above, Nintendo's Wii has revolutionized the gaming world with its focus on kinetic gaming. The user-sensitive technology that this system employs may very well have changed the way gaming interactivity is defined. No longer are players merely clicking and scrolling their way to success within a game, but, rather, experiencing and interacting with the game as a whole-body experience.

Adobe's Flash software offers one point of entry into the practice of digital animation production, and its use is proliferating in a range of fields (animation, gaming, advertising, films, etc.) (Vander Veer & Grover, 2007). Flash animation is the creation of digitally animated material using Adobe's Flash animation software. If you have ever explored the internet for more than an hour or so, you have seen examples of work created using Flash software. It is becoming increasingly difficult to find a website that—for better or for worse—doesn't use Flash animation in some way. Whether it is in the use of a dynamic menu system or the playback of a short video clip, Flash is online everywhere (MacGregor et al., 2002).

The versatility and accessibility of this software are what makes Flash such an exciting and engaging resource. Flash animation does not look much different than other types of more time-and-labor intensive animations. Indeed, the more skilled the producer, the less the animation can be identified as being created using Flash. When viewing Flash files online, one can identify them by simply right clicking on the object in question. All Flash elements will display the option "About Flash Player."

Creating original digital animations and interactive texts (e.g., games, narratives) is something that previously could be done only by the serious programmer with extensive technical knowledge and skills. Flash provides that same level of creative power for amateurs through its well-designed and carefully structured software interface. Users can see clearly the breakdown of an animation project into its component features and, through practice, develop a broader understanding of how animation in general works, and how it can be innovated upon. This software provides a means to engaging in better art, better work, and better play.

It all started in 1994 when a small company called FutureWave Software created a product called SmartSketch (Gay, 2009). Seeing the potential for computer graphics applications, this small six-man team of programmers set out to make drawing on a computer easier than drawing with a pen and paper. Facing stiff competition from other software developers, FutureWave never quite got SmartSketch off the ground, but it nonetheless became the seed for the creation of Flash. Once it became evident that animated internet content was the wave of the future, the SmartSketch programmers focused their energies on adapting the drawing software they had developed to allow for the creation of animated graphics. The result, FutureSplash, was released in 1996 and the first two high-powered clients to use this software were Microsoft Network (MSN) and Disney Online. Shortly thereafter, Macromedia, a large and successful graphics and web development company, bought FutureWave and the first iteration of Flash was released (Gay, 2009). This first iteration enabled basic editing techniques and the use of a timeline to organize graphics as the animation grew and developed. In April 2007, Adobe Systems Incorporated, after buying out Macromedia, released Flash CS3 with improvements that allowed for the integration of other Adobe graphics products like Photoshop, Illustrator, and Dreamweaver. This meant users could more easily share artworks between these various specialized software programs and, as a result, create more dynamic media projects.

The latest version of Flash serves a wide variety of functions. The first of these functions is the creation of animation. Using the drawing tools, users can create graphics and then bring them to life using the animation tools. This may involve text manipulated to look like it is spinning or a character that is animated to walk across the screen. There are many ways Flash can be used to bring movement to different types of original art and many useful applications for the resulting animations as well.

At the most basic level, animation can be defined as a collection of still images or frames viewed at a rapid speed in order to create the illusion of movement. While this definition applied originally to cel-based animation, it still holds for digital animation, too. With Flash, a user can manipulate still images on his or her computer screen to create various effects and movement (e.g., expanding and shrinking, rotation, circular or to-and-fro movement). To a certain degree, Flash is designed to take full advantage of digital technology to help automatically fill in the appropriate images needed for creating a smooth-running animation and thus to eliminate the otherwise painstaking process of creating each individual frame that comprises the animation. In order to best understand the impact of this type of technology on the world of animation, it's useful to understand some of the basics of Flash animation. The lowest frame rate that will effectively create the illusion of animation is 12 frames per second (this is the default frame rate in Flash). A frame is defined as one still image on a strip of film. Therefore, a one minute long animation would involve 720 frames and a ten minute long animation would require 7, 200 frames, and so on. Before computer animation, an artist would have been responsible for the creation of each individual frame. Now Flash can be used to make this process easier through automating certain processes or by enabling other shortcuts with respect to reproducing and tweaking artists' graphics quickly and efficiently.

Professionally speaking, Flash animation features are used to create advertisements or promotional shorts, as well as material for online and television broadcast programming. Integrating Flash animation with live action video is also a popular option. For example, Flash can be used to show an animated character interacting with a real person during a live action scene. To the average consumer, the same Flash software offers a user-friendly workspace for do-it-yourself creations of short animations for presentations, and visual demonstrations, and can be a marvelous storytelling medium.

Flash is used to create many of the animated television series that air today; including, for example, the popular *Little Einstein* series (Weiner, 2005), *Wordgirl* (Gillis, 2007) and *Foster's Home for Imaginary Friends* (McCracken, 2004). For more examples of television programs created using Flash visit: http://coldhardflash.com/series. Links to profiles of and the work of some of the most knowledgeable and well-known professional Flash animators can also be found at ColdHardFlash.com (see: http://coldhar dflash.com/animators). Visit their websites and see a multitude of really good examples of the kinds of high quality animation that can be created using Flash.

For some excellent examples of DIY Flash animations created mostly by amateurs, visit: http://www.guzer.com/category/flashanimations.php. This section of the popular video hosting site—Guzer.com—archives a large variety of short animations submitted by users. In the center of the page, there is a box containing a list of the latest Flash animation shorts that have been posted to the site. Click on the film title to view or interact with each animation. Updated often, this is an excellent site for newcomers to Flash animation to visit in order to become more familiar with the variety of ways in which Flash can be used to create animation.

Flash can also be used to create video files that are formatted in a way that enables better accessibility by a wider array of potential viewers than was previously possible. In fact, all types of video (e.g., *.mov, *.avi, *.wmv) can be converted to a Flash file type. This file format is not strictly reserved for animation. Video sites like YouTube and MySpace all use the *.swf files that are created in Flash. These files allow for higher quality image resolution, more fluid online playback, and easier viewing across computer platforms than do most other video file types.

One very popular dimension of Flash software is the possibility of user interactivity. Interactivity, in a Flash sense, describes materials/resources with which the user interacts in order to make certain actions occur. One very basic example of this is a Flash menu system. This can include a simple pull-down menu system that appears when the user rolls the mouse over it (i.e., the rollover effect), or more elaborate menus that respond to user input in more customized and unique ways—such as miniature animations with sound effects embedded into a webpage. Examples of Flash menu systems can be found at http://www.flashmenus.net. This site provides the user with the opportunity to see and to interact with different Flash menu styles. Click on the tab "Button Themes" in the top left corner and choose a theme. A preview of the menu you are creating will be generated and is enabled for testing the interaction afforded by this menu.

The interactive possibilities of Flash mean that online games can also be created in Flash. This requires a somewhat more complex design process than does Flash animation, but it is still relatively user friendly. Examples of this type of interactivity include online multiple-choice quizzes in a multitude of subject areas, puzzles such as Tetris or Peg Solitaire, and all types of other games (i.e., action games such as Fancy Pants Adventures, arcade games such as Bloons or Bubble Struggle, sport games like Stunt Dirt Bike, to name but a few. For more, see Au, 2008).

Guzer.com also hosts a wide range of good quality Flash games submitted by members (see: http://www.guzer.com/category/flashgames.php). In the text box in the center of the Flash games page, the latest games uploaded to the site are listed. This is a good place from which to start exploring (as with Flash animation on this site, simply click on the game title to play the game). FlashArcade.com is another user-generated Flash game hosting site. The site is organized according to game categories. Choose a category and the top-rated games in that category will appear in the first box on the page. For examples of student-created Flash games, visit the gallery section of FlashClassroom.com (see: http://www.flashclassroom.com/cms/flashclassroom/index.php).

All this is made possible by the programming language used within Flash called ActionScript. The more the user understands about ActionScript the more intricate the interactivity can be, but Flash in many ways simplifies this element for the average user. Certain templates and pre-set elements within Flash allow even the most casual user to create elaborate interactives. (For examples of what ActionScript programming language looks like, visit: http://www.actionscript.org/actionscripts_library/Misc_Scripts). For the more technically adventurous, ActionScript.org provides a forum where ActionScript programmers can share information and templates, post questions for each other, and read the latest industry news and job postings. There is a wealth of information here for do-it-yourselfers interested in honing their Flash skills and insider knowledge.

Flash can also be used to create media for hand-held portable devices such as phones and PDAs. Flash content created with these delivery devices in mind requires a greater flexibility of design and the elimination of the large file size of a standard Flash file. Hence, the name "Flash Lite" given to the software used to develop "portable" Flash files. Using Flash Lite, users can create all the same content as described previously but with a much more simple interface and presentation. A good online resource—albeit one targeting the industry—for this type of Flash product can be found at http://flashmobilegroup.org.

The versatility and applicability of what is now Flash CS4 are close to impossible to dispute. The next section demonstrates the very real accessibility of Flash animation for even beginners by presenting a step-by-step guide for creating a simple, but nonetheless satisfying, animation.

SECTION TWO

Flash fundamentals: A quick introductory tutorial

This tutorial offers a walk through of some of the basics involved in creating a simple animation using Flash CS3 (the same principles apply to Flash CS4). Users will create a smiley face graphic and make it move back and forth. Learning points include:

- Creating a new Flash file
- Using the drawing tools to create simple shapes and change properties
- Using the pen tool to draw simple shapes
- Building an understanding of object grouping
- Building an understanding of basic timeline function
- Defining keyframes
- Using shape tweening to create movement
- Saving and sharing a Flash project

Flash software is available for purchase and can run on both PC and Mac computers. You can download a free trial version from Adobe.com (visit: http://www.adobe.com/downloads/ and click on the "try" option for Flash CS4).

The Flash CS3 software window is made up of many important elements. It is important to understand the basic function of each element, as well as its location (se Figure 8.1). A timeline (1) appears across the top of the screen as a row of small, numbered boxes. The purpose of the timeline is to lay out each frame of an animation so that users can visually and sequentially see each still image that will be displayed in a frame-by-frame manner (this is similar in function to the timeline in movie editing software; see Chapters 7 and 9 in this volume). The toolbox (2) appears down the left-hand side of the screen, and contains a column of different buttons that activate the many drawing and effects tools available to the user. In the center of the window is the stage area (3). This is where the content of the timeline is displayed. Directly below the stage is the properties panel (4), which contains the controls and editing options for the objects contained in the stage above. The panels along the right-hand side of the window can be customized to display whatever options the user wants to access quickly (Gunter, 2007). A video tutorial created by Greg Rewis (no date) also provides an excellent introduction to these same key components.

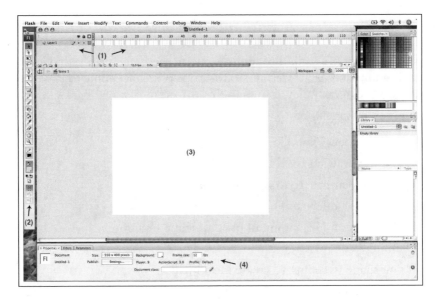

Figure 8.1: The Flash CS3 workspace window

Now that you are familiar with some of the central elements of the Flash workspace window, let's begin to build a short animation of a bouncing, smiley face.

1. Open a new file

- Click on "File" in the menu bar along the top of the workspace.
- Click "New."
- Choose the first file type listed: "Flash File (ActionScript 3.0)."

2. Create an oval

- In the toolbox, look for the icon that appears as a small rectangle.
- Click and hold the left mouse button above this tool and several more tools will appear in a drop down menu.
- Highlight the Oval tool, and then let go of the mouse button. (The Oval tool should now be your active tool.)

- Look further down the toolbox and you will see a small paint bucket icon with a black box below it.

- In order to change the color of the fill for the oval, click on the black box and choose another color from the menu that pops up. This will be the face color of your smiley-face circle so choose accordingly (e.g., yellow is a popular choice). Please note: directly above this tool is another black box with a pencil above it. This tool can be used to change the color of the outline of the oval (by default, the outline is black).

- Using your newly defined oval tool, click in the center of the stage area and drag out an oval of a large enough size to contain two eyes and a mouth. Release the mouse when the oval is the desired size and shape (you can click "Edit" in the menu bar across the top of the workspace and then "Undo" if you're not happy with your initial oval, and then try it again).

3. Create two eyes

- Click on any other tool in the toolbox and then return to the Oval tool. This allows for the creation of a new oval with new properties separate from the large one just created.

- Change the fill color back to black by clicking on the colored box below the paint bucket icon and choosing black.

- Click on the existing circle in the spot where an eye should be and drag out the shape and size of the first eye.

- Repeat this step to create a second eye.

- If you would like to arrange the newly created eyes in a different place on the face, click on the first tool in the toolbox that appears as a dark arrow. This will allow you to directly select the eyes separately in order to drag and drop them to a different location.

4. Create the mouth

- Click on the pen tool, the fifth tool from the top of the toolbox that appears as a pen tip.

- Roll the point of this pen tip over the area on the face in which you would like the left corner of the mouth to begin and click once.

- Roll over to the point where the right corner of the mouth should be, and click and hold the mouse button. Still holding the left mouse button down, move the mouse until the mouth line you have just created is in the appropriate shape for your smiley face. Release the mouse button.

Since each of these shapes has been created separately, before moving forward to animate your smiley face you must combine all the elements into one graphic image. Otherwise, you'll run into trouble with only some parts becoming animated and bouncing right off your smiley face.

5. Combine the separate elements

- Click on the selection tool (the black angled arrow) from the top of the toolbox.

- Click-and-hold on the stage in an area above and to the left of the smiley face and drag out to the right so that a selection box appears around your entire smiley face image. This large selection box should fully contain all of the previously created elements of your smiley face. The smiley face should now appear with selection boxes around each of the separate elements as well.

- Click on the "Modify" button in the top menu bar.

- Click "Combine Objects."

- Click "Union." This combines all the elements of the smiley face into one object.

Now it's time to use the timeline. You have created the object that will be animated and it resides in the first frame of the timeline. In order to animate it, the object must appear in consecutive frames, in strategically different locations in order to create the illusion of movement of the smiley face across the screen. Keep in mind that the default frame rate in Flash is 12 frames per second (for every 12 frames you create there will be one second of animated footage).

6. Animating the smiley face, Part One

- In the timeline, highlight frame number 24 by clicking on it.

- Click on "Insert" in the main menu at the top of the window.

- Click on "Timeline."

- Click on "Keyframe" (a keyframe is a frame that indicates a change in animation, be it movement or appearance). This adds a duplicate of frame 1 at frame 24.

- With frame 24 still highlighted, move the smiley face to the upper right corner of the screen so that the edge of the oval just touches the edge of the stage area.

- Click on any frame in between numbers 1 and 24.

- Look below the stage, in the properties window and find the scroll menu labeled "Tween."

- Click-and-hold on the blue scroll menu indicator and release the mouse button when the "Motion Selection" option appears. This property indicates that Flash is to create frames in between the two existing keyframes (1 and 24) in the timeline. These added frames will generate movement of the object from one position to another.

- Test your animation by clicking on the orange box above the timeline and rolling it back and forth. The animation you created will preview in the stage area. If you click through each frame, you can see how Flash filled in the frames to create the movement.

- Repeat this process in order to make the smiley face bounce off the edges of the screen.

7. Animating the smiley face, Part Two

- In the timeline, click on frame number 48 to highlight it.
- Click on "Insert" in the menu bar along the top of the window.
- Click on "Timeline."
- Click on "Keyframe."
- With frame 48 still highlighted, move the smiley face to the next place where you think it should bounce off of. Be sure the edge of the object touches the edge of the stage.
- Click on any frame in between numbers 24 and 48.
- Look below in the properties window and find the scroll menu labeled "Tween."
- Click-and-hold on the blue scroll menu indicator, and release the mouse button when the "Motion Selection" option appears.
- Repeat this process a few more times, skipping 24 frames each time, in order to continue the animation of the smiley face bouncing off multiple (implied) walls.

8. Viewing the animation

- Click on "Control" in the menu bar along the top of the window.
- Click on "Test Movie." A new window will open and playback your animation.

9. Saving your Flash file

- Click on "File" in the top menu.
- Click on "Save."
- Type in a name for the file and choose its location.
- Click "Save."

Users may come back to this saved file in order to keep working on this project at a later date.

10. Sharing your animation (that is, sending or publishing Flash files online)

- Click on "File" in the top menu.
- Roll the mouse cursor over "Export."
- Click on "Export Movie . . ."
- Type in a name for the file and choose its location (if you would like to save your animation as a file type other than *.swf—the Flash default—you must change the format at this point using the drop down menu found at the bottom of the export window).
- Click "Save."

The movie file created in this last step can be viewed easily by others using the free Flash player provided with most web browsers, or by means of the free download available here: http://www.adobe.com/products/flash player/. For additional tutorials on basic Flash production, visit: http://www.a dobe.com/designcenter/tutorials/.

SECTION THREE

Flash as an educational tool

It is undeniable. Media and digital technology have become so much a part of the world that one can no longer afford to minimize the impact they have on our daily lives. The insatiable appetite of modern culture for media and the momentous speed of technological growth have led to increasingly media-saturated workplaces and lifestyles within most developed countries. It is understanding the significance of the ubiquity of media and digital technology that fully justifies a major shift in the way that the education system in developed—and increasingly in developing—countries approaches media and technology studies. It is no longer acceptable to merely instruct students in traditional discipline-bounded subjects or to have them master, say, the business-oriented Microsoft Office suite of software programs. As the world becomes more and more digitally mediated, it is the exceptionally media literate students who will be the most successful (and not those who can only create PowerPoint presentations or fill in spreadsheets).

In a very real sense, technological evolution can be directly linked to the demands of the users or viewers. Steven Johnson, in his book *Everything Bad Is Good for You* (2006), suggests that it is the consumers who are demanding more and more from the source material as time goes by. The momentum of progress is actually creating a voracious need for new and more challenging media and applications. This has led, for example, to the morphing and expansion of the variety and scope of television and internet media (e.g., open-ended television narratives like *Lost,* which spill over onto the internet where viewers revel in making logical connections between seemingly disparate events and pieces of information). Hand-in-hand with such demands, of course, comes the need for people who can further the development and creation of new digital technologies, programming, and applications.

With respect to education, it is important not to think only about those few students who will become software programmers and hardware specialists but, rather, to recognize that there is no part of the professional world that does not in some way require the use of—or at least the understanding of—different forms of media and technology. No business, organization, community group or school can subsist today without some sort of connection to the technological community. From the creation of interactive promotional materials to online forums for parents and teachers, digital technologies and networks are relied upon to a large degree for mass communication purposes, for maintaining a range of social relationships, for accessing distributed expertise, and for disseminating information.

Henry Jenkins suggests in his book, *Convergence Culture* (2006a), that as digital technology becomes more widely accessible, more people will become more directly involved in media production. The role of producer will no longer be specialized. Indeed, the creation and distribution of consumer-generated multimedia, such as the do-it-yourself Flash media that are already proliferating online, mean a greater variety of voices will be influencing and affecting change in media industries and wider societies (e.g., Flash animation is a popular medium of choice for many political commentators, such as JibJab. See, for example: http://sendables.jibjab.com/originals).

The accessibility and versatility of Flash can only further these trends. Flash offers users an important and unique way to break down the steps involved in creating animated and online media. Understanding the production process and having the wherewithal to produce one's own media is fast becoming an essential asset for students and the world at large. Imagine what would happen if students tried to study literature without ever having written their own material: Would they be able to fully understand and appreciate the skill it takes to construct dynamic written works? Would they be able to fully comprehend the content and structure? Would they understand, without lots of practice and guidance, how to best compose their own texts? Students are constrained by limited experience with the written word and it is the same for digital production. Experience with Flash does not merely enhance the educational experience of students, it is fast becoming essential for the development of a firm understanding of the backbone of a wide range of digital media production processes.

One very important factor in this discussion is the understanding that many youth are already engaging in a variety of different forms of media production. Acknowledgment of these existing interests and skills is unavoidable for the modern educator. A visit to http://www.youtube.com offers myriad examples of the types of do-it-yourself media productions being created by young people (i.e. school projects, music videos, personal reflections, response videos, activist media). In their everyday lives, many people work-play as animators, video editors, creative producers and equipment technicians (Lankshear & Knobel, 2006). Harnessing, encouraging and celebrating this existing knowledge and skills are the keys to creating the most dynamic and effective media education program possible.

In one sense, it takes less effort to see how animation and interactives can offer opportunities for learning when they are produced by professionals and educators with specific curricular intentions. Some excellent educational Flash interactives can be found at:

- http://nobelprize.org/educational_games/
- http://www.bestflashanimationsite.com/archive/educational/

These games cover a wide variety of topics across a rich array of subjects including literature, biology and economics. Users can test their knowledge of *Lord of the Flies*, learn how to defeat a bacterial infection, and explore international economics. These games are thorough, engaging and offer unique ways to explore different subjects.

The *process* of developing these types of resources is also very important in terms of how functional and valuable the final product will be (Kerlow, 2004). User-created videos in general have already impacted the world of television and film, changing the way professionals view licensing and marketing as well as affecting production styles and even movie scripts. A good example of this is the film, *Cloverfield* (Bad Robot, 2008). The cinematic style of this Hollywood film deliberately mimics the filming style of the handheld camera used by the main characters to record the monster's attack on New York City. Additionally, most of the marketing for this film used viral videos, tapping into video meme practices and networks to help advertise the movie. Similarly, developing Flash skills during early schooling could have a significant effect on future productions. As it becomes easier for the average user to create his or her own interactive Flash games, for example, the world of game design will be affected in a similar fashion. Certainly, it can be argued that the portability, interactivity and small file sizes made possible by flash animations have significantly impacted the kinds of applications people are everywhere developing for Apple's iPhone and iPod Touch.

In this era of media immersion, the need for media literacy programs is becoming stronger and stronger (Semali, 2000; Jenkins, 2006b). What must not be forgotten is the fact that media literacy involves the understanding of how media is produced and constructed and *not* something that should focus only on audience reception and "reading/viewing" media. Students who have the opportunity to develop this understanding and build their own production skills will have a much easier time seeing beyond the surface of the multi-media world around them.

When using Flash to create media, each frame must be thought about individually and at the same time in relation to other frames in this animation. This therefore induces a creative process that implicitly addresses a lot of the questions raised earlier, and engages even the uninformed user in a process of discovery with respect to the building blocks of media production. Learning how to make even simple Flash animations builds a skill and knowledge set that carries over into other applications, including all sorts of image, video and audio editing which operate on simple principles (e.g., using timelines, palettes of different features, selecting and cropping and clicking and dragging items, etc.)

All moving images—be they film, television or animation—are composed of several sequences of still images. This is immediately clear within Flash, since all work is broken down into individual still images or frames in the timeline. Users can draw images for each frame, slightly altering the image from the previous frame in the sequence, in order to create animations using a method similar to traditional, sequential, non-digital animation. The same animation can be built using the special tweening function found in Flash, which allows the program to guess at the content of several frames in *between* two frames that have been selected by the user. In either case it is easy enough to click anywhere on the timeline and see the individual still images that make up the final animation. With the understanding that all moving image media are made up of thousands of unique frames, students can begin to understand the core of media production as well as develop their ability to construct and deconstruct it.

Flash also clearly distinguishes between the different elements that make up any or all of the frames within a project. Each frame can be made up of one or more layers of objects that can each be manipulated separately throughout a sequence. These layers might include the background image (location, scenery), a foreground image (foliage, props), and any number of characters. This allows for the careful evaluation of the appropriate placement and arrangement of the various layers throughout a sequence and therefore forces experimentation with different layouts. The important learning here lies in the exploration of the changes in meaning that occur when these elements are manipulated: How are the elements arranged? What is the most prominent feature? Is there movement of the layers throughout the sequence? What impact does the movement have on the meaning or the intention? Moreover, once exposed to this frame-by-frame breakdown of production, students will not be able to read media the same way they did before.

Analyzing media involves breaking down a final piece into its smaller parts and determining their individual meaning as connected to the meaning of the whole. The following is a list of questions that can help this process:

- How does the frame separate the real world from that on the screen? (This can apply to videos and interactives alike. Is it immersive or a more removed experience?)
- How do the composition and design of the elements within the frame alter its meaning/context? (Are things laid out as expected or do they distort conventions? What is in the foreground and background? What are the important elements?)
- Is it more stylized or more realistic?
- What types of shots and angles are used? (Are the images used close up or far away? Is the viewer looking up at or down at the images?)
- Is it dark or light? (How bright are the images?)
- What colors are used and what meaning do they bring? (What do different colors evoke in viewers/users?)
- What type of movement is being used? Is it strong or subtle?
- How quick are the transitions and cuts? (Is it hard to keep up with or does it drag along?)
- Is there sound? Is it loud or quiet?
- What is the overall purpose of the production?

This same type of deconstructive analysis is important to think about when building interactives. The process still includes many of the same important elements that generate meaning, but there may be a stronger emphasis on designing for function. Designing and programming interactives require the evaluation of the relative function of all the elements of a project. This process must also take into account the existing knowledge of the intended users and the degree of technological literacy that they may or may not already have. On a very basic level, all this really means is that certain types of actions will be located in certain places and appear in certain ways that will help to solidify their meaning for the user who has certain expectations of the way these types of projects behave. A user with previous experience with gaming may look for certain conventions in order to best know how to proceed (Gee, 2003). For example, a change in the design of a certain section of a virtual wall may indicate a secret lies behind it. Only a practiced gamer would know to investigate this abnormality. It may also be important, then, to think about the way users unfamiliar with gaming might interact with the projects. This might entail designing an interactive that scaffolds learning in such a way that users develop a stronger understanding of how to engage as they move forward through the game.

Game design in Flash also forces students to think both critically and logically about the meaning of all the elements of a game. FableForge.org, for example, offers a free tool for constructing games that use Flash animation. Some important questions to ask when building interactive games include:

- What is the purpose of the game?
- How does the user win?
- What type of game is this: a memory game, drag and drop game, a target game, a maze, etc.?
- How will the instructions be delivered to the user?
- How does the game itself teach the user to play the game?
- How should the different elements interact with each other?
- How should the different elements appear?
- What is the best tool for controlling moving elements or interacting within the game; the keyboard or the mouse?
- Will there be music or sound effects?

Thinking about the end user/viewer during the design and production of interactives and animations is a very important skill for students to develop. The practicality of this skill is limitless on both professional and amateur levels. Without carefully considering the various elements discussed above, the impact and functionality of any project can easily be lost. It is this most important process that exposes students to the dynamic efforts that are necessary for building effective and entertaining interactive games.

Research conducted by the Lifelong Kindergarten group at the MIT Media Lab indicates that children who are exposed to basic programming and design techniques develop a broad array of skills relevant for their success in the future (Rusk, Resnick, & Maloney, no date). These skills include:

- Media literacy—students understand the process of selecting, creating and managing multiple forms of media
- Communication—students understand how to choose, manipulate and integrate media in order to express themselves
- Critical thinking and systems thinking—students directly experience sensing, feedback, and other fundamental system concepts
- Problem identification, formulation and solution—students can immediately experience the effects that various changes have on a problem
- Creativity and intellectual curiosity
- Interpersonal and collaborative skills
- Self-direction
- Accountability and adaptability
- Social responsibility

The less tangible facet of the argument for the use of Flash in education involves the use of the software as a means of personal expression. In a world that still struggles to ensure funding for the arts in schools and often ignores the value of understanding the basics of musical and visual art, this argument may seem far fetched. In actuality, it is these unfortunate and widespread limitations that further reinforce the need for more diverse and widespread art programs.

Humans, at all ages and in all socio-economic situations, need to be able to express themselves through art. This does not mean that everyone should go out and start painting or sculpting. While an artist is traditionally thought of as someone who creates "fine art," all things made through the process of creative expression is art. For some people this may be writing, dancing, composing, knitting, or even driving. Whatever the medium, everyone needs a way to access their own creative energy and develop a way to communicate that energy to the world around them. It is the job of the education system to engage students in trying out as many different forms of creative expression as possible in order to ensure a well-rounded, functional, and healthy future for our society (Florida, 2002).

Flash can be a simple way for students to experiment with using digital technology as a medium for personal expression. Animating shorts and programming interactives can be a great way to explore different styles of conveying meaning and sharing experiences. As a medium of personal communication and a means for developing and exploring well-rounded characters, Flash can offer a forum for the digital manifestation of the internal passions or curiosities of the creators. As such, it should not be ignored as an important artistic tool.

Flash animation offers easy access to the building blocks of digital production, gaming technology, and web design that comprise essential knowledge for our media-centric future. No matter what the final product, developing skills that enable the use of Flash as a tool to communicate and engage with others in some way is an invaluable process and challenges students to think about their own education and their future place in the world from a unique and creative perspective.

References

Au, J. (2008). 10 most popular flash games of 2008—Mochi Network. *Gigaom.* Dec. 15. Retrieved February 15, 2008, from http://gigaom.com/2008/12/15/10-most-popular-mochi-network-flash-games-of-2008/

Florida, R. (2002). *The rise of the creative class.* New York: Basic Books.

Gay, J. (2009). The history of Flash. Retrieved February 15, 2009, from http://www.adobe.com/macromedia/events/john_gay/

Gee, J. P. (2003). *What video games have to teach us about learning and literacy.* New York: Palgrave Macmillan.

Giannetti, L. (1999). *Understanding movies.* Upper Saddle River, NJ: Prentice Hall.

Gillis, D. (Executive Producer). (2007). *WordGirl.* [Television series]. Watertown, MA: Soup2Nuts.

Goetzman, G., Starkey, S., Teitler, W., & Zemeckis, R. (Producers), & Zemeckis, R. (Director). (2004). *The Polar Express* [Motion picture]. USA: Warner Bros.

Gunter, S. K. (2007). *Teach yourself visually: Flash CS3 Professional.* Hoboken, NJ: Wiley Publishing, Inc.

Jackson, P., Osborne, B. M., Sanders, T., & Walsh, F. (Producers), & Jackson, P. (Director).(2001, 2002, 2003) *The Lord of the Rings: The Fellowship of the Ring, The Lord of the Rings: The Two Towers,* and *The Lord of the Rings: The Return of the King.* [Motion picture]. USA: New Line Cinema.

Jenkins, H. (2006a). *Convergence culture.* New York: New York University Press.

Jenkins, H. (2006b). Confronting the challenges of participatory culture: Media education for the 21st century. A MacArthur Foundation Occasional Paper. Retrieved November 25, 2008, from http://digitallearning.macfound.org/atf/cf/%7B7E45C7E0-A3E0-4B89-AC9C-E807E1B0AE4E%7D/JENKINS_WHITE_PAPER.PDF

Johnson, S. (2006). *Everything bad is good for you.* New York: Riverhead Books.

Kerlow, I. (2004). Creative human character animation: *The Incredibles* vs. *The Polar Express.* Retrieved November 25, 2008, from http://vfxworld.com/?sa=adv&code=319b255d&atype=articles&id=2306&page=1

Lankshear, C., & Knobel, M. (2006). *New literacies: Everyday practices and classroom learning* (2nd ed.). New York: Open University Press.

MacGregor, C., Waters, C., Doull, D., Regan, B., Kirkpatrick, A., & Pinch, P. (2002). *The Flash usability guide.* Birmingham, UK: Friends of ED.

McCracken, C. (Executive Producer). (2004). *Foster's Home for Imaginary Friends.* [Television series]. Atlanta, GA: Cartoon Network.

Rewis, G. (no date). Using the drawing tools. *Adobe Video Workshop.* http://www.adobe.com/designcenter/video_workshop/?id=vid0119

Rusk, N., Resnick, M. & Maloney, J. (no date). Learning with scratch: 21st century learning skills. From the Lifelong Kindergarten Group, MIT Media Lab. Retrieved
November 25, 2008, from http://info.scratch.mit.edu/@api/deki/files/637/=Scrat
ch-21stCenturySkills.pdf

Semali, L. M. (2000). *Literacy in multimedia America*. New York: Falmer Press.

Thomas, F., & Johnston, O. (1981). *The illusion of life: Disney animation*. New York: Walt
Disney Productions.

Vander Veer, E. A., & Grover, C. (2007). *Flash CS3: The missing manual*. Sebastopol, CA:
O'Reilly Media, Inc.

Weiner, E. (Executive Producer). (2005). *Little Einsteins* [Television series]. Burbank, CA:
Disney Channel.

Chapter 9

AMV Remix: Do-it-yourself anime music videos

Michele Knobel, Colin Lankshear and Matthew Lewis

SECTION ONE

Background to AMV as a cultural practice: Setting the context with "Konoha Memory Book"

The catalyst for this chapter is a 4.25 minute fan-made anime music video called "Konoha Memory Book" (DynamiteBreakdown, 2008a). This was created over 4 months during 2005 by one of the present authors, Matt Lewis—also known online as Dynamite Breakdown, Maguma, and/or Tsugasa—when he was 15 years old. It was sourced by Michele Knobel and Colin Lankshear in 2006 while doing work on "remix" in relation to the theory and practice of "new literacies." Artifact led to creator and ongoing email communications, resulting in this chapter.

"Konoha Memory Book" is set to Nickleback's song, "Photograph," and contains hundreds of video clips taken from across the first series of the Japanese anime *Naruto* (DynamiteBreakdown 2008b). The lyrics speak of someone looking through a photograph album and how the photos jog long-forgotten memories about growing up poor, skipping out on school, getting into trouble with the law, hanging out with friends, first love, etc. The narrator is leaving his hometown. Despite all that's happened, he's leaving reluctantly and with at least some fond memories.

Matt uses this basic thread to follow Naruto—the principal protagonist in the series—through a range of adventures. The first verse of the song is accompanied by clips presenting the main characters—Naruto Uzumaki, Sasuke Uchiha, Sakura Haruno, and their ninja *sensei*, Kakashi Hatake—and conveys a sense of some of the mischief and danger Naruto and his fellow ninjas-in-training enact and encounter while developing their skills and characters: e.g., playing truant from school (synchronized clips show students escaping through a school window and running outside) and getting in trouble with the law (clips show someone holding up a record sheet to a sheepish Naruto).

The initial segue to the chorus moves from bright, yellow and red colors—matching the singer's comment that life is better now than it was back then—to darker, more muted images emphasizing bittersweet memories recounted in the song. At this point the video includes many close-ups where an individual is standing at a remove from others, often with text (e.g., "Time to say it" and "Good-bye") superimposed over images and aligning with the lyrics as they're sung. The initial chorus closes with scenes from a beloved elder's funeral. "Good-bye" does double work here, synching with the song and saying farewell to the master *sensei*. The remainder of the song follows a similar pattern. At times there is a literal synching between lyrics and images (e.g., mention of cops in the lyrics is matched with images of law keepers in *Naruto*). At other times the "synch" between lyrics and images has a kind of frisson to it, like the image of Naruto kissing Sasuke (a boy) as the singer recalls *his* first kiss. This "move" references the corpus of Naruto/Sasuke relationship fiction and music videos made by fans. Sometimes, the synch between lyrics and images is more conceptual—as when the lyrics speak of missing the sound and faces of childhood friends, while the clip sequence emphasizes how Naruto, Sasuke, Sakura and their *sensei*, Kakashi, have formed a close bond over the course of living and training together. Second time round the chorus is used to "up" the visual tempo with a bricolage of images that suggests time passing. This bricolage includes pages of the original print-based *Naruto* manga series superimposed over images from the *Naruto* anime series. This speaks directly to *Naruto* having both manga and anime forms, and links to the concept of the photo album at the heart of the song. An image of Naruto running away from the reader is superimposed over other clips, again emphasizing the sense of time passing. This same animation of Naruto is repeated in the closing bars of the song as the singer explains that it's time to leave his hometown and move on.

Matt first uploaded "Konoha Memory book" to AnimeMusicVideos.org (aka AMV.org), the premier website for anime music video creators and aficionados (http://www.animemusicvideos.org). AMV fans found it and subsequently uploaded it to YouTube for others to view. "Konoha Memory Book" has now almost two million views across these accounts. It won all sections at the 2007 Anime Expo in Los Angeles, although contest rules permitted just one official prize: the Popular Vote Award. It has spawned copycat videos using the same song and Naruto video clips. Many fans on YouTube identify it as their "all-time favorite AMV." Possibly, though, the stand-out fan tribute is a *karaoke* version of "Konoha Memory Book" on YouTube. "Konoha Memory Book" remains one of Matt's favorites among his 45 published AMVs to date.

Time spent watching anime music videos online opened up the world of anime to Matt, who is now an avid fan of a range of series.

> The first AMV I officially saw was "Narutrix" [an AMV faux movie trailer parodying the Matrix movies] which is what got me into *Naruto* [the anime series] and downloading anime in general. After that I saw an AMV for *Azumanga Daioh* [another anime series] and decided to give it a shot.

When Matt first began making AMVs in 2005 he'd produce "like one a night, but they weren't amazing. After 'We Will Fight for Her,' one of my first major AMV projects, I spent a LOT more time on AMVs." It's not unusual for Matt to spend hundreds of hours remixing an AMV, particularly if he plans to submit it to a competition, on top of hundreds of hours spent watching anime online, downloading resource files, searching for appropriate scenes, and so on, before starting production and subsequent editing iterations.

Matt mainly creates in-canon fan videos: situated within a single anime universe, like *Naruto*, rather than constructed from clips taken from different series. To date most of his creations have used the *Naruto* series and movies as their anime source, although he's also used *Street Fighter Alpha, Tengen Toppa Gurren Lagann, Digimon, Fullmetal Alchemist, Tenjou Tenge, and Azumanga Daioh*. He categorizes the bulk of his work posted to his AMV.org account as "action" genre (34 of 45) and the remainder as comedy, parody, sentimental, or drama AMVs (many are assigned to multiple categories). As Matt explains, "I really enjoy making action AMVs due to the rush one can get from it; I like that feeling in the back of my head that just goes 'Woah . . . !'" He also enjoys making drama AMVs "cus with it you can try to express a storyline or bring out a trait of a character that not many notice or get to see."

Many of his AMVs are accompanied by "spoiler" alerts, warning viewers that key plot points to the anime series featured in the AMV will be given away. Matt remixes his AMVs with audience strongly in mind. This includes using superimposed text or other devices within the AMV itself to help viewers interpret his video clips. In "Before We Were Men,"

> I wanted to show all the things that the two had gone through up to the fight
> that they have near the end of the series. Also I tried to throw in a bit of fan
> service with the text [i.e., words like "passion," "angst" appear at specific points
> in the video] and the ending along with keeping the theme of the video feed
> effect at the beginning and end [i.e., a visual effect that makes the video look like
> it's playing on a television monitor].

Matt's information page for this AMV (posted to AnimeMusicVideos.org) concludes with the all-caps text "WARNING YAOI-ESQUE ENDING!!!" "Yaoi" is a term used outside Japan by fans of Japanese manga and anime to describe a genre of manga and anime focusing on male/male love (Wikipedia, 2008). Yaoi texts are not necessarily sexual in nature or necessarily considered "gay" texts. Matt describes this particular AMV as yaoi because "The AMV overall has that kind of passionate feeling of the two longing for each other kind of sense. And in the end they're just practically face to face in the rain, and with the lack of a visual and the rain still running it leaves you to think what might happen."

Music videos

Anime music videos are a subset of music videos, which came into their own in the 1980s and have a long and interesting history. During the 1920s and 1930s, music and moving images began to be combined by professional movie makers and music producers to create what are typically referred to as "musical short films" and Vitaphone films (Wikipedia, 2009). These short music films were produced expressly to showcase new bands, vaudeville acts, and opera singers as well as to promote more established artists and their performances (Vernallis, 2004; Wikipedia, 2009). These films were played mostly in cinemas. By the 1940s, jukeboxes were playing "soundies"—a song combined with moving images printed on celluloid film. Produced primarily to promote musical artists, soundies largely presented artists performing their songs in studio settings (Austerlitz, 2007).

In the 1960s, major artists, including The Animals, The Kinks, The Beatles, and Bob Dylan, were experimenting with "song films." Performers lip-synched their songs in the studio or real-world settings. Audio and film were then edited together to produce the song film (Wikipedia, 2009). Producers began experimenting with camera shot types and angles, with editing sequences within the song film, and with color. The launch of the television shows, *Countdown* and *Sounds* in Australia in the early 1970s and *Top of the Pops* in England in the late 1970s, signaled and stimulated the growing popularity of music videos as a distinct form of entertainment. Their fare included music videos showcasing up-and-coming artists and established bands and singers from different parts of the world (Wikipedia, 2009), as well as live performances. Music video-focused television shows became popular in many countries subsequently.

In 1981, MTV was launched in the U.S., offering 24/7 music on television. The music video genre had become mainstream (Wikipedia, 2009), and music videos were carefully edited in synch with the music, lyrics, mood or theme of the song. Music videos soon became expected components of any mainstream music album launch. Increasingly, music video directors began experimenting with visual effects, adding animation and newly-invented editing effects (e.g., visual overlays, quick-cut editing, inserting photographs and found footage, experimenting with film effects) (Vernallis, 2004). There also was a noticeable shift in orientation, away from highly "representational" videos showing the artists and documenting their performance (ibid.), toward greater use of non-representational music videos. The latter included fully animated music videos and live action videos in which the artists did not appear. Some music videos began assuming explicit narrative forms; "telling a story" that added depth or intrigue to the song (ibid.) (e.g., Bonnie Tyler's "Total Eclipse of the Heart" and its multiple layers of interpretation). The 1980s also saw many music videos becoming more conceptual in orientation, often defying narrative conventions altogether; such as Bowie's "Ashes to Ashes" music video, where none of the characters in the video feature in the song, and the main character in the song (Major Tom) is absent in the video.

Current music videos draw on this varied history. They can be representational or non-representational, narrative or non-narrative, and draw extensively on pop culture trends (use of machinima, stop motion filming, anime conventions, etc.). Today's music videos still employ a wide range of filmic and editing techniques, albeit more like those used in television commercials and movie trailers than in feature films (Vernallis, 2004): sudden shifts in shot length, unusual angles and framing devices, reversed film, tracking shots, slo-mo, unusual uses of focus, monochrome or saturated colour, atmospheric lighting, and so on.

As MTV's emphasis shifted in the early 2000s away from continuously airing music videos towards "reality" shows, fan-made music videos—or "songvids"—seemed to gain momentum (Austerlitz, 2007), abetted by affordable or free access to easy-to-use digital video and audio software and networked spaces like YouTube for sharing fan works. Today, countless thousands of fan-made music videos span every conceivable music genre, running alongside commercial professional music video production. Bands recognize the importance of fan-made videos in terms of pleasure and promotion alike, often hosting music video contests and incorporating fan footage into commercial DVDs (Catone, 2008, p. 1).

Part of the pleasure of fan music video creation appears to be its DIY nature: exploring the meaning of the song through images to create one's own interpretation or narrative or commentary. While some fan-made music videos are highly representational, others reflect a much more experimental spirit. Some game and music fans use video game engines to film and create machinima music videos (e.g., Paul Marino's "Still Seeing Breen"; see also, Chapter 6 in this volume). Others synch still images to a favorite song, film themselves lip synching to a favorite song (cf., Gary Brolsma in "Numa Numa Dance"), or create kinds of fan fictions, where favorite movies (e.g., *Lord of the Rings*), movie genres (e.g., kung fu movies), or television shows (e.g., *Star Trek*) provide the source video to be synched with a chosen song.

Anime music videos

Anime music videos are fan-made music videos that use only clips from anime movies and series. Anime—animated Japanese cartoons—come in a range of genres (e.g., comedy, drama, adventure), storylines (e.g., saving villages from demons, saving the world from mecha-robot domination), themes (e.g., coming to terms with one's own character flaws, loyalty, environmentalism, the human cost of wars, dealing with bullies), and orientations (e.g., *shonen* anime targeting boys, *shoujo* anime targeting girls). Creating an AMV involves taking small clips from anime productions and splicing them together in new sequences synched to a chosen song.

The anime clips used as source video bring with them the universe, characters, storylines and themes of the series from which they came. This is often used deliberately by the remixer to add layers of meaning to the AMV itself. Viewers not familiar with the *Naruto* anime series when they first watch Matt's "Konoha Memory book" will likely miss much of its symbolism and many relationship references. The use of anime means that AMVs are mostly non-representational of the bands whose music is being used, although this is not hard and fast. For example, the winner of the 2005 "best video" award on AnimeMusicVideos.org was "Jihaku" by Tyler, set to the Foo Fighters' "Best of You," and included footage of the Foo Fighters performing live.

No definitive account exists to date of how and why anime music videos became a widespread fan practice. Some suggest they were developed initially by anime club members to show previews of movies or new series to attract new fans (Springall, 2004). Others suggest anime music videos are an outgrowth of fansubbing practices, where anime fans add English subtitles to original—often bootleg—copies of Japanese anime (Kirkpatrick, 2003). Some think AMV is a logical outcome of MTV music videos mixed with adolescent interests and experiences (Milstein, 2008). Whatever the original impetus, AMVs are massively popular do-it-yourself fan productions.

YouTube—currently the best-known user-made video content hosting website—simply states "millions" in response to the search term: "AMV" (YouTube, May 1, 2009).

Like music remixing (see Chapter 2 in this volume), anime music video making began well before digital technologies were readily and widely available. During the 1980s and well into the 1990s, creating AMV involved manually working two analog video recorders cobbled together with audio and video cables (Springall, 2004). While one recorder played the source videos, the other captured clips from the sources on a single video tape, building the AMV in a linear way, one small clip at a time. The music soundtrack was added when the clips were finally in place. Synchronization between song and clip sequence was often clunky at best (Springall, 2004). Digital technologies have made the AMV remixing process much easier, more affordable and widespread. An anime fan can now use the free video editing software that ships with most standard computers (e.g., Windows Movie Maker on PCs and iMovie on Macs) to create a good quality AMV. The creation of online fan communities like AnimeMusicVideos.org, and AMV competitions hosted at high-profile anime conventions, have also helped establish anime music video remixing as a well-recognized and widespread DIY fan practice.

Tim Park (2008), founder of AnimeMusicVideos.org, identifies the first recognized AMV as a 1983 creation by Jim Kaposztas, who remixed segments from *Gundam* and synched them with the Styx song, "Mr. Roboto." Early AMV remixing was largely "underground." Occasionally shown in British dance clubs in the early 1990s (Milstein, 2008), AMVs remained culturally marginal until quite recently. Park dates AMV's coming of age to 1999, when Kevin Caldwell's "Engel" scooped the prize pool in three major categories at a premier U.S. anime convention. "Engel" broke new ground with its flawless synchronization between song and the on-screen action, achieved with a laser disc machine and a VHS insert editor (Springall, 2004, p. 41).

2001 was a landmark year in AMV development and direction. "Odorikuruu," by Jay R. Locke, spearheaded dance/fun AMV, which has become very popular within the AMV community. Locke spliced segments from 34 different anime and set them to the wildly infectious dance song, "Elissa," by Mamboleo. "Odorikuruu" continues to set the technical and artistic benchmark for many dance genre AMV remixers (Park 2008). 2001 also brought quantum advances in technical sophistication within AMV productions. For example, E-Ko merged two different anime into the same frame in his "Tainted Donuts" AMV, using Photoshop, After Effects, and Final Cut Pro software to achieve this effect (Park 2008).

2003 brought the release of Koopiskeva's "Euphoria," still ranked the all-time Number One anime music video on AnimeMusicVideos.org. Paradoxically within a fan practice, many AMV exponents claimed they would stop making AMVs because Koopiskeva's AMV had raised the bar too high (Park, 2008).

The range and styles of fan-produced AMVs have continued to grow and broaden, albeit within one or other of two general forms: AMVs that remix clips from a single anime series (e.g., *Naruto*, *Evangelion*), and AMVs that remix clips from multiple anime series and movies. Within these two broad categories, popular types of AMVs include tributes to series or movies, character profiles or biographies, non-narrative or conceptual music videos that focus on a particular dimension of an anime series (e.g., loyalty or betrayal), videos promoting an anime series, compilations of specific events from different anime (e.g., characters falling down, characters kissing), celebrations of multiple anime series set to a favorite song, parodies of social or political events or of AMV making itself, and remixes used to tell stand-alone stories not necessarily connected to the anime from which the clips were borrowed (Springall, 2004; Park, 2008).

Popular genres include drama, action, horror, comedy, dance, romantic and sentimental AMVs (see AMV.org, 2008a; Springall, 2004). Matt describes "Konoha Memory Book" as being principally "sentimental" in intent because it focuses on "all the trials and tribulations, difficulties and memories that the characters of *Naruto* gain and share." "Engel" falls into the drama category, with its depiction of strong, warrior-like Japanese school girls, its fight scenes and its heavy metal soundtrack. This contrasts with the comedy of, say, "AMV Hell," which focuses on slapstick moments set to an eclectic and eccentric soundtrack comprising snippets from sources as diverse as the soundtrack to *The Passion of The Christ*, Lords of Acid's "Spank My Booty," and Shania Twain's "Man! I feel Like a Woman."

SECTION TWO

Creating an AMV

Becoming a good AMV remixer requires watching a *lot* of AMVs. Matt recommends that beginners "watch LOADS of AMVs." He gets "a lot of inspiration from other videos on technical stuff and effects. Just because someone else uses an effect doesn't mean you can't." Watching AMVs helps with working out personal preferences and dislikes with respect to video effects, transition effects, sequence editing, synching between images, music and lyrics, and so on. Reading comments left for anime music videos on YouTube by (re)viewers provides rapid entrée to what insiders consider good and bad quality editing and remixing (e.g., avoid "cheesy" transition effects like the over-used checkerboard effect).

Matt arrives at developing a new AMV by different routes. Sometimes a song strikes him as eminently "AVM-able." Other times, he has an idea that has grown out of an anime series that he would like to explore but keeps on the backburner until he hears a suitable song. The match between the selected song and the anime used in conjunction with the song is crucial: "If you use a Linkin Park song with shows like *Azumanga Daioh*, it's totally pointless," explains Matt. Linkin Park is a hard rock band; *Azumanga Daioh* is a light-hearted, humorous anime. Then,

> Once I get the song I listen to it over and over again so I can get a sense of the song and am able to work with the clips without having to play the song at the same time, which makes it very hectic [i.e., listening to the song and editing clips simultaneously can be hectic].

Matt began remixing AMVs using Windows Movie Maker software and still considers it a useful starting place for beginners: "I always tell people use Movie Maker. Lots of people don't think you can make a good AMV [using this software], but almost ALL of my [early] AMVs are made with it, and my recent ones use it to some extent too. Learn to use it, tamper with the effects and invent new things. I've found ways to create effects in movie maker that [expensive] programs like Adobe Premiere can do." Good quality AMVs also can be made easily using iMovie. The principles for both movie editing programs are much the same. We focus on Windows Movie Maker here to make the most of Matt's expertise. (For a range of excellent tutorial videos for using the latest iMovie release, that can serve in place of our technical descriptions below, see: www.apple.com/ilife/imovie.)

Source anime to be used in the AMV project can be ripped from a DVD or downloaded from the internet (copyright issues are discussed later). "Ripping" requires special-purpose software that copies the video file to one's computer harddrive and converts it into an editable format (e.g., an *.avi file, a *.mov file). Popular DVD ripping software includes DVDFab (for PCs) and Handbrake (for Macs and PCs). Video downloading sites can be used to capture video from YouTube and other video hosting websites, like KeepVid.com and SaveVid.com.

Original, free-to-use-with-attribution anime can be found via CreativeCommons.org. Click on the "Search" option at the top of the page, then on the Blip.tv tab. Key "anime" into the search window and hit "Go." Another option is to search Aniboom.com for anime, find animators whose work you like and then search for them on YouTube or other video hosting sites (e.g., Break.com, Revver.com, Vimeo.com, OurMedia.org) in order to download their videos and use them, after obtaining their permission to do so. A third option is to visit Newgrounds.com, a user-created flash animation portal, and hand search their anime category: newgrounds.com/colle ction/anime.html.

Once the source anime is downloaded to the harddrive, it needs to be stored in a single resource folder to help keep the AMV project stable while working on it inside Windows Movie Maker or iMovie. It pays to keep careful note of where this folder is, in order to be able to access it from "inside" one's video editing program. Setting up this folder under "desktop" makes it easy to locate. Likewise, setting the destination of downloaded files to the desktop makes it easy and quick to drag them to the resource folder and not lose track of what resource is where. Windows Movie Maker only works with Windows Media files (e.g., *.wma, *.wme, *.avi), and some *.mpg file types (but not *.mp4 or *.mov files). Zamzar.com is a useful free service for converting short video clips from one file format to another.

It is important to keep file formats consistent. When using Windows Movie Maker, the project will crash less frequently if all the video clips share the same file type or format. This same resource folder should include the song file as well. Songs downloaded from iTunes will not work with either Windows Movie Maker or iMovie since copyright restrictions are built into the song file. Original free-to-use-with-attribution songs and soundtracks can be found via ccMixter.org, FreePlayMusic.com, Opsound.org, and elsewhere.

Finally, it is important to ensure there is plenty of free space on the computer harddrive because video editing projects can gobble up computer memory quickly.

Building the project

We will focus here on the principles involved in creating a short AMV.

1. Import resource files into Movie Maker.

We open Windows Movie Maker (hereafter, "Movie Maker"), click on "File" in the top menu bar, and select "Import into Collections" (or just press the keys Cntrl + I) (see Figure 9.1). This opens up a file selection window. We locate our resource folder and click on one of our movie resource files inside it. We can also import video files by clicking on the "Import video" hyperlink in the task pane located on the left-hand side of the Movie Maker window (covered by the drop-down menu shown in Figure 9.1). It doesn't matter in which order we import our movie files.

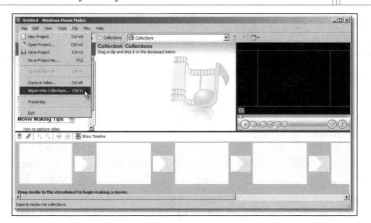

Figure 9.1: Importing the first file into a new video editing project using Windows Movie Maker software

An information window pops up to show file progress as each is converted into a format with which Movie Maker can work. Successfully imported files appear as thumbnail images in the "Collection" space between the task pane and the video player in the top half of the Movie Maker window (see Figure 9.1). If we import a number of collections or sets of video files we can move between them using the drop-down menu in the Collections section. This importing process is repeated until all the movie files we plan to edit at this stage are imported into Movie Maker. We can easily add more later.

This is a good time to first save the project. Saving a project at regular intervals is invaluable for guarding against losing work should the video editing software crash. There is a very important distinction to keep in mind here when saving the project: between "Save project as" and "Save movie file."

Clicking on "File" in the top menu bar and selecting "Save Project" or "Save Project As . . ." saves your file as a Movie Maker project file. This is an editable file that will only play *inside* the Windows Movie Maker software. (It cannot be uploaded to YouTube or OurMedia.org or burned to a CD that can be played as a movie on another machine.) We *must* use this option while we are still working on our AMV: to add or delete files, edit files, move files around, add in transitions and effects and so on. Once our AMV is complete, and we are happy with the final results and want to publish it as a stand-alone movie clip, we can *then* click "File" on the top menu bar and select "Save Movie File. . . ." This will convert our project into a single movie clip that *can* be uploaded to YouTube, emailed to friends, and burned to a CD that will play on compatible media players on any computer. We cannot, however, go back "inside" this *movie* file to edit and tinker with things. If we want to make further changes we just open the project file inside Movie Maker and tinker there, before saving it as a *new* movie file. (The analogy here is saving a text document as a Word file, which can be opened up and edited etc., and then converting this same file to a portable document file, or "pdf." This pdf file can be read in Adobe Reader software, but the text cannot be edited.)

2. Storyboarding clips.

Now we have a pool of video clips imported into Movie Maker from which to draw. For the audio we will use The White Stripes' song "Why can't you be nicer to me?"

Movie Maker provides a storyboard for sequencing clips. Its layout is linear and runs along the bottom of the Movie Maker window (see Figure 9.1). To begin adding clips to our AMV project we simply locate each one we want within the collections pane and click-and-drag it into position on the storyboard, using the mouse and cursor. We can preview clips in the collection pane using the video player in the right-hand top corner of the Movie Maker window. This same video player can be used to review the AMV as we build it.

Ours will be a *compilation* AMV, drawing from a diverse range of different anime. The idea we want to realize in this anime music video is a montage of rather violent mecha-robots who are wondering why people aren't nicer to them. The message of the video portion will be in tension with the song itself. Rather than portraying a solitary figure who is treated unkindly by others, it will suggest that people try and do nasty things to these robots because they are not being nice to others. The White Stripes open their song with three sets of heavy electric guitar downbeats immediately followed by a quick bridge to a repetition of these same sets of beats. The third beat in each set is slightly louder and held slightly longer than the other two beats. So, in our video, the first two beats of the song are synched to a clip of a normal, very static everyday scene, and on the third beat, this shifts to a clip of a mecha-robot stomping emphatically on a car. This same pattern—an everyday, fairly tranquil scene followed by a robot doing serious damage—is repeated for the entire opening sequence of the song.

As we work through this sequence, we find that our resource clips are way too long for our needs; they also contain a lot of extraneous footage that doesn't suit our purposes. We need to clip them and make them shorter. There are various ways to do this and a quick Google search will pull up any number of how-to tutorials. We will begin by clicking on "Show Timeline," an option found in the storyboard function menu (see Figure 9.2).

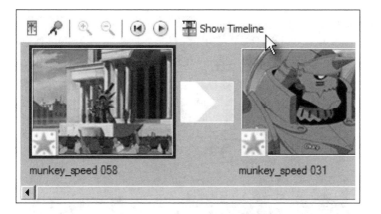

Figure 9.2: Switching between the storyboard view and the timeline view in
Windows Movie Maker

The timeline view displays the actual run-time per clip in seconds, and this is where we work on refining the synch between clips and, later, between clips and our audio track.

In the storyboard we highlight the clip to be trimmed by clicking on it (once selected it will be surrounded by a heavy black outline). Placing the cursor over one side of this highlighted video clip changes the cursor to a red, double-ended arrow. Clicking-and-holding-down the left mouse button when this red arrowed cursor appears, then dragging the cursor, moves the video playhead (which appears as a blue horizontal line) to where we wish to cut the video (see Figure 9.3).

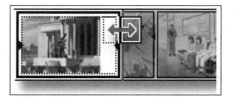

Figure 9.3: Clipping a video file to make it shorter or to remove extraneous footage

We release the mouse button once the playhead is where we want it, and this "breaks" our original selected video file into two clips. The clip segment to the right of the playhead automatically deletes itself. If we make a mistake, we can immediately reinstate this deleted portion by clicking on "Edit" in the Movie Maker main menu bar and then "Undo Trim Clip."

If we want to use a portion of a trimmed clip elsewhere and want to *split* the clip into two, rather than *cut* it and *delete* a portion, we first highlight the clip we want to split. Using the video preview window, we then play the clip to the point where we want to split it, and press the "Stop" button (marked by a square icon, and found next to the "Play" button). Still working in this preview window, we click the "Split" button (see Figure 9.4), and now have two clips instead of the one in our timeline or storyboard sequence.

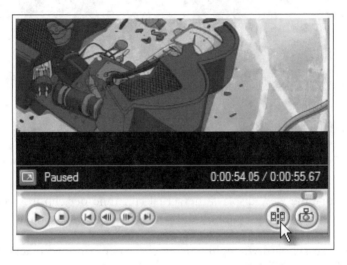

Figure 9.4: Splitting a video into two clips

To rearrange the order of clips, we click-hold-and-drag them to where we want them in the sequence (this can be done in either the storyboard view or the timeline view).

Once we have roughed out a version of our overall concept using the clips to hand, we work methodically through our timeline, selecting each clip and then clicking on "Clip" in the top menu bar of Movie Maker, choosing "Audio" then "Mute." This suppresses the soundtrack for each storyboarded video clip so that it doesn't interfere with the song. Meanwhile, we are saving our project regularly.

Now it's time to import our song and begin working more closely between the rhythm of the song, the song lyrics, our AMV concept, and the video files.

3. Importing our song.

We import our song into Movie Maker by clicking on the "Import audio or music" hyperlink in the task pane located on the left-hand side of the Movie Maker window. This opens a file location window. We locate our resource folder and click on our song file. The song file needs to be in a format such as *.wav, *.aif, *.snd, and *.mp3 (not *.m4a, for example). Once we've imported our song, it will also appear in our collections window pane, marked with a musical note icon. We switch to timeline view for our project and click-and-drag the music file onto the timeline. The audio file now displays as a separate "track" beneath our video clips in the timeline (see Figure 9.5).

Figure 9.5: Adding a song file to an AMV project

Clicking and highlighting our music track means we can also listen to it using the same preview pane used for watching and editing our video clips. We use the "shape" of the sound waves in our audio track to help synch clip transitions. We pay attention to the rhythm of the action *within* each clip—if there's running or other consistent movement we want to aim at lining this up with the beat of our soundtrack. Our music track can be clipped and split, just like a video clip and using the same processes. We can also add effects to the track, like fade out at the end of the song (see Chapters 2 and 3 in this volume).

4. Refining synch.

The process of creating an AMV now becomes quite recursive. We listen to snatches of song and fine tune where one clip ends and the next starts. We may go off in search of new clips that better match the lyrics or to fine-tune our narrative. We might find we need more video clips to match the length of the song. We experiment with transition effects (see below) and find that it throws our timing out, so we tinker with clip length, and so on, in iterations. Refining the synch between music rhythm, lyrics, mood (e.g., slowing clip transitions down during sad patches of music; increasing the rate of clip changes during frenetic bursts of music) is a trial-and-error, "let's-see" process. We trim, split, and move clips until we're happy with the project's overall look, sound and feel.

We also leave some music at the start of our AMV for our title and enough at the end for credits.

5. *Adding transitions and effects.*

We can add two key types of effects to our video: transition effects and video effects. Transition effects govern the different ways one clip can change to the next (e.g., bars, bow tie, horizontal, circle out, fade). Anyone familiar with creating PowerPoint presentations will know about adding transition effects between slides. Video effects added to each clip itself can include fog effects, sepia toning with scratchy old-film effect, grayscale, slow down half, watercolor, etc.

To add transitions and video effects to our video we must be in "storyboard" mode. We click on the second entry—"Edit Movie"—in the Movie Task box on the left-hand side of the Movie Maker program. We then click on "view video effects." This brings up a palette of different effects in the center of the Movie Maker window. By clicking on each effect icon we can preview the "look" of the effect in the preview window (where we earlier previewed video and sound). When we find a suitable effect we click on it and drag it down on top of the clip to which we want to add that effect. A small blue star appears in the bottom left-hand corner of each clip in the storyboard that has had an effect added. When we've finished adding effects, we play our AMV through to check that the effects do not distract from or undermine the mood or idea of the video overall.

To add a transition effect between clips we stay in storyboard mode. Between each clip there is an icon that looks vaguely like a ship's semaphore flag (see Figure 9.2 above). This is where we click-and-drag our transition effects to when we decide which transition we want. The generic transition icon will change to match the icon for the transition effect we've selected and added (e.g., a successfully added keyhole transition effect will be indicated by a keyhole icon appearing between the two clips).

Staying with the "Edit Movie" portion of the Movie Tasks pane, we click on "View video transitions." The palette of video effects is now replaced with a palette of transition effects. We preview each by clicking on the effect and clicking the "Play" button in the preview pane. Transition effects keep the AMV flowing smoothly from one clip to the next. They need to be in keeping with the music and concept of our music video (e.g., lots of gentle fade transitions won't work so well with a fast-paced rock anthem). The trick here is to have watched lots of AMV beforehand and made a note of transitions we found particularly effective and then recreate them within our own AMV. The same holds for transitions (and video effects) that annoyed us because they were so common, clumsy, or over-wrought. We avoid them here since they will likely annoy others too.

For additional help with effects and transitions we can click on "How to add titles, effects, transitions" in the Movie Task box on the left-hand side of the Movie Maker window.

6. Finishing touches: Title and credits.

The title is usually the name given to the final AMV by the remixer and doesn't have to match the title of the song or any titles of anime it has used. For example, we can call our AMV simply "Be Nice" or "Robo-Love," or whatever we like. Having a specific name, like "Konoha Memory Book," makes it much easier to talk about one's AMV as distinct from the song and the original anime on which it drew. It's considered good etiquette to also list the name of the band and the song title somewhere in the AMV, such as in the final credits. Credits typically include the AMV source videos, the AMV remixer's online alias or real name, a website where more AMVs can be found, and sometimes a list of acknowledgments of people who have helped produce the AMV.

Staying with the "Edit Movie" portion of the Movie Tasks pane, we click on "Make titles or credits" and then on the "Add title on the selected clip on the storyboard option" above. This will display the title as soon as our AMV starts rather than creating a separate title sequence. Once we've clicked on the hyperlink, a text box appears and we key in whatever information we want to appear (e.g., name of the AMV, the band and song). We next click on "Change the title animation" and scroll through the different effects we can add to the title text. We choose the "Ticker tape" title animation, which will scroll our information across the bottom of the AMV when it starts to play. Making sure we have the first clip on our storyboard highlighted, we click on the "Done, add title to movie" hyperlink. We preview our title to ensure it hasn't thrown any timing or synching out.

Adding credits at the end requires a similar process. Returning to the "Edit Movie" portion of the Movie Tasks pane within the main window of Movie Maker, we click on "Make titles or credits" and choose the "Add credits at the end of the movie" option. We enter text into the text box columns (e.g., Anime used—*Mobile Suit Gundam, Evangelion, Giant Robo;* Software used—Windows Movie Maker, etc.). We play around with how the credits will appear at the end of the video by clicking on "Change the title animation" and then scrolling down to the "Credits" subheading. We choose "Credits: Scroll, Up Side-by-Side"), so the credits look a little like 1950s movie credits. Clicking on "Change the text font and color" allows us to change the background color of the credits clip. Happy with how the credit sequence looks, we click "Done, add title to movie." Movie Maker automatically adds this credit sequence to the end of our movie.

7. It's a wrap!

We watch our video a few more times once everything is in place to check for smoothness of transitions, that video effects add to rather than detract from the work overall, and that synching hasn't come a little askew when we tinkered with different things. We invite feedback from family and friends. We can also post an in-process copy to YouTube, hoping to attract useful viewer feedback on a work in progress.

When happy with the final video, we click on "File" in the main menu bar in Movie Maker, and choose "Save Movie File . . ." This brings up a dialogue box asking whether we want to save our movie to the harddrive, burn it to a CD-ROM, email our movie, save and upload it immediately to the internet, or use a tape in a hooked-up video camera to record it. Since the file size is quite large, we save it to an external harddrive attached to a USB port. We select the "My Computer" option and click the "Next" button, key in a title of the final movie (e.g., "Robo-Love"). Then we click the "Browse" button and locate our external harddrive in the drop-down file directory and click "Okay." We double-check the destination for the movie file, then click the "Next" button. We're asked to verify file quality wanted—which we do. Clicking "Next" again, sets the ball rolling and our file is converted from a Movie Maker project file to a neatly transportable *.wmv file.

SECTION THREE

Copyright issues

AMVs currently appear to be running beneath the copyright radar of music and other media companies (Lessig, 2008). Milstein (2008, p. 32) suggests this "industry ambivalence" is because companies see AMVs as providing free marketing for anime series as well as constituting resources through which to recruit "editors for making [movie] trailers and DVD extras" (ibid.). DIY anime music videos are actively promoted at anime conventions, and YouTube is loaded with AMVs using commercial anime and music without visibly attracting "cease and desist" orders from media company lawyers. This could change, but at present AMV creation seems relatively immune from the scale of litigious copyright and IP infringement bullying that plagues other areas of young people's popular cultural engagement. Instead, what seems more likely to be a pressing concern for AMV remixers is the use of peer-to-peer filesharing networks for sourcing anime footage. Peer-to-peer networks are increasingly subject to corporate and legal surveillance, especially in the U.S.

Useful educational responses within classrooms to copyright law can include discussion of fair use guidelines for teachers and students (see, for example, Gardner, 2008; Salpeter, 2008). Informed discussion can draw attention to how copyright laws function, how these laws can indeed protect creators' work and earnings—which is necessary—and how corporations should make a fair proportion of their stock available for cultural creativity (see also Chapter 3 in this volume). It is important, however, to ensure that discussion is genuinely *informed* and not *dominated* by "the school's position" on copyright, which may have been shaped more by fear, by convenience, or by being ill-informed than by considerations grounded in the mission to *educate*.

Important ground can be laid in such discussions for helping learners and teachers alike to appreciate the ways in which overly restrictive copyright law and law enforcement can *and does* harm cultural development by removing important resources from the pool of "fair uses." The landmark work of Lawrence Lessig (2005, 2008) is essential reading here. It illuminates how today's generations of digital youth are being denied rights to create that previous generations (whose medium was print) took for granted. Any school failing to deal with these issues is reneging on its responsibilities with respect to literacy education specifically, and education for productive and creative citizenship more generally. Within such discussion, promoting awareness of the Creative Commons system of author-assigned copyright licenses is an important educational contribution. Encouraging learners and colleagues to search for materials bearing such licenses helps sidestep copyright issues—especially with respect to using commercial music files. ccLearn licenses, in particular, are intended to help educators and students locate learning resources (see: discovered.creativecommons.org/search). This kind of educational work will (further) encourage participants to put their own work out there for free use, subject to proper attribution—thereby helping break the stranglehold corporations currently wield over cultural ownership and use. With many young people this will simply involve nurturing an extant disposition.

AMV meets language arts

Interestingly, Matt's creative engagement as an AMV remixer involves him in understanding, appreciating, and doing many of the things English Language Arts educators ideally aim to encourage and develop. He consciously designs his AMVs to be interpreted on multiple levels. In his 2007 "Shinobi Ballad" AMV, for example, he aimed to "grab the emotion of struggle and triumph through the clips I put in, timing them well with the lyrics and making sure that I chose the right clips to pull out the most emotion for each section." He wanted to focus primarily on "the symbolic aspect" of the characters' struggles and triumphs "but also have many scenes that literally express the lyrics." Likewise, Matt pays careful attention to narrative structures. His AMVs typically summarize key storylines from some anime series whilst simultaneously standing as complete self-contained stories. He identifies major elements in complex and episodic stories and melds them into engaging condensations of the original, much larger sequential story. Attending to mood, symbolism, theme, multiple layers of meaning, narrative structure, key character traits, etc., are as integral to Matt's AMV remixing as they are esteemed understandings within language arts and English classes at school.

Explicit pedagogy and media education in schools

Cases like Matt's challenge various established curriculum orthodoxies about media and literacy instruction. Some of these can be grouped around the idea of "explicit pedagogy." In its widest sense, perhaps, it refers to focusing students' attention on very specific tasks and concepts within a structured setting with a view to producing specific learning outcomes. As a "pedagogy" it begins from stating a specific goal for the immediate context and telling learners what they are to do and moves to demonstrating how it is done and then to guiding students' practical efforts to apply the new concept, skill or technique. At the other extreme, "making it explicit" may involve little more than drawing attention to a concrete instance of what is being talked about, or taking the guesswork out of a moment in classroom life, pointing directly to what is relevant and separating it out from other contextual thoughts or talk. With a student like Matt, a teacher might make a link between the learner's "optimizing synch" or "establishing mood" in an AMV and what is immediately at stake in an English literature lesson.

In media and literacy education, theoretical and analytical work done in research often provides motivation and means for importing substantial explicit pedagogy into curriculum and foisting it on learners. A typical example is the long-running fetish for teaching young people how to identify stereotypes in advertisements. It is assumed that young people *need* to be *taught* how to do this, and contexts are contrived—"learning opportunities" are created—for teaching them. Examples like those provided by Matt's experiences with AMV throw this assumption into doubt. Such experiences, born of engaging as an "authentic professional" (Gee 2007) in the world of fan-based, amateurs-working-to-professional-standards (Leadbeater & Miller, 2004) AMV remixing, would call at most for the lesser strain of explicitness distinguished above: leveraging knowledge acquired within contexts of authentic social practice for "scholastic" learning being undertaken within settings that are very often anything *but* authentic. Within media and literacy education it is widely assumed that young people need to be taught key elements of design features, text structures, interpretive strategies, and critical analysis processes, among other things—the best countervailing efforts of popular culture resources like *South Park* and *The Simpsons* notwithstanding.

Obviously, clarity and focus are virtues in *any* context where meaning and purpose are at stake. The point, however, is that in many cases the perceived need to make things "explicit" in classrooms is a consequence of learning situations lacking the kind of authenticity within which facility and competence can be acquired in the ways Matt acquired them—whereupon all that is required is to make relevant connections and to transfer or leverage existing knowledge and competence for formal (analytic, critical, etc.) educational purposes. Furthermore, just as "making it explicit" can work *back* from something that is extant, it can also point learners *forward* to things they are likely to encounter within hands-on engagement in meaningful learning activities. In this sense, making something explicit takes the form of alerting learners to something that will likely lie ahead, so that when they see it they will be able to recognize it as an example of X (which may be educationally important or valid because of Y). There will be no need to *instruct* the point in a decontextualized manner before the event. Learners can make the connection *themselves* at points of application with minimal teacher intervention.

The key to this—a key that comes at educators in waves from accounts of young people surpassing themselves as learners within affinity spaces—is ensuring as far as possible that classroom learning meets the principle of "efficacious learning" that a sociocultural approach to media and literacy education insists upon.

> In a sociocultural approach, the focus of learning and education is not children, nor schools, but human lives seen as trajectories through multiple social practices in various social institutions. If learning is to be efficacious, then what a child or adult does now as a learner must be connected in meaningful and motivating ways with "mature" (insider) versions of related social practices (Gee, Hull & Lankshear, 1996, p. 4)

It is relatively easy to see what this involves when we look at cases of young people's DIY media activity within affinity spaces like AnimeMusicVideos.org or in other popular cultural affinity spaces (see Black, 2008, for fan fiction; Gee, 2007, for video games).

Learning and identity: ProAms, affinities and appreciative systems

Dedicated and strongly invested AMV remixers like Matt aim to become what Charles Leadbeater and Paul Miller describe as "ProAms": "innovative, committed and networked amateurs working to professional standards"

(Leadbeater & Miller, 2004, p. 9; see also Gee, 2007, on "authentic professionals"). Even where their remixes fall short of the ideal, they nonetheless
know what makes an AMV excellent. They are alert to the musical, lyrical and
mood dimensions of *"synch"*—the connections between music and video,
without which there is anime and music but no real connection between
them. They appreciate the importance of *"concept"* as one's vision for the
video, what one wants viewers to think and understand, or how one wants
them to feel. And they are attuned to the role of *"effects,"* with respect to
their meaning, composition, appearance, and so on (Kalium, 2006). Matt's
concept of a high quality AMV emphasizes:

- Good quality video resources (e.g., within the AMV community, using
  footage downloaded from the internet—rather than ripped from
  DVDs—is frowned upon for quality-of-resolution reasons)
- Relevance of the song to the anime resource(s) used
- Excellence of the correlation between the song and the video clips; this
  includes synching lyrics with the video effectively
- Not using clips containing subtitles, series titles, or final credits

Matt's understanding of what constitutes a good quality AMV has been
gleaned from participating in a range of anime and AMV remixing "affinity
spaces" (Gee, 2004). Affinity spaces are places of informal learning—physical,
virtual, or a mix—where people come together and interact around and
through a shared interest, common goal, or collaborative endeavor (Gee,
2004, p. 98). They comprise resources on which this group draws and that it
shares, ways of providing feedback and responding to other members, collective expertise and troubleshooting advice, and networks wherein newcomers
and experts alike work together in collegial and supportive ways. According
to Gee, within affinity spaces "knowledge is both *intensive* (each person
entering the space brings some special knowledge) and *extensive* (each person
entering the space shares some knowledge and functions with others)" (original emphases; Gee, 2004, p. 98). Matt participates actively in spaces like Ani-
meMusicVideos.org, regularly watches and provides constructive feedback on
other people's AMVs, submits AMVs to anime convention contests, and participates in a range of anime cosplay and manga drawing discussion boards
and art-related community sites (e.g., DeviantArt.org, Megatokyo discussion
forums). For Matt, these activities are part and parcel of being recognized as
someone "in the know" (who has intensive knowledge of AMV remixing)
and whose work and opinions "count" among members of the affinity space.
Participating in these spaces also enables Matt to draw on the extensive, collective knowledge and expertise of others in developing his own work.

Gee (2007, p. 172) elaborates upon these ideas in terms of learning contexts where one takes on a new identity and acquires an "appreciative sys-

tem." The point about identity puts the emphasis on learning to be a particular kind of person-practitioner rather than on "learning *about*" or "learning *a subject*." Matt has engaged in learning *to be* an AMV remixer, and at every point his quest has been to become *more of* and *better as* an AMV remixer. As Gee (2007, p. 172) puts it:

> Learning a new domain, whether physics or furniture making, requires learners to see and value work and the world in new ways, in the ways in which physicists or furniture makers do. . . . [I]n any domain, if knowledge is to be used, the learner must probe the world (act on it with a goal) and then evaluate the result. Is it "good" or "bad," "adequate" or "inadequate," "useful" or "not," "improvable" or "not"? . . . Learners can only do this if they have developed a value system—what Donald Schön [1983] calls an "appreciative system"—in terms of which such judgments can be made. Such value systems are embedded in the identities, tools, technologies, and worldviews of distinctive groups of people—who share, sustain, and transform them—groups like doctors, carpenters, physicists, graphic artists, teachers, and so forth through a nearly endless list.

AMV remixers are just such a distinctive group, and their affinity spaces are, precisely, contexts where "identities, tools, technologies, and worldviews" are taken up, enacted, and negotiated within immersive and embedded practice. Participating in AMV affinities and taking on the identity of an AMV remixer aspiring to ProAm proficiency involves coming to realize that AMV remixers "look at and act on the world in quite distinctive ways because of their values and goals and [moreover] these values and goals are supported by and integrally expressed through distinctive tools, technologies, skills, and knowledge" (Gee, 2007, p. 172). As Gee notes, the same holds true for any kind of science (e.g., being a physicist, chemist, biologist) and, we would add, for mathematics and any kind of social science or humanity (e.g., being a literary critic, a poet, a creative writer, an historian, etc.).

Conclusion

This chapter does not imply that AMV remixing should simply be imported into school curriculum and classroom practice, any more than the fact that good commercial video games have sound learning principles factored into their designs means we should give classrooms over to game playing. Rather, the point is to understand how and why cultural practices like AMV remixing constitute social and learning systems that are conducive to learning effectively and that foster high levels of personal investment in achieving success. We can then try to apply these insights to educational purposes in ways that maximize opportunities for students to leverage their own social and learning systems in school-valued ways.

References

AMV.org (2008a). Interviews. *AnimeMusicVideos.org*. Available from: http://www.an imemusicvideos.org/members/interview_list.php (accessed 7 March, 2008).

AMV.org (2008b). Site FAQs. *AnimeMusicVideos.org*. Available from: http://www.an imemusicvideos.org/help/ (accessed 7 March, 2008).

Austerlitz, S. (2007). *Money for nothing: A history of the music video from the Beatles to the White Stripes*. New York: Continuum.

Black, R. (2008). *Adolescents and online fan fiction*. New York: Peter Lang.

Catone, J. (2008). Radiohead Looks to Fans for Music Video Production. *ReadWriteWeb.com*. available from: http://www.readwriteweb.com/archives/radi ohead_music_video_contest.php (accessed Jan. 30, 2008).

DynamiteBreakdown (2008a). The Konoha memory book. *YouTube.com*. Available from: http://www.youtube.com/watch?v=u-12_2peCMg (8 March, 2008).

DynamiteBreakdown (2008b). Video information: The Konoha memory book. *AnimeMusicVideos.org*. Retrieved from: http://www.animemusicvideos.org/me mbers/members_videoinfo.php?v=101473 (8 March, 2008).

Gardner, T. (2008). Fair use and copyright for educators. *NCTE Inbox*. Available from: http://ncteinbox.blogspot.com/2008/11/fair-use-and-copyright-foreducators.html (accessed 4 April, 2009).

Gee, J. (2004). *Situated language and learning: A critique of traditional schooling*. New York: Routledge.

Gee, J (2007). *Good video games and good learning*. New York: Peter Lang.

Gee, J., Hull, G. & Lankshear, C. (1996). *The new work order*. Boulder, CO: Westview.

Kalium (2006). Kalium's AMV Theory Primer. *AnimeMusicVideos.org*. Retrieved from: http://www.animemusicvideos.org/guides/kalium/index.html (March 7, 2008).

Kirkpatrick, S. (2003). Like holding a bird: What the prevalence of fansubbing can teach us about the use of strategic selective copyright enforcement. *Temple Environmental Law & Technology Journal*. 21: 131–153.

Leadbeater, C. & Miller, P. (2004). *The pro-am Revolution: How enthusiasts are changing Our Economy and Society*. London: Demos Publishing.

Lessig, L. (2005). *Free Culture: The nature and future of creativity*. New York: Penguin.

Lessig, L. (2008). *Remix: Making art and commerce thrive in the hybrid economy*. New York: Penguin.

Milstein, D. (2008). Case Study: Anime Music Videos. In J. Sexton (ed.), *Music, sound and multimedia: From the live to the virtual*. Edinburgh, UK: Edinburgh University Press. 29–50.

Park, T. (2008). Otaku Remixes: Anime Music Videos. Curated screening and commentary presented to the 247 DIY Video Summit. Institute for Multimedia Literacy, University of Southern California. February 9.

Phade (2002). Phade's guide to good anime music videos. *AnimeMusicVideos.org*. Available from: http://www.animemusicvideos.org/guides/PhadeGuide/ (accessed 7 March, 2008).

Salpeter, J. (2008). The new rules of copyright. *Tech & Learning*. Oct. 15. Available from: http://www.techlearning.com/article/14522 (accessed Feb. 14, 2009).

Schön, D. (1983). *The reflective practitioner*. New York: Basic Books.

Springall, D. (2004). "Popular Music Meets Japanese Cartoons: A History of the Evolution of Anime Music Videos." Unpublished undergraduate Honors Thesis. Birmingham, Alabama: Samford University, 2004.

Vernallis, C. (2004). *Experiencing music video: Aesthetics and cultural context.* New York: Columbia University Press.

Wikipedia (2008). Yaoi. *Wikipedia.org.* Retrieved from: http://en.wikipedia.org/yaoi (December 12, 2007).

Wikipedia (2009). Musicvideo. *Wikipedia.org.* available from: http://en.wikipedia.org/wiki/Music_video (accessed Jan. 30, 2009).

Afterword: Communities of Readers, Clusters of Practices

Henry Jenkins

This book is at once a "How to" guide to various emerging cultural practices and a "Why to" guide to the reasons you should bring them into your class-room. Throughout, you've learned from expert practitioners what to do if you want to become more adept at music sampling, podcasting, vidding, photo-shopping, flash animation, or machinima and you've learned why these prac-tices matter to those already participating in them and how they might enhance formalized education. This is urgent work, especially at a time when so many schools have cut themselves off from participatory culture. Too many educa-tors are determined to protect youth from exposure to Facebook and MySpace, Twitter, Wikipedia, and YouTube, as if these were threats rather than resources. Those who want to lock them out argue that they constitute dangerous dis-tractions from formal education; many who favor them still talk of making learning more "fun" or "entertaining" for students who grab their iPods the minute the school bell rings.

These approaches are two sides of the same coin and largely miss the point: for the generation which has come of age alongside networked computing, these practices do not simply represent "entertainment" or "distraction." These practices are important gateways into larger learning cultures that help support young people as they construct their identities and navigate their social surroundings. Bringing some of these meaningful practices into the classroom allows young people to deploy more effective learning strategies and to take greater control over their education. Educational reformers have long argued that schools need to break down the walls that isolate classroom teaching from the larger learning ecology surrounding schools, incorporate outside perspectives, connect textbook knowledge with real world contexts through authentic inquiries, and link emerging expertise to the meaningful performance of social roles. Incorporating DIY practices into your teaching is a huge step toward such a more integrated approach.

Carol Jago of the National Council of Teachers of English told *New York Times* reporter Motoko Rich (2008, no page), "Nobody has taught a single kid to text message . . . When they want to do something, schools don't have to get involved." I'm not sure what this implies about the content we *do* need to teach through schools, but I reject this laissez faire approach to the new media literacies. Even if some children learned the needed skills on their own, these practices, and the skills and mental habits associated with them, are unevenly distributed across youth culture: some young people amass diverse "portfolios" of experiences (Gee, 2004), moving across a range of different communities and practices, both acquiring mentors and mentoring others. They have had rich and meaningful online experiences and they have found ways to connect these experiences to knowledge they are acquiring through school. Incorporating these practices lets them strut their stuff, allowing them to tap into the power and status they've acquired online, and it also helps them to articulate more fully what they have learned and why it matters.

But, many other young people have little or no opportunities for such empowering experiences outside of school, lacking access not only to the core technologies but also to what Ellen Seiter (2008) has identified as the economic, social, and cultural capital required for full participation. We might characterize the limits on technological access as "the digital divide" and the limits on social and cultural experiences as "the participation gap." Schools have sought to address the digital divide by insuring that every school and library provides access to networked computing; the best way to address the participation gap may be for schools to assume a similar responsibility for integrating many of these DIY practices into our pedagogies.

From do it yourself to do it ourselves

The book makes a second important assumption that you cannot fully understand the value and significance of these practices without participating. Teachers need to get their hands dirty (at least figuratively) by working with the tools, platforms, and processes fundamental to these new forms of cultural production and circulation. Through doing these things, you learn what it is like to tap a larger community of expertise around your activities. Do It Yourself rarely means Do It Alone. For example, much of what youth learn through game playing emerges from "meta-gaming," the conversations about the game play. Trading advice often forces participants to spell out their core assumptions as more experienced players pass along what they've learned to newcomers. This "meta-gaming" has many of the dimensions of peer-to-peer teaching or "social learning." As John Seeley Brown and Richard P. Adler (2008, p. 18) explain, "social learning is based on the premise that our *understanding* of content is socially constructed through conversations about that content and through grounded interactions, especially with others, around problems or actions" (original emphasis). To call this "learning by doing" is too simple, as we will not learn as much if we separate what we are doing— making a podcast, modding a game, mastering a level—from the social context in which we are doing it.

I have always felt uncomfortable with the phrase "Do It Yourself" as a label for the practices described in this book. "Do It Yourself" is too easy to assimilate into some vague and comfortable notion of "personal expression" or "individual voice" that Americans can incorporate into long-standing beliefs in "rugged individualism" and "self-reliance." Yet, what may be radical about the DIY ethos is that learning relies on these mutual support networks, creativity is understood as a trait of communities, and expression occurs through collaboration. Given these circumstances, phrases like "Do It Ourselves" or "Do It Together" better capture collective enterprises within networked publics. This is why I am drawn towards concepts such as "participatory culture," (Jenkins, Purushotma, Weigel, Clinton, & Robison, 2009) "affinity spaces," (Gee, 2007) "genres of participation," (Ito et al., 2009) "networked publics," (Varnelis, 2008) "collective intelligence," (Levy, 1999) or "communities of practice" (Lave & Wenger, 1991).

Although each reflects a somewhat different pedagogical model, each captures the sense of shared space or collective enterprise which shapes the experience of individual participants/learners. Each offers us a model of peer-to-peer education: we learn *from each other* in the process of *working together* to achieve shared goals. Many of these models emphasize the diverse roles played by various participants in this process. It is not that all participants *know* the same things (as has been the expectation in school); success rests on multiple forms of expertise the group can deploy "just in time" by responding to shifting circumstances and emerging problems. It is not that all participants *do* the same things; rather, these practices depend on the ad hoc coordination of diverse skills and actions towards shared interests.

We need to understand the specific practices discussed here as informed by norms and values that emerge from their community of participants. We see different things if we focus on the practices or on the communities that deploy them, and in my remarks here, I hope to shift the lens onto the communities. Focusing on practices first, the editors write in this book's introduction, "Podcasting, for example, involves using particular kinds of tools, techniques and technologies to achieve the goals and purposes that podcasters aim to achieve and to use them in the ways that people known as podcasters recognize as appropriate to their endeavor in terms of their goals and values." While saying something important about the nature of these practices, this description assumes that the operative identity here is that of the podcaster and that podcasters enjoy a shared identity as parts of a community of practice regardless of the content and functions of their podcasts. And this may be true for some, especially at the moment they are first learning how to podcast or are passing those skills and practices along to others, but for many, podcasting is a means to an end.

Otaku, fans, hip hoppers and gamers

On the ground, these practices get embedded in a range of different interest-driven networks and what motivates these activities may be less a desire to make a podcast than an urge to create a shared space where, for example, fans can discuss their mutual interests in Severus Snape, or where church members can hold prayer circles, or where comic book buffs can interview writers and artists. The Digital Youth Project (Ito et al., 2009) drew a useful distinction between "messing around," tinkering with new tools and techniques to see what they can do, and "geeking out," going deep into a particular interest that may, in turn, lead you to engage with a range of social networks and production practices. There is some risk that as educators organize class projects around the production of podcasts, they risk divorcing these practices from the larger cultural contexts in which they operate.

We might think about different interest-driven networks as mobilizing somewhat different clusters of interlocking and mutually reinforcing practices. Consider, for example, Mimi Ito's (2005, no page) description of the literacy skills within otaku culture, the fan community around anime and manga:

> Anime otaku are media connoisseurs, activist prosumers who seek out esoteric content
> from a far away land and organize their social lives around viewing, interpreting, and
> remixing these media works. Otaku translate and subtitle all major anime works, they
> create web sites with hundreds and thousands of members, stay in touch 24/7 on hun-

dreds of IRC channels, and create fan fiction, fan art, and anime music videos that rework the original works into sometimes brilliantly creative and often subversive alternative frames of reference. . . . To support their media obsessions otaku acquire challenging language skills and media production crafts of scripting, editing, animating, drawing, and writing. And they mobilize socially to create their own communities of interest and working groups to engage in collaborative media production and distribution. Otaku use visual media as their source material for crafting their own identities, and as the coin of the realm for their social networks. Engaging with and reinterpreting professionally produced media is one stepping stone towards critical media analysis and alternative media production.

Certainly, within otaku culture, one can gain an identity as a fan-subber, a vidder, a fan fiction author, a community organizer, or an illustrator, but these practice-based identities do not supersede one's larger identity as an otaku.

What Ito observes about otaku culture is consistent with what researchers have observed in a range of other subcultures. Consider this description from my fieldwork on female-centered science fiction fandom in the early 1990s (Jenkins, 1992, pp. 152–3):

Four *Quantum Leap* fans gather every few weeks in a Madison, Wisconsin, apartment to write. The women spread out across the living room, each with their own typewriter or laptop, each working diligently on their own stories about Al and Sam. Two sit at the dining room table, a third sprawls on the floor, a fourth balances her computer on the coffee table. The clatter of the keyboards and the sounds of a filktape are interrupted periodically by conversation. Linda wants to insure that nothing in the program contradicts her speculations about Sam's past. Mary has introduced a southern character and consults Georgia-born Signe for advice about her background. Kate reviews her notes on *Riptide*, having spent the week rewatching favorite scenes so she can create a "crossover" story which speculates that Sam may have known Murray during his years at MIT. Mary scrutinizes her collection of "telepics"(photographs shot from the television image), trying to find the right words to capture the suggestion of a smile that flits across his face. . . . Kate passes around a letter she has received commenting on her recently published fanzine. . . . Each of the group members offers supportive comments on a scene Linda has just finished, all independently expressing glee over a particularly telling line. As the day wears on, writing gives way to conversation, dinner, and the viewing of fan videos (including the one that Mary made a few weeks before). . . . For the fan observer, there would be nothing particularly remarkable about this encounter. I have spent similar afternoons with other groups of fans, collating and binding zines, telling stories, and debating the backgrounds of favorite characters. . . . For the "mundane" observer, what is perhaps most striking about this scene is the ease and fluidity with which these fans move from watching a television program to engaging in alternative forms of cultural production: the women are all writing their own stories; Kate edits and publishes her own zines she prints on a photocopy machine she keeps in a spare bedroom and the group helps to assemble them for distribution. Linda and Kate are also fan artists who exhibit and sell their work at conventions; Mary is venturing into fan video making and gives other fans tips on how to shoot better telepics. Almost as

striking is how writing becomes a social activity for these fans, functioning simultaneously as a form of personal expression and as a source of collective identity (part of what
it means to be a fan). Each of them has something potentially interesting to contribute;
the group encourages them to develop their talents fully, taking pride in their accom-
plishments, be they long-time fan writers and editors like Kate or relative novices like
Signe.

At the time, I was interested in what this scene told us about how fans read television and how they deployed its contents as raw materials for their own
expressive activities. Rereading the passage today, I am struck by how fully the
description captures the strengths of a DIY culture as a site for informal learning. Sometimes the women are working on individual, self-defined projects and
sometimes they are working together on mutual projects but always they are
drawing moral support from their membership in an interest-driven network.
Each plays multiple roles: sometimes the author, sometimes the reader, sometimes the teacher, sometimes the student, sometimes the editor, sometimes the
researcher, sometimes the illustrator. They move fluidly from role to role as
needed, interrupting their own creative activity to lend skills and knowledge
to someone else. Their creative interests straddle multiple media practices: they
write stories; they take telepics; they edit videos; they publish zines. Each
activity constitutes a complex cultural practice combining technical skills and
cultural expertise. Leadership, as Gee (2004) tells us, is "porous": the space is
Signe's apartment; Kate is editing the zine to which they are each contributing; and Mary has the expertise in fan video production which she shares with
her circle in hopes of getting more of them vidding. And we see here a conception of culture as a series of "processes" rather than a set of "products." Fan
work is always open to revision, expansion, and elaboration, rather than locked
down and closed off from others' contributions. As a more recent account of
fan cultural practices (Busse & Hellekson, 2006, p. 6) explains:

> *Work in progress* is a term used in the fan fiction world to describe a piece of fiction still
> in the process of being written but not yet completed . . . The appeal of works in
> progress lies in part in the ways . . . it invites responses, permits shared authorship, and
> enjoins a sense of community . . . In most cases, the resulting story is part collabora-
> tion and part response to not only the source text, but also the cultural context with-
> in and outside the fannish community in which it is produced . . . When the story is
> finally complete and published, likely online but perhaps in print, the work in progress
> among the creators shifts to the work in progress among the readers. [original italics]

Similarly, Kevin Driscoll (2009) has discussed how Hip Hop's diverse
practices around music, dance, the graphic arts, video production, and entre-
preneurship associated with Hip Hop encourage participants to master a range
of cultural and technological skills. He describes, for example, the different par-

ticipatory practices that got mobilized around the circulation of a single song:

> As the figurehead of 2007's "Crank Dat" phenomenon, Atlanta teenager Soulja Boy exploited social-networking and media-sharing websites to encourage a widespread dance craze that afforded him a level of visibility typically only available to artists working within the pop industry. "Crank Dat" . . . began as a single commodity but grew into a multi-faceted cultural phenomenon . . . Within just a few months of the first "Crank Dat" music video, fans had posted countless custom revisions of "Crank Dat" to media-sharing sites like YouTube, SoundClick, imeem, and MySpace. In each case, the participants altered the original video in a different manner. They changed the dance steps, altered the lyrics, created new instrumental beats, wore costumes, and performed in groups. Some created remix videos that borrowed footage from popular TV programs and movies . . . "Crank Dat" welcomed diverse modes of participation but every production required considerable technical expertise. Even a cursory exploration of the various "Crank Dat" iterations available on YouTube provides evidence of many different media production tools and techniques. The most basic homemade dance videos required operation of a video camera, post-production preparation of compressed digital video, and a successful upload to YouTube. For some of the participants in "Crank Dat," the dance craze provided an impetus for their first media projects. This lively media culture is representative of a spirit of innovation that traverses hip-hop history. (Driscoll, 2009, p. 61)

As a former classroom teacher who worked with inner city and minority youth, Driscoll directs attention towards the technical proficiency of these Hip Hop fans to challenge assumptions that often position African-American males on the wrong side of the digital divide, assuming that they have limited capacity and interest for entering STEM subjects. Rather, he argues that educators need to better understand the ways that their cultural attachments to Hip Hop often motivate them to embrace new technologies and adopt new cultural practices, many of which could provide gateways into technical expertise.

Or consider what James Paul Gee (2007, p.100) tells us about the "affinity spaces" around on-line gaming:

> A portal like AoM [Age of Mythologies] Heaven, and the AoM space as a whole, allows people to achieve status, if they want it (and they may not), in many different ways. Different people can be good at different things or gain repute in a number of different ways. Of course, playing the game well can gain one status, but so can organizing forum parties, putting out guides, working to stop hackers from cheating in the multiplayer game, posting to any of a number of different forums, or a great many other things.

Indeed, for Gee, the idea of multiple forms of participation and status are part of what makes these affinity spaces such rich environments for informal learning. Unlike schools, where everyone is expected to do (and be good at) the same things, these participatory cultures allow each person to set their own goals, learn at their own pace, come and go as they please, and yet they are also motivated by the responses of others, often spending more time engaged with the activities because of a sense of responsibility to their guild or fandom. They enable a balance between self-expression and collaborative learning which may be the sweet spot for DIY learning.

These examples represent four very different communities, each with their own governing assumptions about what it means to participate and about what kinds of cultural practices and identities are meaningful. Yet, all of them embody the pedagogical principles I have identified within participatory culture: "A participatory culture is a culture with relatively low barriers to artistic expression and civic engagement, strong support for creating and sharing one's creations, and some type of informal mentorship whereby what is known by the most experienced is passed along to novices. A participatory culture is also one in which members believe their contributions matter, and feel some degree of social connection with one another" (Jenkins et al., 2006, p. 3).

Challenging the "Learning 2.0" formulation

There has been a growing tendency to describe the application of these participatory culture principles to the classroom as "education 2.0" and as we do so, to take the highly visible corporate "web 2.0" portals not simply as our ideal model but also as the source for these new participatory practices. Look at the way Brown and Adler's (2008, p. 18) influential formulation of "Learning 2.0" ascribes agency to corporate platforms and technologies rather than to communities of participants:

> The latest evolution of the Internet, the so-called *Web 2.0, has blurred* the line between producers and consumers of content and *has shifted* attention from access to information toward access to other people. New kinds of online resources—such as social networking sites, blogs, wikis, and virtual communities—have allowed people with common interests to meet, share ideas, and collaborate in innovative ways. Indeed, the *Web 2.0 is creating a new kind of participatory medium* that is ideal for supporting multiple modes of learning [italics my emphasis].

The DIY ethos, which emerged as a critique of consumer culture and a celebration of making things ourselves, is being transformed into a new form of consumer culture, a product or service that is sold to us by media companies rather than something that emerged from grassroots practices.

For this reason, I want to hold onto a distinction between participatory cultures, which may or may not be engaged with commercial portals, and web 2.0, which refers specifically to a set of commercial practices that seek to capture and harness the creative energies and collective intelligences of their users. "Web

2.0" is not a theory of pedagogy; it is a business model. Unlike projects like Wikipedia that have emerged from nonprofit organizations, the Open Courseware movement from educational institutions, and the Free Software movement from voluntary and unpaid affiliations, the web 2.0 companies follow a commercial imperative, however much they may also wish to facilitate the needs and interests of their consumer base. The more time we spend interacting with Facebook, YouTube, or LiveJournal, the clearer it becomes that there are real gaps between the interests of management and consumers. Academic theorists (Terranova, 2004; Green & Jenkins, 2009) have offered cogent critiques of what they describe as the "free labor" provided by those who choose to contribute their time and effort to creating content which can be shared through such sites, while consumers and fans have offered their own blistering responses to shifts in the terms of service which devalue their contributions or claim ownership over the content they produced. Many web 2.0 sites provide far less scaffolding and mentorship than offered by more grassroots forms of participatory culture. Despite a rhetoric of collaboration and community, they often still conceive of their users as autonomous individuals whose primary relationship is to the company that provides them services and not to each other. There is a real danger in mapping the web 2.0 business model onto educational practices, thus seeing students as "consumers" rather than "participants" within the educational process.

Participatory culture has a history—indeed, multiple histories—which is much larger than the history of specific technologies or commercial platforms. This book's introduction offers one such trajectory, starting with a consideration of how the DIY ideals took root through the countercultures of the 1950s and 1960s, which, as Fred Turner (2008) has suggested, exerted powerful influences on the development of cyberculture in the 1980s and 1990s. We might imagine another history that goes back to the emergence of the Amateur Press Association in the middle of the nineteenth century as young people began to hand set type and print their own publications, commenting on culture, politics, and everyday life (Petrik, 1992). These publications were mailed through elaborate circuits that resembled what we would now call social networks. This same community was among the early adapters of amateur radio in the early part of the twentieth century at a time when it was assumed that there would be almost as many transmitters as receivers (Douglas, 1989). Or we might consider, as Patricia Zimmerman (1995) does, the emergence of amateur camera clubs in the nineteenth century or the growth of home movie production in the twentieth century. Amateur media production got labeled as "home movies" (and locked from public view) within a culture based less on grassroots production than on the professionalization associated with mass media. Rather than participants, mass culture turned fans into spectators.

We might pay attention along the way to the emergence of science fiction fandom in the 1920s and 1930s. Hugo Gernsbeck, the father of modern science fiction, was a major advocate of ham radio. Gernsbeck saw fandom very much as an extension of his pedagogical mission to use his publications—whether focused on real world science or on the imaginings of what he called "scientifiction"—to create a space for expanding popular access to information and insights about the scientific and technological revolutions taking place around them. He saw the fan community as a space where people could debate ideas found in his pulp magazines and thus explore the limits of current scientific understandings (Ross, 1991). Fans quickly adopted the amateur publication and circulation practices of the early Amateur Press Association to connect with each other across geographic distances around shared affinities and to support each other's creative growth and intellectual development. Over the course of the twentieth century, almost every major science fiction writer and artist got their start through producing and publishing amateur work through fanzines or participating in other kinds of fan practices. Forrest K. Ackerman, editor of *Famous Monsters of Filmland*, inherited many of the values of the science fiction fan culture, focusing them on the horror genre and using his publication to encourage his readers to construct models, apply monster makeup, or produce their own horror films, again providing a training ground for many future professionals as well as providing the basis for an autonomous fan culture (Yockey, 2009). Television fandom in turn provided a supportive context through which many women, excluded from the male-only club that science fiction fandom had largely become, could develop their skills and hone their talents, not to mention build a following for their output. By the 1970s, these women (Bacon-Smith, 1992; Jenkins, 1992; Coppa, 2008) were remixing television footage to create their own fanvids, writing and editing their own zines, creating elaborate costumes, singing original folk songs, and painting images, all inspired by their favorite television series. With the rise of networked computing, these fan communities did important work in providing their female participants with access to the skills and technologies as these women took their first steps into cyberspace, reversing early conceptions about the gendering of digital culture as a space of masculine mastery. These female fans were early adopters of social network technologies such as Live Journal and Facebook. In short, this female-led fandom adopted the practices of early male science fiction fans and the resources offered by new media technologies to create their own distinctive forms of participatory culture. Fans were quick to embrace the value of podcasting, given how much their history was linked to earlier forms of amateur radio production. The return to this earlier moment of fan engagement with radio is especially suggested by recent fan projects to resurrect the traditions of radio drama as an extension of fan fiction.

These participatory cultures embraced each new technology as it emerged whenever it offered them new affordances which could support their ongoing social and cultural interactions. The practices associated with specific forms of cultural production, similarly, got taken up by a community which could trace its core identity back to the middle of the nineteenth century. The availability of new media has allowed this community to dramatically expand the scope of its membership, allowing much quicker interactions between members, creating greater cultural visibility for its productions and enabling more opportunities to participate, yet the core logic of participatory culture remains surprisingly unchanged despite the constant churn of tools and platforms. And interestingly, at each step along the way, there were educators who sought to harness the community's practices—amateur printing, radio production, or home movies, among them—as a means of motivating learning, as well as those who resisted such moves as distracting from formal education. All of this points to the need for us to explore continuities within participatory culture and commonalities across creative communities alongside our current preoccupations with technological and cultural innovations. It is an open question as to how many of the "new media literacies" are in fact new and how many of them have simply gained new visibility and urgency as digital culture has enabled diverse communities of practice to intersect and interact with each other in new ways.

In their earlier book, *New Literacies: Everyday Practice and Classroom Learning*, Colin Lankshear and Michele Knobel (2006) draw a productive distinction between new literacies as responsive to a set of new technologies and new literacies as responsive to this larger "ethos" of participatory culture. In my own work, I have placed much greater emphasis on bringing that "ethos" into the classroom than on integrating specific tools and practices, though the ideal is to do both. Otherwise, we may bring podcasting into the classroom and do nothing to alter the cultural context that surrounds contemporary formal education. Without that ethos, podcasts become one more thing we grade, one more way of measuring whether everyone in the class has learned the same material and mastered the same skills. Having students make videos rather than write book reports may shift the mechanisms of learning but may not alter the hierarchical and pre-structured relationship between teachers and learners.

Project New Media Literacies: Bringing participatory culture into the classroom

Over the past few years, Project New Media Literacies (NML), first at MIT and now at the University of Southern California, has taken what we know about participatory culture and applied it to the development of curricular resources for use in both in-school and after-school based programs. Our work has included the development of the Learning Library, a robust set of tools and media-focused activities, which are designed to get learners (teachers and students alike) exploring and experimenting with the new media literacies and in the process, producing and sharing media-related activities ("challenges") with each other; The Ethics Casebook, developed in collaboration with Harvard's GoodPlay Project, which encourages young people to reflect more deeply on the choices they make as media producers and members of online communities; and a series of Teachers' Strategy Guides intended to encourage teachers to rethink how they would teach traditional school content differently in a world which embraced a more participatory model of learning. Our work has been informed both by my own scholarship on participatory culture and by the applied expertise of Erin Reilly, who had previously helped to create Zoey's Room, a widely acclaimed on-line learning community that employed participatory practices to get young women more engaged with science and technology. Our team brought together educational researchers, such as Katherine Clinton, who studied under James Paul Gee, with people like Anna Van Someren, who had done community-based media education through the YWCA and had worked as a professional videomaker, Flourish Klink, who helped to organize the influential Fan Fiction Alley website which provides beta reading for amateur writers to hone their skills, or Lana Swartz who had been a classroom teacher working with special needs children. The work of Project New Media Literacies, thus, emerged from multiple expertises and many different practices, much like the informal learning cultures we drew upon as our model. Much of our work took shape through collaborative authoring tools, such as GoogleDocs and Ning, as we sought ways to embed these technologies and their affiliated practices into our day-to-day operations. And our development and deploying of these curricular resources involved us in collaborating both with other groups of academic researchers, such as the GoodPlay Project at Harvard or Dan Hickey, an expert on participatory assessment, at Indiana University, with youth-focused organizations such as Global Kids and Zoey's Room, and with classroom teachers in New England and the Midwest who were rethinking and reworking our materials for their instructional purposes.

Here, I want to use the Teachers' Strategy Guide we developed around "Reading in a Participatory Culture" to explore what it might mean to bring the "ethos" of a participatory culture into the English/Language Arts classroom. The Learning Library introduces a range of different participatory practices—from Djing to Podcasting, from Graphiti to Cosplay—and encourages young people to go out and explore the web, "messing around" with new tools and platforms, even as they are developing a conceptual vocabulary for linking what they learn at a particular location to their larger acquisition of core social skills and cultural competencies. The Teachers' Strategy Guides adopt a more conservative approach on the level of content, reflecting the current constraints on what can be incorporated into formal education, but propose a radical reconceptualization of what it means to engage with literary texts.

Jenna McWilliams (2008, p. 1), a researcher on the Project NML team, captures many of our goals in this statement from the Teachers' Strategy Guide:

> This model embraces the traditional model—which conceives of a literary text as a living presence imbued with deep cultural meanings—and works to enhance active engagement with the text through integration of participatory practices and skills. The participatory model of reading harnesses the activities that many kids already engage in when participating in online and offline communities. The unit also emphasizes that **reading can be a generative process**, one in which the work of understanding a text can serve as a launching point for creative work and a cultural conversation, one in which they may take on the role of authors who help keep the book alive through appropriation and remixing it for a contemporary audience.
>
> This unit highlights **the concept of purpose-driven reading**: that depending on the role different readers play, they will be driven to engage with a text with different purposes. In other words, purpose is both individual and social: Each student engages with the text in a slightly different way, and these different modes of engagement can enhance a collective understanding of the work.
>
> The goal of this unit is to help students **identify individual motives** for approaching a creative text and to use those motives for **collaborative problem-solving**—working in cooperation with a community of readers to develop an enhanced understanding of the text. [original emphases in bold]

You can already see from this description how we sought to embed what we know about "affinity spaces" and "participatory culture" into a reconfiguration of what it means to study literature in schools. One key way we have done this is to call attention to what we describe as "motives for reading," recognizing that when we read a text for different reasons in the service of different goals and interests, we read it in different ways, asking different questions, noticing different things, and generating different responses.

In school, there has too often been a tendency to reify one kind of reading—one that can easily be reduced to SparkNotes—as if that was the natural or logical way of responding to particular texts. Students aren't asked to think about why they, personally, individually or as members of a larger learning community, might be reading *Moby-Dick*; they have simply been assigned a book, and they are reading it because the teacher, the school board, or the national standards dictate that they should do so. This cuts reading in the literature class off from the other reasons young people might choose to read outside of the classroom and thus diminishes the relevance of the skills we are teaching for the rest of their lives. It has been suggested that if we taught sex education in schools the same way we taught reading, the human race might die out in a generation. Literature professor Wyn Kelley (2008), a key collaborator on this project, describes two very different modes of reading, one Romantic ("we are drawn irresistibly into the text, seduced, horrified, or intoxicated by something greater than ourselves") and one critical ("a left-brain navigation of the text, complete with charts, guides, and lists"). She argues:

> Students, in my experience, approach reading with both approaches in mind. They love the experience of losing themselves in a text, and they also savor the joy of discovering themselves and mastering their world. We do them a disservice if we try to separate those two modes of reading or prioritize them, suggesting that one exists only for private pleasure, the other for public instruction and assessment. One is for enjoyment, we seem to be telling them, the other learning. One is emotional, the other rational. One has no particular meaning; anything you think is fine. The other has a meaning assigned by teachers, critics, and other authorities; whatever you think, you must eventually adopt this authoritative interpretation. (Kelley, 2008, p.12)

The challenge was how to create a context in the literature classroom which supported readers with very different goals and interests, much as Gee (2007) describes the forums around Age of Mythologies as enabling many different forms of status, participation, and leadership. What if young people were asked to identify their own goals for reading this text, to take responsibility for sharing what they learned with each other, and to translate their critical engagement with the text into a springboard for other creative and expressive activities?

You Don't Know Dick!

Our interest in *Moby-Dick* as a specific case study for this participatory model of reading emerged from our interactions with Ricardo Pitts-Wiley, the creative director of the Mixed Magic Theater in Pawtucket, Rhode Island. Pitts-Wiley had gone into an institution for incarcerated youth and helped them to learn to read *Moby-Dick* by encouraging them to identify closely with a single character and to try to imagine what kind of person that character would be if they were living today. In the process, he encouraged them to re-imagine *Moby-Dick* not as a novel about the whaling trade in the nineteenth century but rather as a story about the drug trade in the twenty-first century—both dangerous professions involving men who were on the outside of their society and who formed enormous loyalty to each other and to their leaders in their ruthless pursuit of their economic interests. We might describe this approach as learning through remixing. Pitts-Wiley (2008, p.28) described some of the ways that these young men reconceptualized Melville's characters:

> One of the young men chose Ahab—it was a great story, too! Ahab was at home. He had just come back from a very successful voyage of drug dealing for WhiteThing, his boss. It was so successful that he worried that he was now a threat to the great omnipotent WhiteThing. He was making some decisions that it was time for him to either challenge the boss for control or to get out of the business. He's home, he's got this young wife, she's pregnant, and the drug lord sends agents looking for him. In looking for him, they kill his wife and unborn child. They don't get him. His revenge is based on what they did to him. Another one chose Elijah, the prophet, and the awful dilemma of being able to see the future and no one believing or understanding what you're trying to tell them. "I'm going to warn you about this, but if you don't heed my warning this is what's going to happen," and the awful dilemma that you face. His story was about 9/11. "I'm trying to tell you this is going to happen," and then nobody listened, and how awful he felt that he knew and couldn't stop it . . . Another one chose Queequeg and he made him a pimp. Wow, why a pimp? He says, "Well, when we meet Queequeg he's selling human heads, shrunken heads," so he's a peddler in human flesh. He's exotic. He's tall. He's good looking, and fiercely loyal and dangerous. That's a pimp.

Pitts-Wiley, in turn, took inspiration from the stories these young men created for his own new stage production, *Moby-Dick: Then and Now*. In the process, Pitts-Wiley has become a passionate advocate for getting communities to read and discuss classic novels together as they seek to better understand how these books inform their own contemporary lives and identities. Although Pitts-Wiley saw remixing as an important strategy for constructing a productive dialogue with young people around literary works, he was also emphatic that remixing should emerge from a meaningful engagement with the original and not simply the careless appropriation of someone else's words and ideas for one's own purpose. As an African American, he was very aware of how his culture was often "ripped off" by white artists without any acknowledgment of its original meanings and contexts. He asserted his right to draw on the literary canon but he also insisted that his students pay respect to those who came before. Creative reading worked hand in hand with critical reading; remixing literary texts started with and enhanced what literature teachers have traditionally talked about as "close reading."

We wanted to bring key aspects of Pitts-Wiley's visions and pedagogical practices into our Teachers' Strategy Guide. One way we did this was to offer students multiple models of what it might mean to read *Moby-Dick*. A video (see: http://techtv.mit.edu/collections/newmedialiteracies/videos/410-four-readers), produced by project member Deb Lui and filmed by Talieh Rohani, introduced "Four Readers"—Pitts-Wiley, Rudy Cabrera (a young actor in his troupe), Kelley, and myself, each embodying a very different relationship to the text. Indeed, the video shows that not only do we each read Melville in different ways and for different reasons but that we each may read the same book in different ways on different occasions. Kelley, for example, describes how she reads the novel as a scholar and as a teacher and how these different goals shape what she pays attention to. I discuss what it means to engage with a book as a fan (in this case, using the Harry Potter novels) and as a media scholar. Pitts-Wiley discusses what he looks for in translating a literary text for the stage, while Cabrera discusses how engaging with a text as an actor helped him develop a deeper understanding of Melville's words through the eyes of a particular character. Another resource called attention to the range of different goals and interests reflected in fan websites around popular television shows: a medical student's website on *House* that "nitpicks" its representation of medicine; a *Survivor* fansite that explores why particular contestants lost the competition; a Patrick O'Brian site that draws together information about nineteenth century ships and their procedures, and so forth. Through these examples, students were encouraged to reflect on reading as a process and a practice, identifying the goals and strategies different readers applied to texts.

Students were also asked to take an inventory of their own reading practices, inside and outside the classroom. Jenna McWilliams, Katherine Clinton, and Deb Lui developed an activity where young people charted various aspects of their lives and then identified the different kinds of texts they tapped in their daily activities. As McWilliams (2008, p. 9) tells teachers:

> Though traditionally, reading has generally "counted" if it's a book that you read cover to cover, over the next several weeks the class will be encouraged to expand its concept of what counts as "reading a text"—you can read a website, for example, or read text messages, or even read a movie or a TV show or a song. The class will be . . . reading lots of different things, including but not limited to the main text. The teacher should model these ideas by drafting his or her own Identity Map and engaging in a discussion about what else might be considered within each identity the teacher identifies.

One Somerville-based teacher, Judi, brought a box of materials from her everyday life and asked students to guess what they had in common. Our team member Hillary Kolos (in Clinton, McWilliams, & Kolos, 2009, no page) observed Judi's activity:

> At first, they group the items together in categories like "maps," "menus," and "bills." Judi then led a group discussion about what all the items had in common. With a little help, one student guessed that you read all of the items. Judi explained that she reads items like these constantly throughout the day, in addition to reading books.

Judi described how this one activity started to change her students' understanding of reading. One student, for example, had been told for most of her life that she was not a good reader, but through filling out the activity, she came to realize that "I read all the time." This expanded conception of literacy, thus allows students to understand the reading they do in the classroom as a particular reading practice with its own rules and goals rather than creating a hierarchy where they were taught to devalue their own relationship to texts simply because it "falls short" of their teacher's exacting standards.

Learning is messy business

Teachers and students alike were encouraged to think of the classroom as a "community of readers," a metaphor running through Pitts-Wiley's descriptions of his theater practice. He had launched a campaign to get adults to read Melville's novel so that they might engage in meaningful conversations with younger readers in their community. This is very similar to what the Digital Youth Project (Ito et al., 2009, p. 39) found in interest-driven networks more generally:

> In contexts of peer-based learning, adults can still have an important role to play, though it is not a conventionally authoritative one . . . Unlike instructors in formal educational settings, however, these adults are passionate hobbyists and creators, and youth see them as experienced peers, not as people who have authority over them. These adults exert tremendous influence in setting communal norms and what educators might call "learning goals," though they do not have direct authority over newcomers.

A "community of readers," like the fan communities described above, offers a supportive environment through which individual students might develop their own expertise and share what they discover about the book and themselves with the group as a whole.

One way that students came to share their emerging expertise was through the annotation and illumination of Melville's text. Kelley introduced our team to the recently recovered marginalia which Melville produced as he read some of the books—fiction and nonfiction—and which informed his writing of *Moby-Dick*. Literary scholars are now exploring how these clues into Melville's reading process might shed light on his creative process. As she did so, we were struck by how rarely we encourage students to think about "great authors" as themselves readers of other cultural texts. Our approach, on the other hand, saw Melville as a master remixer who took ideas from many sources and mashed them up to create a work which captures the multicultural community that had grown up around whaling.

Having considered Melville's own model, students were then asked to select a page from the novel, blow it up to poster size, and create their own marginalia. Sometimes they might write words, other times draw pictures, but they were encouraged to engage as fully and diversely as possible with what they saw on the page. Because each student brought different motives to his or her reading, each annotation and ornamentation stressed different aspects, and thus as they presented the posters to their classmates, many different possible routes of interpretation emerged. In an exchange at one of our professional development conferences, Wyn Kelley talked with Paula, a teacher who had been using the Teachers' Strategy Guide, about how the classroom dynamic changed under this more participatory model (Clinton, McWilliams, & Kolos, 2009, no page):

> *Wyn*: In our writing of the guide we started with what we spoke of as a traditional model of literacy which you might summarize as mastery of the text. I wondered how you would define the kinds of literacy you are seeing in your students now? I gather not all of them read the whole book or were able to spout facts afterwards as we might expect in some mastery based model but clearly you saw something that looked like literacy to you. How would you describe that? What is that literacy?

> *Paula*: I want to talk about one student's response to the annotation of Moby-Dick he did. Afterwards he came to me and he said, "You know what I figured out from that exercise," and I'm saying to myself, "Not what the text means, that's for sure." It was really messy and I didn't come off of it really thinking that they understood all of the text, you know what I mean. They probably couldn't even tell me the plot line. But what he said to me was, "I think what I learned is that I really should read the classics because there's something in there I don't understand." And I thought, Ahh! When you do the traditional way we teach literature to students, somehow the teacher becomes a conduit of all information, no matter how you do it, whether it's a study guide or this and that. Eventually the teacher tells you how to think about this particular kind of text. What was driving me a little crazy was that I wasn't telling them how to think about anything. The thing I liked was that they came out of it thinking that they better think some more because they really didn't think it through. Eventually, if you are going to be literate, they have to come to the place where they say that "I had to struggle with this text a little bit to find out what it is saying to me."

Read in such ways, the push towards dealing with meaningful chunks from the novel is not about "lowering expectations" but, rather, about "raising expectations;" asking students to engage closely and creatively with specific passages from the text rather than developing a superficial understanding of the work as a whole, asking students to take ownership over what they are learning rather than relying on the teacher to hand them the answers for the exam. It is about intensive rather than extensive reading. As Pitts-Wiley (2008) explains, "Don't make it a test. Make it a lifetime experience. . . . Then the question becomes, 'How do I support you all the way through?' If you start reading *Moby-Dick* in the ninth grade where are you being supported in the tenth grade? Where are you being further supported in the eleventh grade and the twelfth grade?" For Pitts-Wiley, the key comes through constructing a "community" with a shared investment in literary works the student can draw upon for scaffolding and support. Such a "community of readers" has emerged spontaneously around the discussion of popular texts online, but Pitts-Wiley hopes to use his theater work to help foster a similar kind of community around Melville so young people remain connected to the books they read in school throughout the rest of their lives.

Some of our Strategy Guide activities (McWilliams, 2008, p. 25) pushed the idea of a "community of readers" even further, applying models of collective intelligence to think about how young people might pool their different interpretations and reading interests in the book:

> "How to Ace *Moby-Dick*" wall: Students work together to come up with guidelines for how other students can begin to engage in *Moby-Dick*. The class collectively identifies important themes, concepts, symbols, images, and so on from the text; as these are acknowledged, they're posted on a wall for all students to have access to. The purpose of this activity is to show that knowledge-building can be a collective practice and that this built knowledge can live in a shared social space (much as it does online). Because students don't have to worry about memorizing key ideas, they're freed to engage in the text and work with the key ideas in other ways. By asking students to articulate the ways that they've begun to engage with the novel, they can become more self-reflective of the process of studying the text within the framework of participatory culture. Ultimately, this knowledge can be pooled online (perhaps using social networking sites such as ning.com, or a free wiki through such hosting sites as pbwiki.com) with other classes who are working with the same text, with the end result being a fuller set of tools, instructions, definitions, and terms for future students' use.

One Indiana school encouraged students to make their own contributions to the Wikipedia page on *Moby-Dick*. Over the course of the term, their additions faced challenges from others invested in Melville's novels, as is often the case when additions get made to Wikipedia, and the students entered into the discussion forum to defend their claims, and in the end, they were successful in getting many of their contributions to become an accepted part of the shared knowledge Wikipedia provides. Significantly, the school's computers had previously been blocked from adding content to Wikipedia because some user had vandalized the site. Now, the students became valued members of the Wikipedia community and in the process, they saw themselves as having developed a degree of expertise over *Moby-Dick*.

As they worked with the Teachers' Strategy Guides, different teachers deployed a range of different expressive practices to help their students engage more fully with the novels they were reading. (In many cases, the teachers were appropriating the techniques we had developed and applying them to other books they felt were more appropriate to their students' lives and reading levels.). Some had students develop comic strips using tools like Bitstrips; some staged and recorded plays much like Pitts-Wiley's own *Moby-Dick: Then and Now* which emerged from their reinterpretations and appropriations from the novel; some created music videos inspired by M.C. Lars's "Ahab," an example which was often incorporated into their teaching of the book; and some wrote fan fiction which explored the perspective of secondary characters on board the *Pequod*. The choices of these practices emerged organically from the shifts that were taking place in the classroom culture, shaped by a changed understanding of the nature of literacy and expertise, informed by the reconceptualization of the class as a "community of readers" and their recognition that reading is a springboard for many other kinds of cultural expression.

Writing in her blog about the experience, McWilliams (2009, no page) described how "reading with a mouse in your hand" encouraged young people to move from consumption to production and to move outward from the core text to many other cultural expressions:

> "Reading-with-mouse-in-hand" is fundamentally different from the act of "reading-with-pencil-in-hand," a common practice among professional writers and voracious readers. The difference is in what happens to the generative activity linked to reading. When you are reading-with-mouse-in-hand, your writing is "going public" instantly in a way that marginalia never could. Reading-with-mouse-in-hand, therefore, is a practice that requires a deep sense of an intended public, which is much broader than the public generally identified by the school context.

Students and teachers were encouraged to treat even canonical texts as "works in progress," to go back to our earlier discussion of fan fiction, which have informed subsequent generations of writers and artists.

Learning to read in this context is, as Paula and Professor Kelley suggest, "messier" than learning to read in a traditional classroom, much as the mixing and matching of production practice within any given creative community is much messier than trying to deal with the practices individually. Teachers reported struggling with their own entrenched assumptions about what forms of culture or what types of reading were valuable and often got caught off guard by materials students wanted to bring into the discussion that had not yet been vetted for their appropriateness or directions that students wanted to take the conversation that were far removed from the instructor's own expertise and training. Often, our field observations found that students were most engaged when our practices felt least like normal schooling and least engaged when the bureaucratic structures reasserted themselves. And this is a problem we will need to explore more fully if we are going to be able to bring a participatory model of reading and learning more fully into our teaching.

Yet, this approach is also highly generative in the sense that it sparks a range of different critical and creative responses to what is being read and it encourages students to take a much greater pride in what they were able to contribute to the class's joint efforts to make sense of this complex nineteenth century novel. Some of what is valuable here emerges from a "Do It Yourself" ethos where students are encouraged to take greater ownership over their own learning, but it is also shaped by the fact that they are doing it together as part of a larger community of people with diverse interests and multiple opportunities for participation.

We are, however, pushing up against the boundaries of formal education. We are pushing against the time limits of the class period which restricts the ability of students to "geek out" around subjects of passionate interest to them. We are pushing against the hierarchical structure which places obligations of teachers to be "in control" over what happens in their classroom and which thus generates fear and anxiety when discussions move in directions that reflect the intrinsic interests of their students. We are pushing against the requirements of standardized testing which adopt a model radically at odds with our notion of a diversified and distributed expertise, insisting that every student know and do the same things. We are pushing against administrative practices which isolate schools from the larger flow of the culture, and we are pushing against the division of learning into grade levels which rejects the notions of "lifelong learning" that underlie Pitts-Wiley's idea of continuing to scaffold students' relations to literature after course assignments are completed. Project NML has done its best to identify ways that at least some of what we see as valuable about participatory culture can be inserted into current pedagogical practices, but all of us need to continue to struggle with the challenges of how we might more fully align our schooling practices with what we know to be socially, culturally, and pedagogically productive within the field studies that have been done around DIY subcultures.

At the end of the day, the idea of "do-it-ourselves" remains a radical concept—at least where formal education is concerned. Enter at your own risk.

References

Bacon-Smith, C. (1992) *Enterprising women: Television fandom and the creation of popular myth.* Philadelphia: University of Pennsylvania Press

Brown, J. S., & Adler, R. P. (2008) Minds on fire: Open education, the long tail, and learning 2.0. *Educause Review, 43*(1),16–32.

Busse, K., & Hellekson, K. (2006) Work in progress. In K. Hellekson & K. Busse (Eds.), *Fan-fiction and fan communities in the age of the internet.* Jefferson, NC: McFarland

Clinton, K., McWilliams, J., & Kolos, H. (2009) Reading in a participatory culture: A model for expanding the ELA domain by bringing in new media mindsets and practices. Project New Media Literacies, Unpublished manuscript.

Coppa, F. (2008) Women, *Star Trek* and the early development of fannish viding. *Transformative Works and Cultures,* 1. Retrieved Nov. 1, 2009, from http://journal.transformativeworks.org/index.php/twc/article/view/44/64

Douglas, S. J. (1989) *Inventing American broadcasting, 1899–1922.* Baltimore, MD: Johns Hopkins University Press

Driscoll, K. (2009) *Stepping your game up: Technical innovation among young people of color in hip-hop.* Unpublished master's thesis, MIT, Cambridge, MA.

Gee, J. P. (2004) *Situated language and learning: A critique of traditional schooling.* New York: Routledge.

Gee, J. P. (2007) *Good video games and good learning: Collected essays on video games, learning and literacy.* New York: Peter Lang.

Green, J. & Jenkins, H. (2009) The moral economy of Web 2.0: Audience research and convergence culture. In J. Holt & A. Perren (Eds.), *Media industries: History, theory, and methods.* New York: Wiley-Blackwell.

Ito, M. (2005, September 30) Otaku media literacy. Retrieved Nov. 1, 2009, from http://www.itofisher.com/mito/publications/otaku_media_lit.html

Ito, M., Baumer, S., Bittani, M., boyd, d., Cody, R., Herr-Shephardson, B., Horst, H., Lange, A., Mahendran, D., Martinez, K., Pascoe, C., Perkel, D., Robinson, L., Sims, C., & Tripp, (2009) *Hanging out, messing around, and geeking out: Kids living and learning with new media.* Cambridge, MA: MIT Press

Jenkins, H. (1992) *Textual poachers: Television fans and participatory culture.* New York: Routledge.

Jenkins, H., with R. Purushotma, K. Clinton, M. Weigel, & A. Robison (2006) *Confronting the Challenges of Participatory Culture: Media Education for the 21ˢᵗ Century.* Occasional Paper. Boston, MA: MIT/MacArthur Foundation.

Kelley, W. (2008) Reading *Moby-Dick* through the decades: Expert voices. In *Reading in a participatory culture: Teachers' Strategy Guide,* Project New Media Literacies Retrieved Nov. 1, 2009 at: http://newmedialiteracies.org/ExpertVoices_Revised.pdf

Lankshear, C., & Knobel, M (2006) *New literacies: Everyday practices and classroom learning.* London: Open University Press.

Lave, J. & Wenger, E. (1991) *Situated learning: Legitimate peripheral participation.* Cambridge, UK: Cambridge University Press.

Levy, P. (1999) *Collective intelligence: Mankind's emerging world in cyberspace.* New York: Basic.

McWilliams, J. (2008) Motives for Reading. In Project Media New Literacies *Reading in a Participatory Culture: Teachers' Strategy Guide.* Retrieved Nov. 1, 2009, at http://projec tnml.ning.com/page/teachers-strategy-guide

McWilliams, J. (2009, April 8) Reading with a mouse in hand. Message posted to http://jen-namcwilliams.blogspot.com/2009/04/writing-with-mouse-in-hand.html

Petrik, P. (1992) The youngest fourth estate: The novelty toy printing press and adolescence, 1870–1886. In E. West & P. Petrik (Eds.), *Small worlds: Children and adolescents in America, 1850–1950* (pp. 125–142). Kansas City, KS: University of Kansas.

Pitts-Wiley, R. (2008) Reading *Moby-Dick* as a Creative Artist: Expert Voices. *Reading in a Participatory Culture: Teachers Strategy Guide*, Project New Media Literacies. Retrieved Nov. 1, 2009, from http://newmedialiteracies.org/ExpertVoices_Revised.pdf

Rich, M. (2008, July 27) Literacy debate–Online, R U really reading? The *New York Times.* Retrieved from http://www.nytimes.com/2008/07/27/books/27reading.html?_r=2&ex=1 217908800&en=b2960ae3b8cce1b2&ei=5070&emc=eta1&ref=slogin

Ross, A. (1991) *Strange weather: Culture, science and technology in the age of limits.* London: Verso.

Seiter, E. (2008) Practicing at home: Computers, pianos, and cultural capital. In T. McPherson (Ed.), *Digital youth, innovation and the unexpected.* Cambridge, MA: MIT Press/MacArthur Foundation.

Terranova, T. (2004) *Network culture: Politics for the information age.* London: Pluto Press.

Turner, F. (2008) *From counterculture to cyberculture: Stewart Brand, the whole earth network, and the rise of digital utopianism.* Chicago: University of ChicagoPress.

Varnelis, K. (2008) *Networked publics.* Cambridge, MA: MIT Press.

Yockey, M. (2009) Personal communication.

Zimmerman, P. R. (1995) *Reel families: A social history of amateur film.* Bloomington, IN: Indiana University Press.

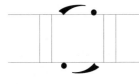

Contributors

Authors

Erik Jacobson is an Assistant Professor at Montclair State University (USA). His research interests center on adult literacy, reading comprehension, and using social networking systems to support teachers and learners. He has published in journals such as *Radical Teacher,* the *Journal of Literacy Research,* and *E-Learning.* He is working on a book to be published by Peter Lang, titled *Adult Basic Education in the Age of New Literacies.* Erik's earliest DIY memories include refashioning his own clothes, being in punk bands in the 1980s, and doing live mixes while on the air as a dj at his college radio station.

Henry Jenkins was until recently the Co-Director of the Comparative Media Studies Program at MIT and is now the Provost's Professor of Communications, Journalism, and Cinematic Arts at the University of Southern California. He is the author or editor of thirteen books, including *The Children's Culture Reader, Textual Poachers: Television Fans and Participatory Culture,* and *Convergence Culture: Where Old and New Media Collide.* He blogs at henryjenkins.org. Henry's earliest memories of DIY culture involve making monster models and play-acting "Batman" and "The Wizard of Oz" in his backyard.

Michele Knobel is Professor of Education at Montclair State University (USA), where she co-ordinates the graduate literacy programs. Her current research focuses on new literacies, social practices and digital technologies. Michele's books include *New Literacies* (with Colin Lankshear), as well as *The Handbook of Research on New Literacies* (co-edited Julie Coiro, Colin Lankshear and Don Leu). One of Michele's favorite DIY memories from country-town, high school days is cutting-and-pasting photos of friends into cruise line catalogues, adding captions and creating jet-set, tabloid lives for them. They did the same for her.

Colin Lankshear is Professor of Literacy and New Technologies at James Cook University in Australia, and Adjunct Professor at McGill and Mount St Vincent Universities in Canada. His recent books (with Michele Knobel) include *Digital Literacies: Concepts, Policies and Practices,* and *A New Literacies Sampler.* He and Michele are currently working on a 3rd edition of *New Literacies,* with a focus on social learning. His favorite DIY memory is building a verandah on the house in Coatepec, Mexico, applying Meccano construction principles to steel, timber, and terracotta tiles.

Matthew Lewis attends College of the Canyons in California, where he is majoring in fine arts. He began using computers at the age of 4 years and always has been fascinated with technology and art. He is also an Eagle Scout. He is deeply interested in anime, cosplay, art, and video gaming. While much of what Matthew does is DIY—everything from creating original manga comics to making anime music videos—the design and art work involved in creating his cosplay outfits is something he finds deeply satisfying.

Susan Luckman is a Senior Lecturer in the School of Communication, International Studies and Languages, and a member of the Hawke Research Institute, at the University of South Australia. Current research explores the use of GIS and mental mapping digital visualisation tools in cultural research interviews. She has authored numerous publications on new media, creative cultures and cultural policy, digital music cultures, and contemporary cultural studies and is co-editor of: *Sonic Synergies: Music, Identity, Technology and Community.* Susan's DIY media directorial debut was a silent Super 8 film fairy tale starring the family guinea pigs.

Guy Merchant is Professor of Literacy in Education at Sheffield Hallam University, where he co-ordinates the work of the Language and Literacy Research Group. He is interested in the digital literacy practices of children and young people, and how their informal uses of these literacies cross into school contexts. Guy's most recent book is *Web 2.0 for Schools: Learning and Social Participation* (with Julia Davies). Once upon a time in the land of

DIY, he invested in a bag full of cold dye and invited all his friends to a "dye-in." It was the summer of '68 and Guy had the most colorful shirts in the neighborhood that year.

Rebecca Orlowicz works in the Technology Teaching and Learning Group at Hunter College, New Jersey (USA), where she is involved with training development, instructional design, and multimedia production of educational technology. Despite limited distribution (to her grandparents), Rebecca's favorite DIY memory is recording Christmas albums with her family, including guitar and recorder accompaniments.

Robin Potanin is a Senior Lecturer in Concept Development at the Academy for Digital Entertainment (mADE) at NHTV University (The Netherlands). She used to produce and write commercial console and PC games. Now she teaches interactive narrative and entertainment theory. Her earliest and strongest DIY experiences are learning how to cook piroshki with her Siberian grandmother and reaching up to the stove from under the barrel chest of Johnny Cash to help create a delicious *chile con carne* while singing "Ring of Fire."

John Potter is a lecturer in new media and education at the London Knowledge Lab, part of the University of London Institute of Education. Currently, he is program leader for the MA in Media, Culture and Communication. As part of the Centre for the Study of Children, Youth and Media, his research interests and publications are in the areas of new media and learning, in formal and informal settings, as framed by media and cultural studies, theories of identity, new literacies and multimodality. John's earliest DIY media memories are of rainy Sundays spent recording ghost stories on a 2 track stereo reel-to-reel tape recorder, using sound effects (clanking chains, howling wind, etc.) from BBC vinyl LPs borrowed from Croydon Public Library.

Christopher Shamburg is an Associate Professor in the Educational Technology Department at New Jersey City University. He is the author of *National Educational Technology Standards for Students: Units for the English Language Arts* and *Student-Powered Podcasting: Teaching for 21st Century Literacy*. His favorite DIY memory is making pear wine in a friend's basement as a teenager—the pears were from a neighbor's tree and the recipe was from the Jersey City Public Library.

Angela Thomas is a Senior Lecturer in English Education at the University of Sydney (Australia). Her research centers around the social and discursive practices in new media spaces, with a particular focus on youth communities in virtual worlds. She is author of the book *Youth Online: Iden-*

tity and Literacy in Virtual Communities, and is currently working on a project exploring children's multimedia authoring with the Australian Children's Television Foundation. Angela has a fond DIY memory of spending many long hours in a darkroom developing her own photographs.

Nicole Tufano is a teacher at Memorial Elementary School, Maywood, New Jersey (USA), where she teaches Kindergarten and Grade 1. Nicole holds a Master of Arts in Reading, and her interests include working with literacy and digital technologies to enhance students' learning. She is currently completing a graduate certificate program in new literacies, digital technologies and learning at Montclair State University. She is looking forward to introducing claymation (stop motion) video making into her Kindergarten class.

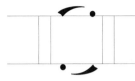

Index

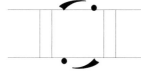

Subject Index

Colin Lankshear, Michele Knobel,
& Michael Peters
General Editors

New literacies and new knowledges are being invented "in
the streets" as people from all walks of life wrestle with
new technologies, shifting values, changing institutions,
and new structures of personality and temperament emerging
in a global informational age. These new literacies and
ways of knowing remain absent from classrooms. Many education administrators, teachers, teacher educators, and aca-
demics seem largely unaware of them. Others actively
oppose them. Yet, they increasingly shape the engagements
and worlds of young people in societies like our own. The
New Literacies and Digital Epistemologies series will explore this terrain with a view to informing educational
theory and practice in constructively critical ways.

For further information about the series and submitting
manuscripts, please contact:

Michele Knobel & Colin Lankshear
Montclair State University
Dept. of Education and Human Services
3173 University Hall
Montclair, NJ 07043
michele@coatepec.net

To order other books in this series, please contact our
Customer Service Department at:

(800) 770-LANG (within the U.S.)
(212) 647-7706 (outside the U.S.)
(212) 647-7707 FAX

Or browse online by series at:

www.peterlang.com